Color Me
Butterfly

Color Me Butterfly

A true story of courage, hope, and transformation

L. Y. Marlow

éL publishing
Bowie, Maryland

ISBN-13: 978-0-9787320-5-9

ISBN-10: 0-9787320-5-7

Library of Congress Catalog Control Number: 2006906076

Printed in the United States of America
Cover and interior design by Lightbourne, Inc.
Cover source photography: gettyimages.com

PUBLISHER'S NOTE

This book spans over a sixty year period and is based on the author's memories, years of research, and stories told to her by her mother and grandmother. As a way to bring life to the story and protect identities, occasionally the author changed names, rearranged dates, compressed events, invented dialogue and scenery, and created certain episodes to accommodate narrative flow. All events described herein actually happened, though on occasion the author has taken certain liberties, and those liberties are not intended to portray actual events; no events of abuse, so integral to the story, have been magnified.

Books are available at quantity discounts when used for domestic violence or women's abuse initiatives, and the promotion of certain products and/or services. For information, please write to èL publishing, Special Markets Department, P.O. Box 2182, Bowie, MD 20718 or email info@elpublishingonline.com.

To Eloise and Mattie,
the two women who gave me life and made
it possible for me to tell our story.

To my daughter—
you are my Treasure.

Some would say that I've lived a sad life, a pained life. The room where I sit is beautiful, blanketed in my favorite colors—lavender and white. Colors that I so often dreamt about since I was old enough to appreciate color, to appreciate life.

I sit at the head of the table, a table surrounded by my most prized possessions, my most precious gifts—my family. The family I have often thought about in my darkest moments, my brightest hours. They are the saving grace that has kept me whole for as long as I can remember.

My mind was once full of memories of times when time seemed to have caved in on itself, like a rainbow that has lost its arch, its color. Memories I recall having been so bad that I once prayed for death. But those times are forever lost in my mind like a tiny dust particle. And as odd as it may seem, it is those memories that I have come to be thankful for. I now know and believe with all that exists within me that certain things are put in your path as a way to strengthen you, to bring you to your center. I have since gained many memories that far surpass those that once lay at the core of my being.

My life? Well, it is one that I cannot explain. You see, my life has never been the kind that one reads about in a romance novel or a Cinderella story. In fact, it is a life that many have shed tears over. But I would say to them, don't cry. Don't cry for me. Don't shed tears for something that I have come to be so grateful for. Yes, I've had my share of ups and downs—more downs than one lifetime might absorb. I've loved. I've lost. I've grieved. I've gained. And for this, I am grateful.

The nonbelievers would call this a sad story; but I like to see it as grace. In my heart of hearts, I am wise enough to know that God don't give you nothin' that don't serve a purpose or reason to make you appreciate all that has come to pass.

I have no complaints about my life, even though there still rests in the deepest part of my soul a craving to have known better things. But each time these thoughts cross my mind, I say a silent prayer and smile. I smile because I've come through the rain, pulled through many of storms, and still I can't help but wonder as I sit here surrounded by my chi'ren, my chi'ren's chi'ren, and their chi'ren, how it is that I can be so blessed. My blessings have been sixty years in the making.

I smile, and through my tears I see the smile in every pair of eyes, feel the love vibrating from each heart. "You are the reason for keeping this family together," my eldest son says to me in a voice that reminds me of his youth. "We love you, Ma, and we thank you for all that you've done for us." This I hear from my eldest daughter as she takes me into her arms. My second son's eyes hold my own as he hands me a single white rose, and all that he wants to say rests solely in his tear-stained eyes. I stand from my seat, wanting so much to lift up and spread all the grace that holds me, as words that are stuck in my heart push their way up to my lips, but I cannot speak. Humility has overtaken my heart and my mind. And it is now my youngest daughter who comes to me and folds me into her arms as she lets this serve as her words to me and my words to her. When her embrace releases me, I turn and look at a table that's covered in a silk white cloth and silver picture frames: frames that hold the photographs of those who are still deep within me, those who I've loved, those who I've lost.

All are here today, in spirit or in flesh. They have all come to celebrate me, to celebrate my life. And today, for this, I am grateful.

I am grateful for living. I am grateful for loving. And most of all, I am grateful for just being who I am.

Who am I? you wonder.

I am Mattie.

COLOR ME BUTTERFLY ❧ *Five Generations*

Eloise & Isaac

2nd Generation

3rd Generation

4th Generation

5th Generation

Deller
Denise
Leonard

Mattie
Roy Jr.
Eileen
Anthony
Lydia
Angie

Lionel
Rochelle

Walton
Starlette

Leona
Terrance
Tiara
Brian

Rollie
Keisha
Rollie, Jr.
Cory

Paulene
Tanya
Gilbert

Charlene
Michael
Sherre

Leonard
Shakeeria

Roy Jr.
Roy Jr. II
Lavar
Maurice

Eileen
George Jr.
Demetrius
Damon

Anthony
Michelle
Zahri
Shakeera

Lydia
Treasure

Rochelle
Kyle
Amber
Marquita

Tiara
Jahnyah

Tanya
Kymere
Mykia
Tahj

Sherre
Tamir
Rahshee

Denise
Louis Jr.

Shakeeria
Johnaysia
Johkei
Iran

Maurice
Selena

George Jr.
Brandon

Roy Jr. II
Kaleem
Samir

Michelle
Tonaija
Charles Jr.
Maurice

PART ONE

Mattie

1

BALTIMORE, MARYLAND: 1941

*T*he cost of the Greyhound bus ticket and his new suit would set him back for weeks, and Isaac Bingham knew it.

From the moment he got the letter from his mother that Aunt Isabel had passed, things had started to deteriorate. *Gon' so quik we ain't ev'n no what ail her,* his mother had written. Now the bus was pulling out of downtown Baltimore at eight p.m., and he was due to arrive in Kingstree, South Carolina, early the next morning, just in time for the funeral.

The night was black and cloudy, thick with a misty rain. The smell of urine and heavy liquor that reeked from the man sitting next to him made Isaac sick. He didn't like riding the bus with its odor, and the way it bounced him around made him feel dizzy. He would have preferred driving home, but it would be a long time before he saved enough money to buy the car he'd been dreaming about since he was a young boy.

7

He was only fifteen when he left home. His friend Willie convinced him to move up north. "You need to go back to Baltimore with me," Willie had told him while home one weekend for a visit. "That NAACP thing done figured a way to make it better for us coloreds, and you'll be able to fend for ya'self with a job in the city." Isaac didn't know the least bit about no NAACP, but Willie had said two words that got him to thinking—*Colored People*—and if this NAACP was something that was gonna help coloreds, then it sounded to him like Baltimore was where he needed to be if he was ever gonna make something of himself.

At first, Isaac's parents wouldn't hear of it. "Boy, we can't afford to lose another pair of farm hands," his father, Jessup, had told him. "Sides, what you gon' do in some big city anyway?" But Isaac convinced Jessup and his mother, Ruby, that he'd be better off up north; he'd make plenty more in a big city than the little he earned sharecropping; he'd even be able to send them something from time to time.

After weeks of pleading and making promises, Isaac had made his case. He worked from sunup to sundown to earn enough cash for a one-way ticket to Baltimore. On the day of his leaving, he packed a small wooden suitcase that his father had lent him and confiscated an old Prince Albert Tobacco can, which he would use to stash all the money he'd managed to save.

Isaac stared out into the blackness. He couldn't sleep, and he couldn't keep his mind off of wanting to get back to Baltimore even though he'd just left. He'd missed his family the six years he'd been gone, but thoughts of returning to a place with few good memories and no future just didn't sit well with his stomach. Still, he'd be there soon. *Fourteen hours from door to door*, the driver had announced before leaving the terminal.

As the bus eased its way along 95 South at thirty-five miles an hour, Isaac stirred from a fitful sleep that had kept him awake most of the night. He stretched the kinks from his neck and back and peered out the window, hoping to recognize someone that could give him a lift into Kingstree, his hometown, about five miles away. He saw many eager faces waiting to welcome loved ones, but no face to welcome him. He figured anyone who might have come was probably over at the church helping to prepare for Aunt Isabel's funeral.

He grabbed the wooden suitcase and walked along the side of the road, passing shanty homes that sat back in the distance and rows of cotton fields and crops that covered the land for miles. To this day, the sight of it still made his knees feel wobbly.

Isaac slowed as he neared his parents' home, a tiny wooden shack surrounded by oak trees and cornfields. He had often shut his eyes to his surroundings and imagined being somewhere else, anywhere other than this place, which had made his heart yearn for something better and his head fill with possibilities. Now he was twenty-one years old. He looked like the man he'd become since he left Kingstree, no longer the boy who was once afraid to dream. He had made a way for himself in Baltimore and managed to push this measly living from his mind. His legs ached and his stomach let out a growl, reminding him that he hadn't eaten since this time yesterday. His mind drifted as he pondered why a death had to be the only reason to bring him back this way.

He poked his chest out a bit when his eyes caught sight of his father rocking slowly on the porch in the same old rustic chair. Jessup Bingham, a man of few thoughts and words, was as stubborn as a mule and as set in his ways as hardened cement. By virtue of the thirteen children he'd reared, and the countless years he broke his back sharecropping somebody else's farm, he didn't see the need for wanting anything much beyond the life he lived. He saw no need in colored folks being overproud or too good for their own senses, he used to tell Isaac. And when Isaac made the choice to seek a better life, Jessup had all but pushed him out of his mind and heart.

Jessup's ashen, gray-brown face revealed his age, as he watched his youngest son approach him. "Looks like you done finally made it, boy. We didn't spect to see you till we done put Isabel in the ground," he said, his words rocking with the motion of the chair.

Isaac gave his father a weak smile. "I took a late bus out last evenin'," he stammered. "I figured I could make it in plenty of time befo' she be laid to rest."

Jessup's eyes swept over his son, inspecting him. "Well, I spose you must be hungry then. Gon' in there and fix you a plate. I reckon the grits should still be warm."

"Yes, sir," Isaac said as he walked up onto the porch and gave his father a nod, the best gesture he could summon to say that he was glad to see him again.

Isaac was sitting in the kitchen slopping up grits and eggs, when his brother Henry came through the door.

"Hey man, it sho' good to see you." Henry grabbed Isaac

in a bear hug as soon as Isaac stood to greet him. "How you
been, city boy?"

Isaac coughed and tried to release himself from his brother's grip. "I'm fine, but everything is so different now." He
looked around, feeling like a stranger. And in a way, he was.

"You almost ready?" Henry asked. "We gon' be late."

"Yeah. I just need to change into my suit."

The funeral was held at the First Baptist Church of
Kingstree, the one Isaac and his family had attended since he
was a little boy, the one he had been baptized in. Isabel
seemed peaceful, lying there in her lavender dress, a wig, and
makeup that made her look better than she did when she was
alive. Isabel was Ruby's eldest sister, the one sister that Ruby
was most fond of, and Isaac would have been banned from
the family if he weren't there. It was a sad funeral, the way all
funerals in the South are—with lots of hollering, Amens, fake
fainting, and prayer, followed by the gathering.

After the burial, they all returned to the house that Isabel
had shared with her husband, Herbert. As was the custom,
the women went to the kitchen to prepare the feast while the
men sat on the porch, smoking cigarette sticks and drinking
moonshine that Henry had made.

Isaac was standing near a tree talking to his cousin Chuck
when he first noticed Eloise. This beautiful young girl was
gazing at him from across the yard, but each time he turned
to look at her, she quickly lowered her eyes. She looked familiar to Isaac, but he just couldn't place her name. He was sure
he'd seen her somewhere before. Maybe in church, just before
he'd left for Baltimore. Most likely, she was one of the many
girls who had chased after him.

"Hey, Chuck, who that gal over there?" Isaac asked.

Chuck turned and looked at the girls standing across the yard from them. "You mean the one in the yellow dress?"

"Yeah, that one," Isaac answered.

"Oh, that's one of George and Affie's girls. You rememba', they have six girls. That one's Eloise."

George and Affie had six daughters and three sons. Eloise was the third eldest daughter. Affie had known Isabel for twenty years, and when she heard about her death, she thought it only proper for her family to attend the funeral. That was the way of life for coloreds in the South. If someone died, every family member and friend within a hundred miles was expected to attend.

A look of surprise flashed across Isaac's face. He had known their family for years but had never much noticed Eloise before. He guessed that she was younger than he, by only a few years perhaps. She was pretty. Pretty in a natural kind of way, he thought.

Eloise was still unaware of the allure and effect she had on men, especially men like Isaac, who knew a good thing when he saw it. Isaac had fancied many girls, but he had never seen one as beautiful as Eloise, with her coppery brown skin and innocent eyes. Her beauty was magnetic. And Isaac was hooked.

After circling the yard like a lion stalking its prey, Isaac worked up enough nerve to approach her. "Hello ma'am. You may not rememba' me, but I used to live in these parts befo' I moved to Baltimore." Isaac flicked the cigarette he was smoking and mashed it in the dirt with the toe of his worn wing-tip shoe. A twinkle sparkled in his left eye. "You one of George and Affie's gals, right?"

Eloise turned to Isaac and nodded. "Yes," she said, her eyes shifting nervously toward the ground as though she were too afraid to look at him. He was the handsome boy that all the girls had a crush on, including her. She used to go out of her way to get Isaac's attention whenever he happened to be at their shared family events; he would always nod and smile at her as though she were a child, which she was. But today was different. Today, he'd been staring at her for the better half of the afternoon, and she had noticed him the moment he walked into the church with Henry.

Isaac smiled boyishly and pressed his hazel eyes into hers. "I'm Isaac," he said. "Isaac Bingham. I'm one of Jessup and Ruby's boys." He stepped in closer and held out his hand. Eloise took it and shook it lightly.

Isaac knew all too well the effect he had on girls. His Cherokee Indian mother had blessed him with unusually long, wavy hair, caramel color skin, and high cheekbones. All the girls in the South, not to mention Baltimore, were always flocking to be his next girlfriend, but Eloise needn't flock. On this day, she had caught his eye and his heart.

"You look very pretty today," Isaac said, turning on the charm he had picked up in Baltimore.

Eloise looked up at him and smiled. "Thank you," she said.

"How old are you?"

Eloise's eyes lit up. "I just turned sixteen," she offered.

"Is that right? Well, you are a very pretty sixteen-year-old." Eloise blushed.

"I rememba' when you were a little girl. Now look at you: all grown up."

Eloise smiled again as she searched for a reply.

"I live in Baltimore now. You eva' been to a city?" Isaac asked.

"Uh—no," Eloise stammered. She remembered seeing pictures in school of Chicago and New York and Philadelphia, but she had never thought seriously about anything beyond Kingstree.

"Baltimore's real nice. Got lots of colored people and things to do. You'd like it there," Isaac went on. "I didn't much think about livin' no where sides here till my friend Willie told me 'bout it."

Eloise nodded politely.

"I'm gonna be going back in a few days. I sho' wish I could take you with me."

Isaac's flirting made butterflies flutter in Eloise's belly.

"Maybe you'd be open to going out for a soda pop or somethin' befo' I go back to Baltimore," Isaac said, after a moment.

"Okay," she replied bashfully. "I'd like that."

The next day when Isaac showed up on Eloise's porch with two daisies that he had picked out of his mother's garden, Eloise smiled from ear to ear. No boy had ever courted her before, and it was clear that Isaac Bingham intended to court her, especially after he asked her father in the proper way.

Eloise was fascinated by Isaac's big dreams. She'd never known anyone who had been places like he'd been, and he dreamed of things she could not even fathom. He told her all about Baltimore and how he longed to save enough money to buy a house, "a big old house," he bragged. "One that have plenty of rooms—and a car, too. I always wanted to get me a car so I won't have to take no train or bus everywhere I go."

Isaac Bingham was different. Different than any boy Eloise had ever laid eyes on. And she liked him, liked him more than he could ever know.

· ◆ ·

Isaac sat alone in the last seat at the back of the Greyhound bus, across the aisle from a young man and woman. He noticed the man fondling the girl's legs and her pushing his hand away. When the girl caught Isaac watching them, he tried to shift away, but she looked right at him and smiled. Newlyweds, Isaac thought. His suspicion was confirmed when the man turned, leaned toward Isaac, and whispered, "This hea' is my wife. We jus' got married." Isaac smiled and nodded, then stared into the night through the darkened window. He could still see their reflections, so he closed his eyes and thought of Eloise and how he was missing her already as the bus slowly made its way out of the terminal and headed back to Baltimore.

The past few days had been the finest Isaac had experienced in a long time. Being home made him realize how much he missed family and the simpler things in life. Meeting Eloise had stirred up feelings inside of him that had been dormant for a long time. For the first time ever, he thought of what it would be like to have his own family. It brought newfound comfort to his soul and spirit.

The night flickered through the window as he nuzzled deeper into his seat, and his mind drifted to a dream about Eloise.

· ◆ ·

Over the next few months, Isaac and Eloise wrote to each other every week. By spring, Isaac had saved enough money to make a trip back to Kingstree to see Eloise. While there, he told her how much he had missed her and how he wanted to make a life with her. "Maybe we can marry and you can move back to Baltimore with me," he commented one evening while sitting on her porch.

"All my family is here, Isaac," she responded. "I don't know much 'bout livin' in no big city. I like it here. Maybe you can move back to Kingstree and we can have a life *here* together."

Isaac didn't put much stock in what Eloise proposed. Moving back to the South wasn't something he wanted to do. He had worked long and hard to make a life for himself in Baltimore. He'd been working with a local construction company since he arrived. And he was good at what he did. As a young boy, he was always fascinated with fixing things, and it didn't take long for others to notice how skilled he was with his hands. Even though he was a colored man, his boss treated him almost like an equal. He had come to depend on Isaac—asking his advice about almost everything. Isaac liked feeling important, and he liked the way his boss made him feel like a man, no matter his color. Just recently, his boss told him he'd been thinking about promoting him and would do so for sure if they won the new city construction contract that was to start soon. He didn't want to give it all up to move back to a place that held no future for him.

Isaac spent day and night thinking of ways to convince Eloise to marry and move up north with him. But every time he hinted at it in his letters to her, she'd write back that city life was no place for her.

In December 1941, six months after Isaac and Eloise met, the war began. Isaac thought about enlisting, but a leg injury he'd gotten at one of the construction sites prevented him from signing up.

Four weeks later, his boss approached him. "Isaac, I have something I need to talk to you about. Why don't you finish up here and come on into my office."

"Sure, boss," Isaac said. He reached down and picked up the final nail, holding it steady as he drilled it into the board. He checked the angle of the nails, making sure they were just right, then followed his boss to the office.

"I don't quite know how to tell you this. You been a hard worker from the day I hired you. Always on time. Always good work." Uncomfortable, the boss looked out the window at the other construction workers.

Isaac shifted on his bad leg. It always seemed to pain him when bad news was coming.

"You know the war done started, and many of our boys are thinking 'bout enlisting and some may even be drafted." He paused, looking Isaac straight in the eyes. "Well, there ain't no way around this, so I'm just gonna come on out with it." He took a deep breath. "I'm gonna have to let you go. With the war and all, we've been told to cut back. Besides which, the city decided not to go through with the contract."

Isaac felt a small surge of heat rising from his leg to his head. He just stared at the boss man. Not sure what to say or how to say it.

"I know. This comes as a surprise to me, too, but I've got no choice."

Isaac stared out the window at the other men, all of whom favored his boss, and he couldn't help but wonder if they'd gotten the same news. He forced himself to stand tall. *Always stand straight when you confrontin' another man,* he remembered his father saying. But somehow this advice didn't seem to leave the same impression as it did when he was a boy. Today, he couldn't help but let his shoulders slump as he walked out of his boss's office and gathered his things.

"You'll be all right," Willie told Isaac when Isaac showed up on his doorstep. "You'll land on your feet, just like you always do."

Isaac lowered his head and nodded.

"Hey, you know what this might mean?"

Isaac looked up at Willie, giving him an inquisitive look.

"Why don't you do what you been talkin' 'bout for the last few months?"

Isaac's eyes narrowed.

"You know, about marrying that girl you met. The one you always talkin' 'bout, the one you met at your aunt's funeral." Willie paused, letting Isaac gnaw on his thoughts. "You got no reason to stay in Baltimore now. Why don't you gon' back to Kingstree, marry her, and then y'all can move back here afta' you save up some money."

"I already done thought about that, but Eloise jus' don't want to move to no city."

Willie chuckled. "Well, she ain't gonna move nowhere with you if you don't marry her," he said. "You gotta go back there, marry her, and then you can talk to her about movin' back up here."

A smile broke across Isaac's lips. "Yeah, you right. That's what I need to do. I do love her. Love her more than any woman I eva' known."

"Speakin' of women," Willie said, scratching his head. "Maybe you should think about it before you bring her back to Baltimore. Afta' all, you wouldn't want to bring no new wife 'round all the women you done courted here."

Isaac gave Willie a thoughtful glance. "Yeah, I reckon' we can move to Philadelphia. I always liked Philadelphia. Hell, I'd been thinkin' 'bout makin' that my home anyway, afta' that contract ended. Now I got no reason not to do what I've been plannin'."

Less than two weeks later, Isaac sat on the Greyhound bus again, with the receipt for his one-way ticket to Kingstree clutched in the palm of his hand. He had spent the last month clearing out his ties to Baltimore and readying himself to return to Kingstree. He had written Eloise telling her about the recent developments, and her return letter indicated that she was thrilled about his decision to move back.

Isaac closed his eyes and leaned his head against the vinyl seat. He instinctively patted his coat pocket, which held a small tan box with a secondhand silver ring he'd bought with the last of his money, that very afternoon.

2

KINGSTREE, SOUTH CAROLINA: 1946

*E*loise lay in bed waiting for the sun to come up. The thought of moving to a place where she had no roots, a place that already felt foreign to her, was heavy on her mind. She kicked back the sheets. The room seemed still to her, even though she could hear the children playing outside her door. She looked out the window. A single tear rolled down her cheek. Isaac was loading the final bags into his brother's car. Anxious about their move, he had barely slept the past two days. It had all happened so fast. Isaac had wasted no time in asking for her hand in marriage. After they married, Deller, their first daughter, was born. Then, Isaac lost his job and they were forced to move in with Eloise's parents until he found a new one. Not long afterward, Eloise was carrying another child and then another. And now, after living together in Kingstree for five years, Isaac had returned home one evening and announced it was time for them to move.

Eloise gathered the children and dressed them. Then she got dressed and fixed breakfast. She wanted to support Isaac's decision to move, but she couldn't help but feel sad about leaving the only home she had ever known.

"Are you ready?" Isaac asked when he came back inside.

"Yes," she replied, looking around the small trailer as if taking a final mental snapshot and burying it in her mind's eye.

Their belongings were packed in old luggage and large brown paper bags. The trip with an infant and two small children would be long and difficult, but Isaac insisted the north would provide a better way of life for them. The children would get a better education, and he a better job.

"Tickets please. Final call for Philadelphia," the railroad agent called out as he took tickets from the boarding passengers. Eloise reluctantly released her mother's grasp, adjusting baby Lionel in her arms while Deller and Mattie clung to her skirt.

Affie worried about Eloise leaving Kingstree and moving to a place they couldn't even spell. There was all kind of crime and crooked people in them big cities—that's what her church friend Pearl had told her when they learned of Isaac's plans to move his family to Philadelphia.

"You know you always gon' have a home here if things don't work out," Affie said to her daughter.

Eloise nodded. Her eyes filled with tears as she pressed herself and her three small children into her mother's arms.

"Isaac's your husban' and you got to do right by him. You gon' and make the best of it. I know that the Lord gon' see to it that y'all gon' be okay."

"Okay, Mama," Eloise whispered.

"You take care of my grandbabies," Affie said.

"All aboard," the agent called out one last time. Isaac loaded the final packages as Eloise gathered the children and waved a final gesture to her mother before boarding the train.

"How long befo' we get there?" Eloise nervously asked Isaac after they settled into their seats.

"Bout sixteen hours."

Eloise sat next to a window, her head resting against the seat. Lionel lay snuggled in her arms. As the train pulled away from the station and picked up speed, Eloise gazed at the country zipping by and thought about all they were leaving behind. Large clouds began to flood the morning sky, turning gray as the sun slowly moved away. As the clouds thickened, Eloise settled into her seat. Her legs rocked slowly, lulling Lionel into a deep slumber. As she leaned her head back, closed her eyes, and let her thoughts rock along with the rhythm of the train, her mind brought her back to the time that Isaac had first struck her.

Not quite a year after they had married, Isaac came home one evening very angry. He'd learned that the mill—where he worked in the evenings to support his family and save for their move—was releasing many of the colored workers. "Well, maybe we don't have to move to Philadelphia," Eloise had told him, trying to relieve his worries. Isaac's eyes turned hard, and just as she was about to take back what she'd said, he slapped her with such force that it sent her tumbling to the floor.

"I'm sorry," Isaac said, rushing to her side. "I been workin' so hard to save the money we need to move, and this is gon' set us back, Eloise. I'll never touch you like that again. I promise."

Although she forgave him, Eloise had carried an unsettling feeling since then. Isaac had never hit her again, but now that she was leaving behind family, friends, and the only home she'd ever known, she couldn't help but wonder.

Isaac's voice jerked Eloise back from her thoughts. "Are you all right?" he asked, stirring in his seat.

Eloise stared blankly out the window. "Yes, I'm fine. I guess I'm just sad 'bout leavin' is all."

Isaac smiled at her, leaned his head back, and closed his eyes. He was numbed with weary. He had worked around the clock to save for their move. Now exhaustion held onto him so tight, he could barely muster up any excitement. Sleep hit him before he heard Eloise's lingering sighs.

Eloise looked over at Isaac softly snoring. Mattie lay across his lap while Deller snuggled under his arms. Eloise drew baby Lionel closer to her and smothered her thoughts in his scent. She closed her eyes and tucked away any further unpleasant feelings. Then she asked God to deliver them safely to their new home.

· ◆ ·

Eloise gaped out the taxi window, watching the city with its fast-moving cars and people. She marveled at quaint Philadelphia, with its miles and miles of paved roads, wide city streets, rows and rows of homes, clusters of people, and buses and trolley cars that cut from one end of the city to the other. The broad Schuykill River moved diagonally through the city, a large park sitting alongside its banks. Oversized bridges gave way to the city, while ferry boats darted across the waters. The driver slowed the car and stopped in front of a two-story brick rowhouse on a street with the strangest sounding name—Susquehanna. Eloise covered her mouth with her hand and gasped.

The house had been transformed into two apartments, and Isaac had rented the small three-room apartment on the top floor. It wasn't much, with its living room, small bedroom, kitchen with a burner stove, and bath, but Eloise would make do. She'd brought plenty of blankets and towels to create a makeshift bed for the children in the dainty living room.

As night fell, Isaac and his family settled into their new home. Between the giggles of Mattie and Deller, and the loud snoring coming from Isaac, Eloise strained to hear the unusual sounds of the city below.

3

After four years of living on Susquehanna Avenue, Isaac moved the family to a two-bedroom apartment on 15th and Diamond Streets, not far away. Eloise had given birth to two more children, and another was on the way. Isaac had to work two full-time jobs to support his family. And even then, they were barely making it.

Eloise was relieved that Isaac hadn't come straight home this evening, because now wasn't the time to tell him she'd missed her menstrual cycle. Her sister Maybelle had written to tell her that she'd dreamt about fish again. It seemed every time Isaac looked at her, she got caught, just like the fish in Maybelle's dreams. And every time she got caught, it drove a wedge between her and Isaac.

"I don't know why you keep this up," Isaac had said the last time she announced she was pregnant, with their fifth child—as if he had nothing to do with it. Eloise had turned away from the telltale disgust in his eyes. "I ain't move way up hea' to raise all these babies!" Then he stomped out of the room, leaving Eloise standing there with his words stuck in her heart.

Eloise lay down and closed her eyes, but sleep wouldn't come. She sat upright in bed. The sun had long since gone down, and a sliver moon peeked from the sky. She looked at the moon, trying to call up the years that had passed so quickly. She thought about how fast their life had changed and the pace at which Isaac was changing with it. Oftentimes he wouldn't come home at all, and when he did, he barely said two words to her and the children; the few words he did say weren't pleasant. The loving father who once played happily with his children now treated them like little soldiers. It was as if he was running some kind of boot camp and they were his subordinates. Eloise tried to talk with him about it, but he only ignored her. "Don't tell me how to raise my chi'ren," he would scold.

Isaac left work after his shift ended at 11 p.m. and headed straight to Lee's, a makeshift bar buried in the basement of Lee's three-story home on Broad and Dauphin Streets. It was a place where Isaac often went on weekends to bury his troubles in booze and his eyes in other women.

"Hey, Isaac, what brings you out tonight? I didn't expect to see you till Saturday," Lee said, when Isaac entered. He poured him a glass of corn whiskey, his usual.

Isaac took a seat. "I had to get out of the house tonight," he said, taking off his overcoat. "Seem no matter how hard I work to try to get ahead, something always set me back." He chugged the drink and slammed the glass down on the bar, an indication that he wanted Lee to pour him another.

In no time at all, Isaac had slammed the glass down at least six times before Lee told him it was time for him to go home to his family. Isaac put on his overcoat, stumbled out of the basement, and walked outside where the blistering cold air immediately revived his sense of direction. He swaggered home and stumbled into the living room, where Eloise sat waiting. She helped him to the bed and then put a pot of coffee on the stove. Isaac's next shift was less than four hours away, and considering the circumstances, he couldn't afford to lose another job.

Eloise let Isaac sleep for a couple of hours before she woke him. He stirred and shoved her away. "I ain't goin' nowhere," he gruffed before collapsing back into a deep sleep.

Eloise poked and pleaded, but Isaac wouldn't budge.

An hour later, Isaac got up and dragged himself into the bathroom. When he came out, grits and eggs awaited him. He stumbled into the kitchen and sat at the table, barely acknowledging Eloise as she poured coffee into him. After he stormed out the front door, Eloise went to their room to pray. She asked God to bring back the man she had fallen in love with and married nearly eight years ago. She wasn't sure what was happening to her husband, but she knew that whatever it was, it wasn't good.

Isaac returned home unexpectedly, much earlier than his usual time. The children were outside playing. When they saw their father walking up the street, they froze. Despite the fact that he had forbidden them to go outside when he was away from home, Eloise would often let them outdoors to play, warning the children to stay close by so that she could summon them in well ahead of Isaac's return.

Isaac ordered them inside. He slammed the door behind them and rushed to find Eloise in the kitchen. "What them chi'ren doin' outside?" he growled, grabbing her by the arm.

"They only been out there for a short while," Eloise winced, bracing herself.

Isaac released her arm and turned toward the children. "Y'all get on in that back room now! And I want every stitch of clothes removed."

Isaac stormed into his bedroom and fetched the thick leather belt that he kept hidden in his dresser drawer. The children listened to his footsteps, and when they saw the belt dangling at his side, they cried.

Isaac beat each one until fiery welts appeared on their backsides. Eloise could do nothing but watch helplessly. She was as afraid of him as her children were.

After Isaac beat the last child he turned the belt on Eloise, beating her as shamelessly and even more forcefully than he had the children. Once and for all, he wanted to make it known that his rules were not to be broken—that they all knew who was in charge. And he had made it unmistakably clear that it was he, and not Eloise.

4

$\mathcal{M}$attie felt the weight of her eldest sister's leg slung across her stomach, as the two younger girls lay entangled in the blanket, their limbs sprawled across each other. She awoke to the sun beaming on her face in the small room that she shared with her three sisters and three brothers. They all slept in two small beds—the girls in one, the boys in the other. The youngest, a year old, slept between Isaac and Eloise in the narrow bed they shared in the room across the hall.

Mattie pushed Deller's leg from the pit of her stomach, causing Deller to stir. She turned away from the sunlight to salvage a few final moments before the familiar sound of their mother's footsteps approaching their room marked morning. Instead, she was alarmed to hear the thunderous voice of her father—at it again—screaming at their mother for something Mattie couldn't quite make out because Isaac's anger obliterated reason.

She pulled the blanket over her head to silence him, but she could tell from the tone and depth of his voice that today would be a bad day, the kind when she was reminded that he was no longer their daddy. He was Isaac, with a capital *"I."* They no longer thought of him as the father who used to play with them, take them to see a picture show, and lead them in birthday song. Their *Daddy* had disappeared, replaced by this volatile, angry man.

When the loud voices were replaced by loud thumps, they all sat up in their beds and looked at the door, imagining what was happening to their mother on the other side.

After the last thumping ceased, the children heard the swift shuffle of Isaac's feet moving quickly up the stairs and toward their bedroom. The door flew open, and there he stood, in all his fury. "I smell pee way downstairs. Who done wet the bed this time?" he demanded, his anger gripping each child.

As if on cue, they all pointed to Rollie, the youngest son, just three years old.

"I tol' you the las' time, if any one of y'all wet this bed again, I was gon' see to it that it ain't gon' happen no mo',," he shouted across the room, looking at Rollie, but intending it for all of them. "Get dressed and get y'all asses downstairs now!"

While the children dressed, Isaac went to the rat-infested basement and checked one of the large traps he had set. It held the carcass of its victim. Isaac picked up the trap and walked slowly up the dark stairs, the rat's tail swinging alongside him.

Terror shadowed the children's small faces as Isaac came into the kitchen.

"Get over hea'!" he ordered.

The children eased their way closer to the kitchen table. Isaac removed the rat from the trap, skinned it, and sliced it down the middle. Blood dripped on the table and chair. The children watched, horrified, as he filled a cast iron skillet with lard and heated it, then put the skinned rat into the hot fat. He cooked the rat on both sides until the flesh shriveled and the skin became leathery and brown. He tossed the rat onto a plate and shoved it at Rollie.

"Eat it!" he said, daring Rollie to disobey.

Eloise and the other children looked aghast: in the silence, they could hear the rat's skin still sizzling.

"Isaac, no! Please Isaac, no!" Eloise pleaded.

Isaac turned from Rollie only long enough to warn Eloise.

Rollie cried helplessly; though he was too young to fully understand what was happening to him, he understood one thing—he had just watched his father skin the very thing that scared him as it scurried across the bedroom floor each night. The look in Isaac's eyes left no doubt as to what would happen should he disobey. Rollie picked up the rat and bit at its flesh.

The children sobbed; tears flowed down their cheeks and soaked into their clothing. Their eyes pleaded with Isaac, but each knew not to interfere or even speak. Eloise lowered her head and cried.

After Isaac left for work, Eloise went upstairs to her children, who had returned to their room. Rollie lay on the bed, crying. Foamy saliva and remnants of vomit still dripped from his mouth. Eloise held him and cried. The other children stood watching, crippled with grief.

"Mattie and Deller, y'all hurry up and get ready for school and help me get these hea' young'uns ready," Eloise mumbled. There was no need to say how sorry she was; her face conveyed more expressively than words.

The children came to the kitchen table to have their breakfast, but when Eloise put the plates before them, they stared with revulsion, their appetites lost. Today, she didn't lecture them about eating their meal. She just let them linger as long as they needed.

After the five elder children left and Eloise was alone with the three toddlers, she forced herself to try and recall when Isaac had become so evil, but no single incident or reason stood out. She fell to her knees and prayed for the day that her children would forgive her for lacking the nerve to stand up to him, the strength to protect them, and the courage to leave someday. Exhausted and still aching from the beating Isaac had given her before turning his rage on Rollie, she drifted into sleep.

Several hours passed before Eloise gained the strength to get up. When she awoke, Charlene, Paulene, and Rollie were huddled next to her, as though her body could protect them.

Charlene and Paulene, the one- and two-year-olds, didn't understand why their mother held them so close as she repeated, "I'm so sorry. I'm so sorry. I'm so sorry." But little Rollie knew. He understood that his mother wanted nothing more than to protect him from Isaac.

When Isaac returned home from work that evening, the children were already in their room. They had come home from school, done their homework and chores, eaten dinner, and hurried upstairs.

Mattie came downstairs to help her mother clean the kitchen. Isaac sat at the table, eyes buried in his plate.

"Gal, pass me the light bread," he snarled, without looking up at her.

"Yes, Daddy." Mattie fetched the bread out of the cupboard and handed it to him.

While he ate, Mattie snuck glances at him, searching for a hint of remorse, but it seemed that he had none. He sat at the table and ate as though nothing had occurred that morning, as though it were normal to force a three-year-old to eat a skinned rat that had been dead for who knows how long.

Mattie searched for a sign of regret, a hint of kindness. Nothing. She gazed closely to see if he looked disturbed; he did not. She tried to make her eyes penetrate his shirt, skin, and ribcage to see if he still had a heart: she couldn't tell.

Isaac finally stood, leaving his plate on the table so Mattie could clean up after him. He looked like a giant to her—a giant who had invaded their home. She finally got up enough nerve to ask the same question she always asked: "Daddy, are you done?" He ignored her and walked out of the kitchen.

Mattie went back upstairs. She glanced at her sisters and brothers to warn them that Isaac had returned.

"Is Isaac still mad?" little Rollie asked when Mattie shut the door behind her.

"I'ont know, he didn't say much. But he wasn't screamin' at Mama like he did this mornin'. I guess he ain't mad no more."

Rollie looked at Mattie innocently. "Can you help me go to the bathroom tonight so I don't wet the bed again?" he asked.

"Rollie, you're gonna have to learn to be a big boy. You know Isaac warned you before about wettin' that bed. You gotta stop drinkin' so much stuff before you go to bed. I'll help you, but you're gonna have to learn on your own, okay?"

"Yes, I'ma try harder," Rollie promised, blinking his eyes as though that would suddenly make him outgrow his problem.

That night as Mattie lay down, she tried to block out all that had happened that day. She had long known that things had changed, but it hadn't become fully real to her until she'd witnessed the evil in her father's eyes. She pulled the blanket over her face to shut out the glaring moonlight, wanting nothing more than to fall into a deep sleep and wake up to the father she'd had years ago.

The next morning, they arose to silence. No loud voices, no frightening thumps.

Mattie jumped up and immediately ran over to check the spot that Rollie had slept in. Dry. *Thank God!*

She and Deller were laying out clothing for the smaller children when they heard their mother's footsteps. This time, Eloise greeted them with her usual instructions: "Mattie and Deller, y'all hurry up and help me get these hea' young'uns ready."

They moved quickly. As they listened to Eloise return downstairs to the kitchen, they heard their father talking to her. The tone of his voice was even, the depth level. Today would be a good day.

5

It seemed like only yesterday that Eloise discovered she was pregnant with their first child, and now there were eight of them. By now, the family had outgrown the apartments and had moved several times, so Isaac worked three jobs to save enough money to buy a home not far from the first apartment they had rented. It was a brick-front, three-story, three-bedroom rowhouse on Boston Street: a quiet, middle-class neighborhood where many of the homeowners were white.

Isaac was proud to have been able to buy a home for his family in this neighborhood, although during the first year, he'd had to rent out the top floor to make the monthly payments. He didn't let that discourage him, knowing that eventually he would be able to afford the full payments on his own. After all, there weren't too many black families as large as his that could afford a home in a neighborhood as nice as this one.

Though it didn't have much furniture and needed painting, Eloise relished the idea that they had a home of their own. And while Isaac had changed over the years, he still saw to it that she and the children had a home, food on the table, and clothes on their backs—even if the clothes were from a thrift store and the children had to wear the same outfits for an entire week.

With each passing year, Isaac seemed to grow more distant and belligerent. It felt as though Eloise and the children awoke one day to realize the husband and father they had once known was gone. In his place was a man who held his family hostage for his perceived failures.

Isaac had come from a large family and understood the strife of growing up poor with barely enough food to sustain his family; still, he had begun to feel overwhelmed and suffocated by the responsibilities of caring for a large family. Every time he turned around, it seemed Eloise's belly was swelling with the next addition to the family.

• ❖ •

Word had just circulated around town that week: the Supreme Court had reached a unanimous decision in the case of Brown vs. the Board of Education, ruling in favor of the plaintiffs for the desegregation of schools across America.

When the media announced the court's decision on May 17, 1954, the local black churches had gotten together and arranged for a carnival in celebration. Families across the city were planning to attend. Isaac had even decided to take his family. He returned home one afternoon and told Eloise to get the children ready.

Mattie ran upstairs to tell the others the good news. "Y'all get ready," she shouted excitedly. "Daddy said he's gonna take us to the carnival."

They had never been to a carnival but had heard all about it from friends at school. And when they heard their daddy was going to take them, they were elated. They couldn't wait for him to come home.

"What are you gonna wear?" Deller asked Mattie, as she fumbled through the few items of clothing in her dresser drawer.

"I'm not sure, but Mama said we should wear somethin' real nice so we don't embarrass Daddy."

The children dressed hurriedly, ran downstairs, and waited for their father to return from his errand.

"Deller, take Rollie upstairs and find somethin' mo' decent for him to put on. I declare that boy done thrown on anything," Eloise proclaimed.

Little Rollie was confused; he thought he looked pretty darn good, given that he'd gotten dressed all by himself for a change.

"Lionel, run on upstairs and get me my hair brush, and bring the Vaseline jelly so I can clean the ash off y'all faces."

"Yes, ma'am," he replied, leaping up the stairs like he was going to find gold.

While Deller changed Rollie, Mattie helped the girls dress and Eloise brushed the boys' hair and greased their faces with petroleum jelly. When they were all ready, Eloise inspected each of them. "Y'all sit still till Isaac return," she told them.

She had even put on a nice dress, run the hot comb through her hair, and dabbed on a bit of rouge and lipstick. She wanted Isaac to be proud of how nice his family looked.

They all sat tentatively in the living room, patiently awaiting Isaac. After an hour had passed, Eloise went to the door to see if he was coming up the street. She looked out and when there was no Isaac, she worried. He had said he only needed to run a quick errand. He should have long since returned, she thought.

As the hour turned into two and then three, their excitement began to fade. Eloise stood in the vestibule, willing Isaac to come through the door. There was an unaccustomed stillness in their home, as though they thought being quiet would bring their father home. But when the sun began to set and the sky went gray, the smaller children began to cry.

Finally, Eloise relented. "Y'all chi'ren gon' upstairs and change outta your good clothes. Mattie and Deller, y'all hurry up and help me get dinner ready for these hea' young'uns," she said, as though they hadn't been waiting for four hours.

•◆•

Summer, fall, and winter had come and gone and not much had changed. The children were staying out of Isaac's way and he out of theirs. The carnival incident was never discussed—Eloise never asked, and Isaac never told.

Though the children never questioned or openly defied Isaac, they began to talk among themselves about him. Deller and Mattie were old enough to know there was definitely something weird about their family, but neither dared to speak openly about it or even acknowledge it. Lionel, the eldest boy, had just turned nine and was beginning to resent his father. Lionel had been around enough friends to know that something was lacking with the relationship he and his brothers had with Isaac.

Mattie and Deller had come to suspect their mother resented him as well, but she had never said a bad word about their father, at least not in front of them. Eloise was loyal to Isaac no matter how badly he treated them. He'd shown her no more kindness than he had shown them, so when he decided to take her with him on one of his outings, they were suspicious.

Isaac had come home one Friday evening and told Eloise to get dressed—he was taking her to a party. Eloise was thrilled. *Maybe,* she thought, *he tryin' to be nice to me for a change.* She pressed her hair and washed and ironed a dress she'd bought at the thrift store. She even borrowed a pair of shoes from her friend, Lill, who lived on the same block.

"Mama, I found an old necklace in your jewelry box that would look nice with your dress," Mattie said. She wrapped the necklace around her mother's neck and fastened it from the back. She and Deller stood on either side of their mother, and they all stared in the mirror, marveling at how beautiful she looked.

"Come on woman befo' you make us late," Isaac yelled up the stairs. When Eloise finally came down, Isaac peered at her as though something were wrong. "Hurry up and get yo' coat," was all he said to her.

As soon as they arrived at the party, the other women just stared at Eloise. They couldn't believe Isaac had finally brought her along. Eloise was unsure whether they were staring because of her or because of Isaac. She sensed that Isaac probably fancied many of the women there.

"Hello, Eloise. You may not remembа' me, but I used to work with Isaac at the hospital befo' they laid us off," a man said, holding out his hand to greet her.

Eloise was nervous because Isaac never brought her around his friends, nor did he allow her to venture out on her own, except to attend an occasional church event—and even that was rare. "How you doin' suh. I'm not sure I remembа' your name." She fidgeted with an imaginary crease in her dress.

"Oh, I'm sorry. My name is Albert. That there is my wife, Cora," Albert said, pointing his finger at a young, beige-skinned woman with big eyes. "It's her birthday and I told Isaac that he needed to bring you around us sometime. How your young'uns doin'?"

"They all doin' jus' fine. Growin' up real fast. Our eldest girl turned thirteen the month befo' last."

"Well it's nice seein' you again. You enjoy ya'self, and be sure to fix a plate. My wife made all the food he'self."

Eloise felt relieved when Albert finally released her hand and walked away to greet the other guests. She felt odd and out of place, and it didn't help that Isaac had abandoned her as soon as they had arrived.

Eloise was sitting in the same chair peering out the window, when Isaac came to find her and told her to join them in the kitchen.

The men were seated at the table, playing cards, while their women looked on. Eloise followed Isaac to the one vacant chair that she surmised had to be his. He sat down, still wearing his black-brimmed hat, a Marlboro cigarette dangling from his lips. A glass of corn whiskey sat to his left and a can of beer to his right. A stack of bills lay in the center.

"Looka hea' y'all. This my wife, Eloise," he said in the same breath that he asked the dealer for another card. Eloise just nodded, feeling foolish just standing behind Isaac like a lifeless plant that wanted to avoid the heat. She watched Isaac transform as he guzzled down the corn whiskey. Each time he slapped down the empty glass, someone would pour him another drink. She knew that it was going to be a long night.

After a while, Eloise felt like her legs were going to give out from standing so long. Just when she decided to seek refuge, Isaac suddenly leapt from his chair and grabbed her by the arms. "Y'all wanna see somethin' real pathetic?" he boasted, tightening his grip. He tore at Eloise's dress, stuffed his hand down her bra, and pulled out the socks that had given the dress its form. Eloise struggled to release herself from his hold, but it was too late—her shame had been exposed. A few laughed nervously, while others looked away; there was no humor in the way Isaac had humiliated his wife.

Hearing the ruckus, Albert rushed into the room. Seeing Eloise huddled on the floor, holding the dress together and crying like a child, he went to her. "Damn you, Isaac," he said. Then he escorted Eloise from the kitchen. "You want me to take you home?" he asked her.

"No, I'm fine," Eloise said, as she grabbed her coat and left. She knew that Isaac would beat her for leaving without him, but she didn't care. This would be one beating she would surrender to because what she had just endured was far greater than any pain he could inflict.

The children hesitated when they heard the door slam and their mother's cries. Deller and Mattie went to her. Lionel, Walton, and Leona followed.

Eloise sat crying in the dark living room, her dress torn and the necklace missing from around her neck.

"Mama, are you all right?" Mattie asked, her voice quivering.

Looking up, Eloise was surprised to see the children standing there. "I'm fine." She sat up, pulling the torn dress over her bra. "What y'all chi'ren doing up so late? Y'all gon' back up to bed."

Deller and Mattie lay with their backs to each other. Deller cried into her pillow and prayed for the day that she would be able to leave home. Mattie cried and prayed for the man that had sung to her on her birthday.

Eloise froze as soon as she heard the key in the lock. She lay there on the sofa, not breathing, the air trapped in her chest. Not even noticing her, Isaac stumbled up the stairs and collapsed on the bed, too drunk that night to harm anyone.

The only thing that held Eloise together was prayer. She moved through the days like a zombie, her emotional and physical strength depleted. She had barely enough energy to mother her children, and lacked even that at times. Having given up hope that Isaac would change, she lectured the children about trying harder to mind him and encouraged them to stay out of his way. She even considered working, as a way to contribute and to relieve some of the pressure from him.

She had heard that a farm in New Jersey was looking for berry pickers, and she talked to Isaac about it. At first, Isaac wouldn't hear of it, but eventually, he agreed to allow her to work on the weekends. He saw it as a way to minimize his financial burdens. She saw it as a way to get out of the house and away from him. If contributing to the family responsibilities might lessen his hostility, she would work seven days a week if she could.

• ◆ •

On a muggy, overcast Saturday morning, Eloise walked to her sister Ava's house to ride with her to the farm. The dampness in the air promised rain, but still she pushed on. Maybe the gray clouds would fade, and the day would not be lost. They could use the few dollars she would earn at the end of each picking. Deller had just turned fourteen, and Mattie was twelve. They were now old enough to tend to the household chores and the younger children.

Once Isaac had left for his second job, soon after Eloise's departure, the girls got started with their housework. Each of the children was given a task, even Paulene and Charlene, who were three and four. They worked diligently to finish as quickly as they could so that they could get outside to play. They were only allowed to play on the block, but that was better than nothing at all.

Mattie had gone inside for a minute, when suddenly she heard a loud noise. She ran to the door to see what had happened. "What done happened?" she asked, perplexed.

"Lionel and Walton done thrown a rock and broke Miss Ella's window," Deller blurted.

Miss Ella came running outside. "Looka what y'all done. I'm gonna tell Isaac!"

"We sorry," Lionel offered. "We didn't mean it."

"Sorreee, sorreee. Sorreee didn't break my window, now did it?" Miss Ella said and sashayed back inside.

Mattie and Deller knocked on Miss Ella's door. It flung

open, and big ole Miss Ella peered at them over her wide-rimmed glasses.

"We wanna pay for your window, Miss Ella," Mattie said. "The boys are really sorry," Deller added.

"Maybe if we gave you all of our lunch money, you won't have to tell our father," Mattie stuttered.

Miss Ella stood there, her thick arms wrapped into each other, her face poker straight. "You chi'ren should know better than to throw rocks at people's windows. I'm gonna tell Isaac the minute he return."

Realizing that Miss Ella would not budge, Mattie and Deller beckoned the boys inside, where they all sat patiently awaiting Isaac.

As soon as the children heard the pace of Isaac's footsteps the moment he closed the door behind him, they knew that Miss Ella had already gotten to him.

He barged into the room. "Get them clothes off by the time I get back hea'." His voice had that familiar tone that meant, *If you heathens don't learn, then I'll beat it outta you till you do.*

The children stripped naked as soon as Isaac left the room. Deller and Mattie were embarrassed at having to reveal their adolescent bodies.

Moments later, Isaac returned and beat each child, youngest to oldest. He made them kneel down and put their heads between his legs and their hands clamped against their backsides. He lashed the belt until blood flowed from their skin.

After the beating, Mattie put her clothes back on and ran out the front door. Tears streamed down her swollen cheeks, and blood dripped from her arms and legs as she sat on the steps for all the neighbors to see.

Eloise heard the children's cries the instant she stepped through the front door. She rushed to their bedroom and then hurried to the bathroom, filling the basin with warm water and peroxide to wash their battered skin.

The children cried harder as the bubbling peroxide turned pink and their wounds began to sting.

Eloise sobbed, trying to steady her shaking hands so she wouldn't hurt the tender wounds.

Mattie wept, because she knew that she felt something she had never felt before—hatred. Hatred for the man she knew as her father.

Hatred for Isaac.

6

*B*eing thirteen spawned a whole new outlook for Mattie. Her idea that the man living in their home was a surrogate for her *real* daddy had been replaced with a more accurate view: Isaac was her father and there was no changing that fact, or him. It seemed the older she got, the stricter and meaner Isaac became. He was especially so with the girls, because he knew how boys could prey on girls—above all, ones as attractive as his.

It wasn't easy being thirteen and living under the same roof as Isaac. Mattie had come to learn how to stay out of his way and keep out of his reach. She and her siblings had made a pact to do whatever it took to please their father. They walked cautiously through their lives like dancers on a tightrope—always keeping their steps straight, never straying away from the line.

Mattie had grown into a beautiful girl. Her butterscotch skin, innocent eyes, sharp cheekbones, and the black mole that sat at the tip of her smile made her uncomfortable with her beauty. On top of that, she was extremely shy and timid, just like her mother. The other children were equally shy and timid, with the same good looks. They often stayed to themselves, because Isaac wouldn't allow them to play with other children. Most didn't want to play with them anyhow, because they were so different in the way they dressed and because of their strange father.

One wintry Saturday while the boys played in the cellar, they came upon Isaac's Prince Albert Tobacco can, where he stored the money from his weekly paychecks he cashed at a check-cashing service. Isaac was sure that white people found ways to steal from coloreds whenever they could, and since only white folks worked at the local banks, he didn't trust them with his hard-earned pay. Every week, he preferred to pay the five percent service charge in exchange for being his own bank: an old tobacco can stored in a rat-infested basement where he counted every penny before he deposited it.

Isaac had no formal education, but he did have one important self-taught skill—how to add, subtract, roll, and wrap his money in a handkerchief and store it in *his* bank. He maintained deposits and withdrawals, the equivalent of receipts, in his head.

The next Friday after the boys had discovered the can, Isaac went downstairs to his bank to deposit his latest earnings. He noticed the can wasn't exactly in the position he had last left it. He always secured his bank by turning the can at an angle so he could detect if anyone had been messing with his stash. This week, the can tilted slightly more to the right than usual. He suspected that someone had robbed his bank, and his suspicion was confirmed when he meticulously counted every dime. Exactly three dollars and eighty-six cents was missing.

Isaac bolted up the basement stairs, leaping the steps two by two, and headed straight for Eloise in the kitchen. "You been messin' with my money, woman?" he asked, daring her to say that she had.

"Wha'choo talkin' bout? I ain't messed with nobody's money."

"Somebody done messed with my stash, and I'm gon' find out who." Isaac stormed over to the stairs. "I want y'all down hea' right now," he yelled.

The children filed down the stairs, in order of size.

"Now I'm only gon' ask one time, and one time only." His hard eyes locked on the children. "Which one of y'all heathens done messed with my money?"

Without warning, they all began to cry. They knew that no matter who had done it, each one of them would be punished.

"Wee . . . wee . . . wee found the money while wee was playin' in the cel-la," Lionel confessed, staring at Isaac's shoes.

Isaac gave him a scowling look. "Boy, you mean to tell me that you found somethin' you know don't belon' to you?"

Lionel's lips quivered, along with his body. "We ain't tried to take nuttin' from you, Daddy. We thought we had found it."

"Isaac, I'll put every cent of your money back when I get paid next week," Eloise offered.

Isaac's eyes darted toward her. "I don't want your damn money, woman!" He turned back to the children. "Get downstairs now!" He jabbed his stiff finger at the basement door.

The dark, dank basement had one bright lightbulb that hung in its center. They stood in silence, sobbing, their eyes glued to the cement walls. Eloise avoided looking at her children, knowing their eyes would plea with her to stop Isaac. But she didn't have the strength. She was as afraid as they were. And she knew that Isaac would teach them a lesson, because there were two things that he did not tolerate: someone trying to cheat him and someone messing with his money.

As soon as they heard Isaac's heavy footsteps coming down the basement stairs, they all started to strip.

"You gals don't need to take off your clothes. But I want every last stitch off of you," he gestured the belt in the direction of Lionel, Walton, and Rollie.

Once stripped, Isaac grabbed Lionel and pushed him to his knees, then forced Lionel's head between his legs and grabbed hold of the clenched hands behind his back. He wrapped the end of the belt around his right hand and, with the buckle dangling, he lashed it against Lionel's backside. The sound of the buckle hitting flesh nauseated Eloise. Lionel screamed and wiggled to free himself, but Isaac's legs locked around his neck prevented it.

Eloise flinched at every lash, feeling the pain that Lionel endured. After several lashes, when Lionel's body went limp and he no longer cried, Isaac finally released him, letting his bloodied body fall to the cold cement floor.

Isaac moved his rage to Walton and then little Rollie.

Only a vicious, heartless person could inflict that kind of pain on small children, Eloise thought. She had long since stopped loving Isaac, but that night, she detested him.

After everyone had gone to bed, Eloise did as she had always done, the only thing she knew how to do—she got down on her knees and prayed. She begged God to forgive Isaac. "For he know not what he do, Lord," she prayed. "And forgive me, Lord, for hatin' the man that gave me these young'uns."

In the days that followed, Mattie had trouble even looking at her father. She knew that he was evil but never thought him capable of what he had done to her brothers. Every time she was around Isaac, she was jittery, just wanting to do the right thing to avoid his rage.

"Why are you crying?" Deller asked Mattie one evening when they were alone in their bedroom. "Are you all right?"

"No," Mattie responded. She looked down at her intertwined hands.

"I hate livin' in this house with him, under the same roof. I can't wait to leave," Deller confided.

Mattie wiped one side of her face with the back of her hand. "Do you think Daddy hates us?" she asked.

"How could he not? He don't even treat us like we his children anymore. He beat on us for no reason. He acts like he don't want us."

Mattie stared out the window. "I remember the time when he sat me on his lap and sang happy birthday to me. I was six years old," she said, a wide smile breaking over her face. "Do you remember?"

"Not really," said Deller.

Then Mattie whispered a question that had circled her mind a thousand times. "Do you think Mama would ever leave him?"

"I'ont know. I hope so."

Mattie lay down on her side, arms overlapping her chest, trying to still herself so she could fall asleep without thinking and worrying. Deller went to the other side of the bed and lay down next to her.

Sleep fell upon them, and they escaped to their private dreams.

• ◆ •

Away from the Bingham household, Mattie adjusted to junior high. She tried to fit in and appear normal. Although she couldn't change some things, there was one thing she could change: what people thought about her family. The less they knew, the less they could think anything. So she harbored her family's dark secret from teachers and friends.

Mattie and her siblings came home from school each day, did their homework and chores, had dinner, and then went to their rooms, out of Isaac's way. Every now and again, Isaac would call the children downstairs and talk to them, about nothing much really. It was like he was reaching out, trying to connect with them somehow, but he had already lost their trust.

By Thanksgiving, things had gotten no better.

One evening, Isaac returned home in a drunken stupor. Eloise and the children were eating Thanksgiving leftovers at the dinner table.

"You been messin' round with them men on that farm," Isaac accused, swaggering in his stance.

Eloise ignored him, hoping that silence would quiet his wrath. Isaac pulled up a chair to sit down and nearly missed the seat. His arms flailed, practically knocking Deller out of her chair.

"Y'all chi'ren gon' upstairs," Eloise said. The children moved slowly, reluctant to leave the kitchen.

"You think I didn't know, didn't you?" Isaac said, his words partially incoherent. "Well, I do! And I'ma teach you not to cheat on me."

As soon as Isaac threw the first blow, Eloise ducked and ran for the stairs. By the time she reached the landing, Isaac had caught up to her. She tried to fight back, but she was no match for his strength.

The children sat still in their rooms listening, and when they heard a cry come from their mother that they'd never heard before, they ran to her. Lionel and Walton were the first to grab their father when they saw him trying to throw Eloise down the stairs. Then Deller and Mattie joined in. Mattie grabbed hold of her mother to keep her from falling. Deller jumped on her father's back, wrapped her arms around his neck, and dug her long nails into him, drawing blood.

"I'm gon' kill you all," Isaac promised, as he released Eloise and grabbed hold of his neck, searching for the wound.

Eloise quickly collected the children and sought refuge in the basement.

Waiting for Isaac to make good on his threat, they sat quietly in the dark, their breath—the cool air that blew from them—was the only thing they heard.

Half an hour later, when Isaac hadn't appeared, they knew that something about this night was different. In the cool, damp silence and the thickness of their fear, a small sense of victory shadowed them.

Isaac awoke the next morning to a dry mouth, pounding head, and empty thoughts. It wasn't until he felt the moisture on his neck that he vaguely remembered what had happened. He jumped up and ran downstairs.

"Which one of y'all cut me last night?" he asked, his right hand shrouding the wound.

Eloise and the children sat quietly at the kitchen table having their breakfast. No one looked up.

"Ain't nobody cut you," Eloise retorted, a sliver of courage sitting in the creases of her face.

Isaac squinted and glared at each of them. Deller fidgeted in her seat. He glared at her until he remembered that she was the one who had the gall to jump him from behind and use her nails like a weapon.

As soon as Deller saw the evil in her father's eyes, she ran, dodging right past him and out the front door.

"I'm gon' kill you, gal," he barked after her.

Deller ran with just her adrenaline carrying her until she came to her friend Sandra's house. Mrs. Womack, Sandra's mother, opened the door.

"Can I please come and live with y'all?" Deller blurted, practically out of breath.

"Deller, what in heaven's name are you doing out here with no coat on in this cold weather?" Mrs. Womack asked.

"Sorry, ma'am," Deller said. She slowly moved inside, shivering and embarrassed.

"Are you all right?"

"Yes, ma'am."

"Well, what on God's earth happened to you then?"

Deller lifted her chin, and her eyes teared up. "My daddy chased me out the house. He said he gon' kill me."

Mrs. Womack stared at Deller. "Well, you come on in here for a while. Go on in the kitchen with Sandra and fix yourself something to eat."

When darkness fell, Mrs. Womack told Deller that she needed to be getting back home. "Sandra will lend you one of her coats," she offered kindly.

Deller's legs felt like lead as she slowly made her way back home. As soon as she opened the door and turned the corner of the vestibule, she saw Isaac sitting in the living room, the belt in his lap. The other children were sitting with him, as he had instructed.

"Strip!" he ordered.

"Daddy, please don't make me do this in front of them," Deller pleaded. "I'll take the beating, just please don't do this in front of the boys."

The boys beckoned to leave the room.

"Y'all stay right hea'," Isaac snapped, wanting to humiliate her the same way she had humiliated him when she tore her nails through his neck, leaving a scar to carry to his grave.

"I said strip now, or I'ma rip them damn clothes off of you, gal."

Deller slowly removed her clothing, including her bra and panties. She sobbed, imagining she was inside one of her dreams.

She cried not because of the pain, and not even because of how humiliated she felt, but because she knew that she had to find a way to leave that house.

She had to find a way to get out from under Isaac.

•—•—•

Deller and Mattie stood at the mirror and giggled as they applied a small amount of their mother's red rouge to their cheeks. They hurried to put on the simple dresses that hung in their closets. They wanted to leave for the dance before their father had a change of heart. It was Deller's first high school dance, and her father had given her permission to go, but only if she took Mattie along.

"Mama, we're leaving," Deller called out to the kitchen, as she and Mattie rushed to the door.

"Y'all wait a minute. Let me see y'all befo' you go," Eloise said, scurrying from the kitchen and wiping her hands on her apron.

Mattie and Deller smiled as their mother looked them over.

"Well y'all sho' look pretty," Eloise said.

"Thanks, Mama," Mattie replied.

"Y'all gon' and have a good time. Rememba' what your father said. You need to be home by nine."

"Yes, ma'am."

Mattie and Deller barged out the door as soon as they heard their father's footsteps clomping down the stairs.

Shortly after Deller and Mattie arrived at the school dance, Deller noticed a boy staring at her. At some point, she looked up and smiled at him, giving him the nerve to walk over to her.

"Hi, my name is Ben. Would you like to dance?"

"Yes," Deller blurted.

Deller and Ben danced every song while Mattie sat nearby watching them. Ben told Deller all about himself: he was eighteen, a senior in high school, and he had plans to join the army right after graduation.

Deller told Ben only the things she wanted him to know: she was sixteen, had seven sisters and brothers, and they lived on Boston Street. During a break, they joined Mattie, and when it came time for Deller and Mattie to leave, Ben asked if he could walk them home.

"No, our father don't allow us to talk to boys," Mattie and Deller told him straight out. But Ben wouldn't take no for an answer. He walked them to within a block of their home.

"I'm gonna come to your house on Sunday and ask your father's permission to court you," he told Deller before they said goodbye.

Silently, Deller hoped that he'd keep his promise.

The following Sunday, Ben showed up at the Binghams', dressed in his Sunday best. Isaac opened the door and scowled at the stranger.

"Suh, my name is Ben, and I was wond'rin if I can come an' visit with Deller on Sundays. I will be leavin' for the army in July, and I would like to spend time with her before I go," he said.

"How you know Deller?" Isaac asked, curious to know if Deller had been sneaking around with boys.

"I met her at the dance last Saturday, and she told me that she wasn't allowed to talk to no boys. So I thought I'd come and ask your permission, suh."

Isaac looked Ben up and down, doused the cigarette that he'd been smoking, and said, "Well, I reckon you comin' on Sundays won't do no harm. I guess Deller old enough now to take boy company."

The next Sunday when Ben came for his first formal visit with Deller, Isaac greeted him again and showed him to the sofa in the living room. He then sat dead across from them, glaring at Ben the whole time.

In early July, Ben received his orders and was being shipped to New York City for basic training. He promised Deller that as soon as he completed his training he would return to ask her parents if they could marry. Ben knew the odds were against him, because Deller was only sixteen and a junior in high school.

They wrote each other for six months straight until Ben's request to take a leave was granted. He returned home to do what he had thought about every day while he was gone. He had learned a lot during those six months, and the most rewarding lesson was how to confront another man.

On the following Sunday, Ben arrived at the Binghams' at one o'clock sharp, suited in his army uniform, to ask for Deller's hand in marriage. Eloise said yes. Isaac flat out said no.

"It'll be a wintry day in hell, boy, fo' I let my daughter quit school to marry you," Isaac had snapped. Then he stood and threw Ben out of the house. Deller was heartbroken.

Over the next several days, Eloise talked to Isaac about it. Even though Deller wouldn't finish high school, it was a chance for their eldest daughter to marry, she told him, and it would be one less mouth for him to feed. And being that Ben was a serviceman, Deller would be well provided for, and she'd get to go places she'd never been before.

At first, Isaac wouldn't hear of it. But finally, he gave in.

A few weeks later, a justice of the peace married Deller and Ben. Ben's parents attended. Eloise and the children did, too. Isaac stayed home.

The next morning when Deller returned home to pack her belongings and say goodbye to her family, Isaac refused to speak to her. *How dare she think that I would even think about sending her off,* he thought. *Shoot, she better be glad I didn't break her neck for taking the stuff my hard earned money paid for.*

• ◆ •

The eighth-grade graduation ceremony was the talk of the school. Mattie and the other eighth graders were excited about graduating from Gillespie Middle School. The boys talked about who they would take to the graduation dance. The girls boasted about more important matters, like the dress they'd wear and the matching shoes. Everyone bragged about how exciting graduation day would be, with their families in the audience watching them march down the aisle in their fancy outfits.

Mattie returned home one afternoon with a graduation flyer, excited to share the upcoming festivities with her mother. The previous year had been difficult with Deller gone, but she had made a new friend, Ruth. She and Ruth had already talked about the dream dresses they would wear.

Eloise was preparing dinner when Mattie walked in and handed her the flyer. "Mama, this is the information for my graduation. Can I get a new dress to wear?" she asked, her voice filled with anticipation.

Eloise wiped the flour from her hands and took the paper from her. "You gon' have to ask Isaac," she said and handed it back to Mattie.

As soon as Isaac came home that evening, Mattie nervously showed him the flyer. "Daddy, this is for my eighth-grade graduation, and I was wond'rin if I can get a new dress to wear to it."

Isaac grabbed the paper and looked at it, then threw it on the table. "The way I see it, you got two choices, gal," he said, his voice level. "You can either wear one of them dresses you already got, or stay home." Then he turned and walked away.

Mattie's heart sank. She didn't have a proper dress, not to mention matching shoes, so she chose to stay home.

On graduation day, Mattie sat silently in her room and promised she would never forgive her father. Someday, when she was old enough and had the courage to stand up to him, she would tell him how he had denied her so many childhood memories that other families got to cherish. She'd let him know exactly the kind of malicious father he was, when all she ever wanted was for him to be proud of her and love her.

While she sat in that room, cloaked in sorrow and despair, Mattie bravely wiped away her tears, tucked her emotions deep inside her, and wondered how she would ever survive her father.

7

$\mathcal{W}$illiam Penn was one of the few all girls' high
schools in Philadelphia. Mattie found it strange going to a
school with all girls, but at least she wouldn't have to worry
about odd glances like the ones she often got from the boys
in junior high.

Besides, Ruth was also attending William Penn, and
they had become very close. They had done just about
everything together, except share in the junior high graduation. Ruth wondered why Mattie hadn't shown up, but
Mattie just said she had been ill. She was too embarrassed to
tell the truth, because in Mattie's eyes, Ruth's family was a
real family—the kind she often dreamed of having. She
went out of her way to hide her family from Ruth, and for a
while everything seemed to be going well. That is, until one
ill-fated Saturday afternoon, when Mattie decided to go to

Ruth's house for a visit. It was about four weeks after they started William Penn.

Ruth, Mattie, and their friend Barbara had spent the afternoon in Ruth's bedroom trying on Ruth's new clothes and talking about boys. Mattie hadn't been there more than two hours when Ruth and Barbara agreed to walk her home, and she invited them in.

"Gal, where you been," Isaac said, as soon as they entered. He sat on the sofa, the all-too-familiar belt in hand.

"Mama said I could go out after I completed my chores, and I only went to Ruth's house for a little while." The words tumbled quickly out of Mattie's mouth, as though speaking fast would deter her father.

Isaac called Eloise into the living room. "Beat her!" He shoved the belt at Eloise.

Eloise refused. She would much rather take a beating than beat one of her children the way he did.

The more Eloise refused, the angrier Isaac became. Mattie's knees began to buckle. She knew that her mother's defiance would only make it worse for her.

"Strip!" Isaac said.

Mattie's whole body began to shake. Surely, her father didn't expect her to strip naked in front of her friends. She had never confided in them about the things that happened in their home, and she certainly didn't want them to find out like this.

"Daddy, please. Please! Not like this," Mattie pleaded. Her eyes shifted from Isaac to Barbara to Ruth, and then back to Isaac.

"Strip!" Isaac shouted again.

Eloise lowered her head and left the room.

As Mattie slowly began to remove her clothing, Ruth was suddenly reminded of all the times Mattie had come to school with bruises on her arms and legs. It all became clear to her now. And if Mattie's father was going to beat her naked in front of them, she could only imagine what he had done to her in private.

Once stripped, Mattie knelt down before her father. Isaac whacked the belt against her bare flesh. As the blood began to flow, Ruth and Barbara began to cry; they had never seen anything in their young lives as evil as what they were seeing now.

Moments later, Isaac released Mattie and turned to Ruth and Barbara. "Get the hell outta my house," he barked.

Their legs felt like bricks as they slowly walked toward the door. As much as they wanted to stay and console Mattie, the look in Isaac's eyes suggested otherwise.

Mattie stayed in her room all day on Sunday and worried about how her friends would respond to her at school the next day. She was so ashamed about what had happened that she considered packing a small bag and running as far away as she could, but she had nowhere to run. Besides, if Isaac ever found her, and she knew that he would, the consequences would be far worse. So she put those thoughts out of her mind and wondered what she would say to Ruth when she saw her. She cried over the idea of having to tell Ruth that her father had beaten her like this ever since she could remember. She cringed at the thought of having to reveal her family's secrets.

On Monday, Ruth joined Mattie at her locker. The look on Ruth's face was enough for Mattie to know that she was just as embarrassed and ashamed about what had happened as she was. Ruth's expression conveyed a consoling warmth, which told Mattie that everything would be okay. Mattie's eyes filled with tears, silently thanking Ruth for her understanding.

No words were exchanged, but they both knew in their hearts they shared a terrible secret that would forever underscore their friendship.

• ◆ •

A few weeks after Isaac had shamelessly beaten Mattie in front of her friends, Deller and Ben arrived for a visit. They were now the proud parents of a new baby girl.

Since getting married, Deller had written to her mother but didn't dare come home because she worried Isaac was still very angry with her. She missed her family and wanted them to meet their new addition.

Eloise's face lit up the moment she took her first grandbaby in her arms. Isaac barely spoke.

That first night, Deller and Mattie went upstairs and talked for hours. Deller told Mattie all about New York City and how she and Ben had their own small apartment. Mattie told Deller about Isaac beating her in front of her friends. Deller cried, imagining how painful that must have been for Mattie. It was bad enough to endure the beatings, but to suffer it in front of friends was unspeakable.

Isaac's hard voice cut a seam right through Deller and Mattie's discussion. They could tell by his tone that something terrible must have happened. Holding their breath, they rushed downstairs.

"Boy, you done broke my set. Who tol' you to touch it?" Isaac growled, standing over the thirteen-inch, black-and-white TV set. He wiggled the loose wire coat hanger that served as its antenna.

Isaac had recently purchased the used TV from a local thrift store, and although the picture was static and the sound barely audible, he thought it worked just fine until Ben tried to fix it.

Ben was a pretty darn good handyman; at least that's what Deller had told him. He didn't understand why Isaac was so upset, acting as though someone had killed his firstborn.

"You must be stupid boy to make the set worse off than what it was," Isaac ranted. "Do you know how much money that set cost me? Now you've really messed it up."

"I apologize for messin' with your TV, suh, but I'm not gonna stand for you to speak to me that way," Ben asserted.

"You just plain dumb, boy," Isaac continued.

"I said I'm not gonna stand for you to speak to me like that," Ben repeated. "You owe me an apology."

Isaac gave him a hard stare. "It'll be a cold day in hell befo' I apologize to your stupid ass. Matta fact, I want you, your wife, and that child outta my house."

A familiar terror ran through Eloise when she realized that Isaac was about to throw Deller, Ben, and the baby out into the frigid night air.

"Please, Daddy, can we stay? We got nowhere to go," Deller said.

"That's your problem, gal."

"Go and stay with my sister Ava," Eloise whispered to Deller. "She lives just a few blocks away." Eloise shoved a small, crumpled up piece of paper in Deller's hand with Ava's address scribbled on it.

After getting packed, Ben and Deller walked swiftly to Ava's house. Deller held the tightly wrapped baby against her bosom to shield her from the cold, and Ben carried their suitcases.

"Aunt Ava, Daddy threw us out an' we got nowhere to go," Deller said when they arrived.

Ava felt her heart stop when she saw the sadness in Deller's eyes and the way she cuddled the baby. "Damn Isaac," she said, moving aside. "Y'all get on in here out the cold."

The next morning Ava made them a big breakfast and wished them well before they caught the next train back to New York City.

•◆•

Getting through the first year of high school was a relief. Now the incoming freshmen would bear the brunt of the teasing that Mattie and Ruth had experienced when they started William Penn. They were a fine pair. Their friendship had been sealed by the secret they shared. Mattie was indebted to Ruth, because Ruth kept her word and never again discussed that awful day. When further abuse occurred, Ruth would embrace Mattie, telling her that it was going to be okay.

One Monday morning early in the semester, Ruth didn't show up for any of her classes. Mattie went looking for her, but the only thing Ruth's teachers could tell her was that Ruth was absent.

After school, when the bus let Mattie off at Diamond Street, she ran all the way to Ruth's house. She sensed something terrible was wrong.

Mrs. Wallace, Ruth's mother, met Mattie at the door. She looked sad and worn. "Ruth's in the hospital, baby. She took sick," she said quietly.

Mattie squinted when she heard the words *took sick*. "Is she going to be all right? What hospital is she in? Can I go see her?"

"Sure, baby," Mrs. Wallace said. "Come on in and let me write down the information for you."

Mattie followed Mrs. Wallace into the kitchen and watched as she jotted down the information and handed it to her.

"I'm going back to the hospital this evenin'. I'll let Ruth know you came by," she said, giving Mattie a comforting smile.

On Saturday, Mattie felt disconnected as she floated around the kitchen.

After she finished her chores, she told her mother that she was going to the hospital to see Ruth. She would take the bus fare from the little stash she had managed to save from junkin' early that morning. She and her brothers had found some valuable items in the trash that they had taken to a nearby junkyard in exchange for cash. Junkin' had become a way of life for them. Mattie used the money to buy little items that she needed and for emergencies. Today was an emergency.

"Ma'am, I'm here to see Ruth Wallace," Mattie said nervously, as she arrived at the hospital's information desk.

The receptionist looked up Ruth's information. "She's in intensive care on the fourth floor. Take the elevator over there."

As soon as Mattie arrived on the fourth floor, one of the nurses escorted her to a changing room and handed her a blue gown and mask. "Miss, in order to see Ruth, you're gonna have to wear this," the nurse said.

Mattie looked worried. "Why?" she asked.

"Because Miss Wallace has a disease called Tuberculosis, and since it's contagious, all visitors and staff must wear protective gear whenever they go into her room."

"Okay," Mattie said quietly.

Ruth lay in the hospital bed propped up on pillows. Thick plastic surrounded the bed. An oxygen tank and intravenous equipment stood next to it, with lines running from the equipment to Ruth's left arm. A white mask covered her face.

As soon as Ruth saw Mattie, her eyes lit up and she pulled the mask away. "Hi," she mouthed, as she smiled and waved at Mattie. Her gestures seemed clumsy.

Mattie smiled. She fought back the tears brimming in her eyes.

"I know. I look scary, don't I?" Ruth said.

"No, no. You don't look scary," Mattie replied, smiling. "It's okay. You're goin' to be fine. I know it."

Ditching their awkwardness, the girls started catching up on all the school gossip. They carried on like they were sitting in a local park. Ruth never mentioned her condition, and Mattie never pried. It was the same level of understanding they had developed the year before, when Ruth was there for Mattie.

"I promise I'll be back next Saturday," Mattie said when visiting hours were over. She stood and pressed the palm of her right hand to the outside of the plastic covering. Ruth raised her palm and pressed it to Mattie's. The girls remained that way for a while until Mattie felt the tears come again, then she quickly turned and left.

The following Saturday, Mattie rushed to complete her chores, changed her clothes, and started out on her journey to the hospital. This time she had written down every bit of gossip, and she could hardly wait to share it all with Ruth.

A more confident Mattie arrived at the hospital to check in with the receptionist. "Hello, ma'am. I'm here to see Ruth Wallace. She's on the fourth floor in the intensive care unit," Mattie said. She waited patiently while the receptionist looked up Ruth's name in the white binder.

"I'm sorry, miss, but Ruth Wallace is no longer a patient at this hospital," she reported nonchalantly. Then she looked past Mattie to the person that stood waiting in line behind her.

"Are you sure, ma'am? She's in the intensive care unit on the fourth floor. I was here just last week to see her."

"Are you kin to Miss Wallace?" the receptionist asked.

"Yes ma'am. I'm her best friend."

"Best friends aren't kin, and unless you are blood kin to the patient, I can't share confidential information with you. Sorry."

"Please, ma'am. Please tell me if Ruth's all right," Mattie pleaded.

"You'll have to discuss it with her family," the receptionist said.

Mattie's heart dropped. She rushed out of the hospital

and caught the first bus to Diamond Street. She stared out the window and prayed that her friend, her soul mate, would be okay. When the driver finally announced her stop, she leapt from her seat and ran all the way to Ruth's house. She pounded on the door until her knuckles felt sore. Ruth's brother answered.

"Is your mother home?" Mattie asked, breathless.

Mrs. Wallace came out of the kitchen, and when she saw Mattie, she could tell that Mattie must have gone to the hospital.

"Have a seat, baby," Mrs. Wallace said. She took a seat next to Mattie. "Baby, Ruth's condition has gotten worse, and since this Tuberculosis thing is contagious and the doctors don't seem to know much about it, we had to transfer Ruth to another hospital, one that's far away, in the mountains, so others wouldn't catch it. Ruth is going to have to stay there for as long as it will take for her to get better." She stopped talking and took a deep breath. "There's a chance that she may never get better because there is no cure."

Mattie started to cry.

Mrs. Wallace took Mattie in her arms and rocked her. "Ruth wrote a letter and wanted me to give it to you." She pulled out an envelope from her apron pocket and handed it to Mattie.

"I know it hurts, baby," Mrs. Wallace said, taking Mattie in her arms again. "We're all sad about this, but we gotta be strong for Ruth."

"Please tell Ruth that I kept my promise to visit her today, and I'll still be her friend whenever she comes home," Mattie sobbed. She stood and tucked the letter in her pocket.

Mattie sat in her room and stared at the envelope for more than an hour before taking the letter out and reading it.

Dear Mattie,

Today is the saddest day of my life. By now, I'm sure you have heard the news that my illness is very serious and rare and that I have to go away to get better. There is no cure for this disease, so I'm praying, as I'm sure you are, that I will get better and return home soon. I know that you are sad, too. But I ask that you keep the faith. I'm going to get better. Besides, we made a promise that we would graduate from William Penn together. I want to be there to see us walk down the aisle with our caps and gowns and to see you finally get to wear that beautiful white dress and matching shoes. I am going to continue to pray for you. Know that as long as you put your faith in the Lord, he will deliver you. As soon as I'm better and able to return home, you will be the first person I visit. Pray for me, Mattie. We will be friends forever. Keep your courage.

Love always,
Your Best Friend Ruth

A big wave of sadness unfolded in Mattie. So many thoughts turned over in her mind. How was she to go on without Ruth? How could it be that she was losing the one and only friend she'd ever had? It felt like hours had passed before she finally inserted the letter back into the envelope and lowered herself to her knees.

"Please, God, cure Ruth," she whispered into her clasped hands. "Please bring my friend home."

Then she cried herself to sleep.

8

Mattie sat in her last class of the day and waited impatiently for Mr. Carter to make his final announcement: "The math test is tomorrow, so make sure you study tonight. Class dismissed."

She quickly rounded up her things and rushed out into a misty afternoon, inhaling the sweet smell of spring. It intoxicated her, and she truly felt her life was about to change. Or was it simply spring fever? She was so engrossed in her thoughts that she nearly missed her bus and had to run extra hard to catch up to it.

Mattie heard the loud noises coming from upstairs as soon as she arrived home. Her brothers and sisters were sitting in the living room, puzzled looks on their faces. "What's going on?" she whispered to Lionel.

"I think Daddy's packin' his stuff," Lionel replied.

Mattie crept up the stairs to change and peeped across the hall into her parents' room. Isaac was rushing around, throwing all his belongings into a big black trunk.

Mattie tiptoed to her room, quickly changed, and went back downstairs. They sat quietly, listening to their father's footsteps.

Eloise was over at Mrs. James' house, one of the widows whose home she cleaned every week. She had left the farm work several years before when Velma, a lady in church, mentioned that a white family needed an extra pair of hands to clean their large home in South Philadelphia. Eloise jumped at the chance to earn eight dollars a day. That would double the earnings she made every weekend picking berries at the farm. Mrs. James only needed her two days a week, but Velma had told her that there were other families needing the same kind of help.

Before long, Eloise was working six days a week for four different families. They each paid eight dollars a day, except for Mr. Lewis, who only paid her six. He didn't think she deserved more than that. Eloise took the job but only gave him six dollars worth of cleaning. She'd show him who was really in charge.

Isaac grabbed the large trunk by its handle and dragged it down the stairs, practically tumbling along with it. The children giggled as they heard the thumping sounds.

"Damn you," Isaac slurred at the trunk. He straightened up after hitting the bottom step, pulled his handkerchief from his shirt pocket, and wiped the sweat from his head. "I should have done this a long time ago," he muttered to himself.

After catching his breath, he went to the kitchen, grabbed his lunch bucket, and began filling it with leftovers that Eloise had planned to supplement the evening's meal with.

He returned from the kitchen, sat the bucket on top of the trunk, and headed toward the basement door. The children could only guess where he was going—to claim his Prince Albert Tobacco can.

Isaac brought the can upstairs, removed several bills, and inserted them into his handkerchief. He put his lunch bucket on the floor, opened the trunk, tucked the can underneath his belongings, and then dragged the trunk out the door and down the five steps to a car that was waiting outside for him.

"Hey Earl, give me a hand, man," Isaac yelled toward the car.

Earl got out and helped his friend lift the trunk into the car.

Once it was secured, Isaac went back into the house, grabbed his lunch bucket, and walked out the front door without so much as a nod to his own children.

The children listened as the car turned the corner at Boston Street. They sat in silence for a long time, fearing that their father would have a change of heart and instruct the driver to turn back. But when thirty minutes passed, and then another, their silence gave way to relief. They were relieved that the Prince of Darkness had, at long last, left their home.

As soon as Eloise arrived home three hours later and saw the ghostly look on her children's faces, a gnawing feeling took over her stomach. She knew that Isaac was gone. He had been talking about leaving for weeks now, but she thought his words were only empty threats.

The children watched for their mother's reaction—some

kind of a sign that she felt as they did. But her expression conveyed something much further-reaching. It wasn't that she didn't feel relieved, but she knew how nearly impossible it would be to sustain her children and the household on her own.

She rushed to the bedroom, checking under the mattress to see if Isaac had left enough money to make the next house payment. Nothing. She went to the kitchen and checked the drawer where he sometimes left a few dollars for groceries, and then to the basement to see if he might have left the Prince Albert can behind. This last-ditch effort confirmed her worse fear: Isaac had fled without leaving them one red cent.

"God, he even took the leftovers," Eloise whispered when she checked the refrigerator. After she opened the freezer and saw that it contained only two packs of frozen chicken, she collapsed in the kitchen chair, buried her head in the palms of her hands, and let out a wretched cry. "How could he do this to us?" she wailed. "How could he just walk out and leave us like this?"

She cried, not because Isaac had left; hell, she was relieved that she wouldn't have to put up with the beatings anymore. She cried because she didn't know how to survive on a measly forty-eight dollars a week.

From where they sat in the living room, the children watched their mother. After a while, Mattie got up the nerve to go to her. "Mama, do you want me to help with dinner?" she asked.

Eloise looked up and wiped the tears from her face. "No, no, I can do it," she said, putting her hand on the table and leveling herself to stand. "You gon' and help them young'uns with their homework."

As soon as Mattie left the kitchen, Eloise took the frozen chicken out of the freezer box and put it in water for defrosting. She looked inside the cupboard and found a box of grits and flour.

That night, they ate fried chicken, grits smothered in the chicken drippings, and homemade biscuits. There was little to be said at the table, just thanks that they were fortunate to have a blessed meal.

After dinner, Eloise retired to her bedroom. She was exhausted, not from the day's work or from the mundane tasks that usually followed. She was emotionally exhausted. She put on her housecoat and lay in bed. The empty space next to her made her feel hollow inside. No matter how horrible Isaac had been, she still had a man in her bed and someone to provide for her and the children. She finally closed her eyes and willed her mind to a peaceful place, one that carried her into much-needed sleep and dreams of the future.

•◆•

Isaac felt liberated as he boarded the Amtrak train at Philadelphia's 30th Street Station. To be rid of Eloise and all those damn children was a relief to him. He was just plain tired. Tired of working for nothing. Tired of having to sacrifice everything he earned. It had been nothing but nonstop work and headaches ever since they had moved north. He loved Eloise, but moving north and having all those children was not part of his plan. She had to keep popping them children out like little biscuits. And the children were hardheaded, too. No matter how much he disciplined them, it seemed the more heathen they became. They'd had it easy as far as he was concerned. His parents weren't as liberal with him. With her Cherokee Indian upbringing, his mother had reared him and his siblings with a strict hand and heart. They weren't even allowed to look at her for fear she would spit the tobacco juice from her mouth in their faces.

"Shoot, they don't even know what it's like to be whooped," Isaac grunted to himself. His Ma had used a thick switch of branch that she tore from one of the massive trees standing upright in their yard. "Damn Eloise," he whispered.

Then he lay back and braced himself for the long ride back to Kingstree.

•—•

Eloise walked twenty blocks to the public assistance office. She didn't know the first thing about welfare, except for what the ladies at church or the farm talked about. She knew that needy folks could get food stamps and a check from the government. And if ever there were a time she felt needy, it was now.

Eloise waited three hours before her number was called. Timidly, she approached the designated cubbyhole.

"How may I help you?" a young woman asked, smiling.

Before Eloise even took her seat, the words came out. "My husban' done left us, and I ain't got enough money to make the house payments or buy food for the chi'ren. And the electric bill is due, and so is the water. The chi'ren need clothes. I just don't know what I'm gon' do."

The woman gave Eloise a comforting look. "Don't you worry, ma'am. I'm going to see to it that you and your children are taken care of," she said, pulling a Kleenex from the tissue box on her desk and handing it to Eloise. "I just need for you to fill out these forms."

After Eloise completed the paperwork, the woman gave her a book of food stamps and told her she would receive a check in the mail within the next ten days.

Eloise felt a pang of hope as she started on the long walk home. With every step, she held her head high and recited a silent prayer. She thanked God for blessing her and her children. She asked Him for guidance and the strength to raise her children without Isaac. Finally, she thanked Him for relinquishing them from the pain and suffering that Isaac had put them through for the past eighteen years.

During the weeks that followed, Eloise worked twelve hours a day, six days a week to supplement her fixed income. She knew there would be trouble if the public assistance office ever learned about the money she earned, but she had no choice. There was no way she could ever afford to make ends meet on the measly public assistance checks and food stamps. Oftentimes, she worked a double shift on Saturday to pick up extra money so she could pay the mounting utility bills or make the house payment on time.

As the months passed, the bad memories with Isaac began to dissolve, and Eloise took solace in the children who were now more at ease. They didn't seem to mind eating cold grits for dinner, leftovers from the morning's breakfast, or going without lunch. They were happier than they had ever been, even with the marginal life they were living.

• ◆ •

Six months after Isaac left, Eloise received a letter from her sister Maybelle.

"Isaac done return to Kingstree," Maybelle wrote. "He been stayin' with his brotha' Henry and his wife. Isaac done tol' ev'rybody that he back to stay, jus' ti'ed of city life." The letter went on to say that Isaac was running around with every woman he set his eyes on and that he'd been spreading lies around town about Eloise.

Though Maybelle's letter contained only a few words, it was enough to stop Eloise's heart.

Maybelle ended her letter with a single line of scripture: 1 Peter 1:21: *Through Him you believe in God, who raised Him from the dead and glorified Him, and so your faith and hope are in God.* And then she told Eloise to let her know if she needed anything. Anything at all.

Eloise scanned the letter twice. Though she and Maybelle only had a fourth-grade education and so many of the words were as misspelled and convoluted as her trying to pronounce them, still she was able to understand the letter enough to know that Isaac was gone for good, and it was time to push him from her heart.

Eloise folded the letter and wiped away her tears as she thought about her own mother, grandmother, and great-grandmother. She knew that on her shoulders stood a legacy of strength—given to her by these great women. And even though she'd only made it through the fourth grade, she had a strong instinct for survival. And survive she must—if not for herself, then for the children that she so dearly loved.

9

On a beautiful Sunday afternoon, as Mattie sat alone on the front porch, she could feel the young man across the street staring at her. She had seen him around before and had always dodged his advances, but today when he crossed the street and started walking toward her, she remained seated. Besides, she felt bored and could use a little company.

"Do you remember me?" the young man asked, a wide grin spreading across his boyish face.

Mattie rolled her eyes and turned the other way. He grinned harder, as though rolling her eyes indicated that she liked him. When Mattie continued to ignore him, he invited himself to take a seat at the bottom of the steps.

"My name is Roy. What's yours?" he asked, gazing up at her.

Mattie didn't answer.

"All right, then. Well, if I can guess your name, will you at least say something?"

Mattie turned and looked the other way.

"Okay then. Let's see," Roy said, closing his eyes and feigning deep thought. "Mattie, right? Your name's Mattie?"

Mattie kept her eyes diverted, but she couldn't help chuckling.

"All right. I cheated. I didn't guess your name. You want to know how I got it?" Roy gave her a warm smile. "Your brother Lionel told me," he said sheepishly.

Mattie blushed.

"See, I knew I could get you to smile."

Roy went on telling Mattie all about himself. He was twenty years old, born and raised in a small town in North Carolina, and had just moved to Philadelphia with his mother, Miss Esther, and her new husband, Mr. Marshall.

"I was in the war," he said, his voice drifting off. He wanted so much to tell her all about his short time in the war, of how he had seen things that no man should see and heard things that still ring in his ears to this day. How he had been injured, physically and emotionally, and had been given an early discharge. And how today, as he sat at the bottom of the steps staring up at her, he knew that she was all he needed to quiet the strife in his head and heart.

"Were you hurt?" Mattie finally spoke up.

Roy hesitated. "Yes, but I'm all right now. It's good to finally be home."

Before long, two hours had passed, and it was beginning to get dark.

"I have to go inside," Mattie said.

"Will you be out here again tomorrow?"

"Yes," Mattie replied.

"Okay, well I guess I'll see you tomorrow then."

Inside the house, Mattie hurried over to the window and watched Roy swagger across the street. His lively gait reflected the thrill he felt, having finally gotten close up to the girl he'd been trying to meet for a long time.

For several days after, Mattie sat on the steps waiting for Roy to turn the corner when he got off the bus. She was always excited to see him again.

"I started a new job today," Roy said a few days later. "I work there on weekdays and sometimes on the weekends to earn extra money. I'm saving so I can get my own place soon."

"You're gonna live by yourself?" Mattie asked. She made no attempt to conceal the surprise in her voice. She couldn't imagine what it would be like to live away from her family.

"Yeah, I can't wait to move into my own place. I've already talked to the man who owns the building on Wallace Street, and he said he'd rent me a small place when I save enough money for the deposit."

Mattie's disbelief showed on her face.

"What about you? You haven't told me much about you and your family," Roy said. He was hoping that today she would open up to him.

Mattie wanted to tell him everything but was too ashamed. She began slowly. "Well, I have three brothers and four sisters. Mama takes care of us now. My father left about a year ago."

"Where did he go?" Roy asked, puzzled.

Mattie gave a furtive look around. She didn't want anyone to overhear their conversation. "I think he went back down South, where he used to live. One day he just came home and packed his stuff and left. Mama never really told us why or where he went."

"You reckon he's ever comin' back?"

"Nope, I hope not. Isaac was really mean to us," she whispered.

Roy could see that it was painful for Mattie to talk about her father. He wanted to know more but didn't want to upset her. He subtly tried to change the conversation. "What about your friends at school?" he asked.

"What about them?"

"Just wondering who your friends are, is all."

"Oh, I had a best friend named Ruth. We were going to graduate together, but she got sick and had to move away."

"What do you mean she got sick and had to move away?"

After Mattie didn't respond, Roy looked at her and noticed the tears.

"I'm sorry," he said. "I didn't mean to make you cry."

"No, it's okay. I just miss her. She was the only true friend I ever had. She got sick over a year ago, and her family moved away soon after that. I don't know how to reach her. I don't even know if she's still alive."

Roy grabbed Mattie's hand and held it. He had only known her for a short while, but already he saw a world of hurt in her. He wanted nothing more than to protect her from all the hurt and anger she felt toward Isaac and from the sadness she felt about Ruth.

"I have to get ready for school tomorrow," Mattie

announced suddenly. She stood and wiped away her tears.

"Maybe I'll see you tomorrow," Roy said, hoping he hadn't spooked her after finally getting her to open up to him.

"Yes, maybe," Mattie replied. She smoothed out her skirt with her hands.

Roy stood, too. "Well, bye for now," he said, as Mattie went inside.

Roy and Mattie continued to see each other every day. Before long, they began to venture out on small dates. Roy couldn't afford much since he was saving to move into his own place and was helping out his family. But somehow he found a way to take Mattie to a picture show every now and then or to the corner ice cream parlor to buy her a double-scoop cone.

Mattie enjoyed Roy's company and the fact that he liked her despite her frayed clothing and lack of spunk like other girls her age. Roy made her feel special, even pretty. He always complimented her on how nice she looked. Even though she didn't know how to fix herself up with makeup and fancy hairdos, she was naturally beautiful. Roy knew the moment he laid eyes on her that she was special.

•◆•

Nothing could have prepared Eloise for Maybelle's next letter. It arrived on a peculiar day—one that felt like it carried grief. Eloise returned home from work, removed her coat, and headed straight for the kitchen to soak her aching feet—a ritual she practiced every evening to allay the pains from being on her feet all day.

"Lionel, run the hot water in the basin, and pour the alcohol and epsom salt into it," Eloise said. "Mattie, come on down hea' and get dinner ready."

Eloise sat at the kitchen table and rested her feet in the basin Lionel had prepared. Mattie looked at her mother sympathetically when she came into the kitchen. Eloise sat with her arms folded across her chest, her head nodding slightly and her eyes closed. Mattie moved around silently so as not to disturb her mother's rest.

A few minutes later, Eloise stirred in her seat and lifted her head. Maybelle's letter lay on the table with the rest of the mail.

"I declare, Maybelle done wrote another letter," Eloise said, when she noticed Maybelle's handwriting on one of the envelopes. She grabbed the letter from the pile and opened it.

"Somethin' ter'ble done happin, Eloise," the letter read. Eloise poised herself for the news that Maybelle had scrawled on the small piece of paper. As Eloise read the last few words, the letter slowly fell from her fingertips into her lap and her eyes welled up with tears. "No, Isaac. Why?" her strained voice cried out. "Why Isaac?"

She sobbed silently, closed her eyes, and began to pray for the family—pray for Isaac.

10

*H*enry wasn't certain at which point and for what reason he began to despise his brother Isaac.

Henry and his wife, Betty, owned a small piece of land where they farmed cotton, corn, and other small vegetables. Isaac had sent a letter long ago asking if he could come stay with them for a while. Henry replied, telling Isaac they could use an extra pair of hands to help out around the farm. Even though the brothers hadn't spoken or seen each other since Isaac moved back north, he was still family—and in the South, family could depend on each other no matter what.

Henry and Isaac's arrangement started off just fine. Henry would pay him every week and split a small portion of the crop profits—if there were any—at the end of the season.

Every day, Isaac worked his brother's farm like it was his own. He had run Mr. Johnson's farm for years before moving to Baltimore, so it didn't take long to renew his interest in the tasks at hand.

Henry and Isaac worked side by side—planting, hoeing, and picking. The crop would be a good one this year, and Isaac started planning how he would spend his share of the earnings. He was convinced that he would earn enough to move into his own place and possibly enough to buy a small car. A man like him needed a car in the South, especially if he wanted not to rely on others, the way he had to rely on Henry.

Occasionally, during an off time, Henry would concoct a jar of old-fashioned moonshine the way Isaac liked it, and they'd start reminiscing about old times. When Isaac really got going, he'd start in on Eloise and the children and how hard he had worked to provide for his family. He told Henry about the house he owned in Philadelphia and how he was forced to leave it because he couldn't keep up the payments and feed all those mouths at the same time.

Betty noticed Isaac's resistance to talk about Eloise and the children when he had first come to live with them. Whenever she brought up the subject, he would just ignore her. The air around them would fill with tension—the kind that made Isaac shift from one foot to the other. There was a kind of emptiness in his eyes that Betty found disquieting. She felt like he was hiding something, but she let it go because Isaac was her husband's brother and, besides, who knew what was really going on inside him. Eventually, they pieced together that Isaac must have abandoned his family.

As time went on, Isaac started drinking almost every day and staying out till all hours of the night, with little regard for Henry and his wife. He'd even begun to slack off with his duties on the farm.

At first, when Henry learned the truth about Isaac deserting his family, he just let it roll off his sleeve. It wasn't his place to judge him. But he wouldn't stand for the drinking and carousing. Henry threatened to kick Isaac out if he continued to disrespect his home and not earn his keep.

"I done tole you, I ain't gon' pay for no sloppy work," Henry taunted when Isaac showed up late in the field with the smell of alcohol seeping through his pores.

"Man, you ain't gon' tell me how to live my life. If I wanna drink when I feel like it, then I'ma do it. It ain't none of your bizness." Isaac stood his ground.

The brothers had been feuding for weeks, and it was escalating. One day when Isaac didn't show up in the field at all, Henry hit the ceiling and went to find him. Isaac was nearly passed out in his room.

"I want you outta my house tonight," Henry said, barging in. The room reeked of moonshine.

"I ain't goin' nowhere till you pay me what you owe me."

Henry stood there, his mouth set, ready to grab Isaac and throw him out the door. "I ain't payin' you a dime. You get your shit and get the hell outta my house right now."

"You gon' pay me what you owe me or I ain't goin' nowhere."

Neither of them would succumb.

Finally, Henry grabbed hold of Isaac and tried to force him out. Though the potent alcohol that stirred in Isaac's belly left him disheveled, his strength was tenfold. Henry couldn't break his stance. They wrestled around, knocking over everything in their path.

Betty heard the ruckus and left the front porch, where she'd been shelling peas. She gasped when she saw the men brawling. "Please, y'all, stop this," she cried, attempting to force herself between them.

Betty's small frame was pushed away as Henry's strength overpowered Isaac, hurling him to the floor.

"Git the hell off me," Isaac shouted. "You gon' pay me befo' I leave hea' tonight."

"I ain't payin' you a dime. I'ma throw your ass outta my house, is what I'm gon' do."

Isaac struggled to untangle himself from Henry's grip. He ran into the mudroom and grabbed the hunting rifle that Henry kept in the closet.

"You gon' give me my damn money before I leave hea' tonight," Isaac said, pointing the rifle at Henry.

"Isaac, don't do this," Betty pleaded.

Isaac's steely eyes locked on Henry. "He gon' pay me what he owe me."

"I ain't payin' you nothin'," Henry spat, dodging for the gun.

Isaac lowered the rifle and squeezed the trigger. Without warning, Betty jumped in front of her husband. One lethal bullet tore into her chest. She fell limply to the floor, a stunned look clouding her face.

Henry's anguished cry pierced the silence. "Oh my God! Look what you done. Damn you." He rushed to his wife, who lay sprawled on the living room floor. He knelt down, lifted her lifeless body in his arms, and cried into her chest.

Isaac stammered for words, the fear of God rising in him.

"See what you done made me do? I tole you you ain't gon' cheat me outta my money."

Henry turned and set his hard eyes on Isaac. In a voice as cold as ice, he said, "I ain't payin' you a damn dime." Then he lunged at Isaac.

Isaac pulled the trigger again, and another bullet shot out of the rifle's head and ripped through Henry's belly. Henry looked stunned for an instant, before he fell to the floor next to his wife.

Isaac stood there, disbelief covering his face. When his mind came back to what he'd done, feeling no remorse, he put the rifle down. Henry had no right to try and cheat him, he thought. He looked down at Henry and Betty, their bodies showing no signs of life. He knew they were both dead.

After the shock wore off, Isaac went to his room, grabbed his wallet, and returned to the living room. He picked up the rifle, searched Henry's pockets for the keys to the truck, and walked slowly to the front door before turning to look at them one last time.

He got into the truck and drove himself to the sheriff's office.

He was going to tell them the truth.

11

Mattie stood in the yard hanging clothes on the old, weathered clothesline. The air was sweltering as the sun beamed down on her. She squinted her eyes, trying to shield the sun's glare. The heat offered no relief, and her clothes clung to her. Nearly a year had passed since her mother had told her the news of her father. She remembered the day vividly. She and Roy had just confirmed their loyalty to each other, her mother had just accepted that Isaac was not coming back, and they were moving on with their lives. Then another letter arrived from Aunt Maybelle.

Mattie regretted having felt joy when her mother received the first letter from her aunt confirming that Isaac was gone for good. She wanted him gone, but not at the expense of another family's suffering. And not at the risk of his spending his life in prison. She hadn't thought her father evil enough to kill his own brother and his wife. It was beyond her comprehension.

After the killings, they had received word that Isaac had been convicted of second-degree murder and sentenced to twenty-five years to life.

In the worst way, Mattie wanted to know if her father had any remorse for what he'd done. She hoped someday she would have the courage to confront him and ask him why: Why did he do what he'd done to that family? Why did he do what he'd done to them?

There were so many whys, her heart felt heavy.

She sat on the steps waiting for Roy. The evening had cooled enough for Mattie to enjoy what was left of it. Roy had promised to come over as soon as he returned home from work. He had been working days, nights, and weekends to save for an apartment. Mattie encouraged him in the same way he showed compassion for her whenever she felt sad about Isaac or Ruth.

"Are you okay?" Roy asked, as soon as he arrived.

Mattie looked away, embarrassed that he was able to see through her somber mood. She had tried to talk herself into a better mood, but she couldn't. "I'm fine. I thought about my father again today. I've been thinkin' about him a lot lately," she replied in a distant voice.

"Maybe you should write him a letter."

"I can't do that," Mattie said a little too quickly. "He would never read it, no way."

"You never know. He may need to hear from his family."

They sat on the steps with little more to say, each

engrossed in their own thoughts about Isaac.

"I want to marry you," Roy blurted out of nowhere. Mattie didn't know how to respond. She wasn't sure she had heard him correctly. Her mind wrapped around his words.

Roy smiled and awaited her answer.

Mattie momentarily disregarded his proposal, not because she didn't want to give him an answer or because she hadn't fantasized about this very moment many times, but because she didn't expect that he would ask to marry her now, during her senior year in high school.

"I want to marry you, Mattie," Roy professed again. He held her hand and leaned on one knee.

Mattie's eyes teared up, but at the same time, she beamed with joy. Roy looked at her, puzzled. "I'm still in school, Roy. I'll be graduating in January, and that's only three months away. I don't want to quit school now. If we get married, they won't let me graduate," she said quietly.

"We could still get married. No one but our families would have to know."

For a long while, Mattie let his words circle her mind and thought about keeping it just between the families—their little secret. "Yes, Roy. Yes, I will marry you," she suddenly blurted.

Roy stood up and lifted Mattie off her feet and spun her around. "We're getting married!" he boasted. "You're gonna be my wife."

"Ssshhh," Mattie warned, as she held her arms tightly around his neck and buried her tears in his chest.

They broke the news to Eloise's and Roy's families, and they were all thrilled.

"She's gonna make you a fine wife," Mr. Marshall had told Roy. "A very fine wife."

On a warm and bright fall afternoon, Mattie and Roy held a small ceremony in Eloise's living room. Eloise, the children, Miss Esther, and Mr. Marshall all attended. Even Deller and Ben surprised Mattie by showing up for the occasion. Eloise fried up some chicken and made potato salad and collard greens. Miss Esther baked a cake and two sweet potato pies. Mattie's sisters prepared the punch. It was by no means a lavish gathering, but it was special to Mattie. She wore a white dress and veil that Roy had bought for her at the local thrift store.

Mattie nearly fainted when the preacher asked the proverbial: "Do you, Roy, take Mattie to be your lawful wedded wife?" The magnitude of what this meant hadn't hit Mattie until Roy answered, "I do." And when the preacher turned to her for the same conviction, she realized for the first time that when she returned to school on Monday, she would be a *married woman*—a married woman with a secret.

After they celebrated with their family, Roy and Mattie returned to the small apartment he'd rented. A secondhand wooden bed and a small kitchen table and two chairs were the only furnishings Roy could afford. They sat at the table. Both seemed extremely nervous. Roy was nervous because he knew this would be Mattie's first time. Mattie was nervous because she hadn't the faintest idea what to expect; her mother had never explained those sorts of things to her. Neither she nor Roy had experienced much beyond the few kisses they'd shared on the porch when no one was looking or the hug he gave her before he said goodbye each night.

"The wedding was nice," Mattie said, looking down at her trembling hands. "Mama did a great job puttin' it all together."

"Yeah, I really liked the food."

"You ever been to a wedding before?" Mattie asked.

"Yeah, I been to a few down South. But they weren't as nice as ours." Roy noticed how the white dress glistened against Mattie's caramel-colored skin. His eyes didn't shift when Mattie bashfully looked away.

"You nervous?" Roy asked.

"Kinda. I've never done anything like this before. I mean, I've never been away from Mama and my sisters and brothers."

Roy smiled at her. "Don't be nervous. I would never hurt you. I love you."

Mattie allowed herself to smile. "I love you, too," she said. Then she took a deep breath.

Roy finally took Mattie's hand and led her to the small bed. For the first time in her young life, she felt happy— happy to feel loved, happy to feel safe. The loss of her virginity with the man she adored, now her husband, was the way she had always imagined it would happen.

The next morning when they awoke, Mattie bathed, dressed, and went into the kitchen to prepare breakfast. They didn't have much money, but Roy had stocked the refrigerator with enough food to last until his next paycheck. Mattie made grits, sausages, eggs, and biscuits for their first breakfast together as man and wife.

As the weeks went by, Mattie became more comfortable in her new role, and with their secret. She'd return home from school to complete her homework and chores and then prepare dinner for Roy. She enjoyed cleaning the small apartment and preparing a hefty meal for her husband.

"You don't have to make all this food every night," Roy said one evening, fearing they would run out of food before he got paid again.

"Most of this is just leftovers that I threw together. That's one thing my mama taught me—how to stretch food," she said, trying to relieve his worry. She turned and smiled coyly at Roy.

The next morning as Mattie prepared for school, she suddenly felt light-headed and nauseous. After getting dressed, she forced a small plate of grits down and was about to leave the apartment when she felt a sudden urge come over her. She turned and ran straight for the bathroom, throwing up what little she had eaten.

Feeling better, she put on her coat again and walked to the door. When her hand touched the doorknob, the queasy feeling came back. Before she could make her way to the bathroom, she vomited all over the living room floor. Panic struck her in the pit of her belly. As much as she didn't want to go to school, she knew she had to. She would be graduating in less than eight weeks and didn't want to miss a day of school. She had to go on as though her life hadn't changed.

She quickly cleaned the floor and went to the bathroom to brush her teeth and splash her face with cold water. This time when she touched the doorknob and felt the urge take hold of her again, she snatched open the door and let the cool air smack her in the face.

As soon as the school bell rang at three p.m., Mattie ran all the way home. She had been feeling ill most of the day, but she concealed her discomfort. When she arrived home she tried to eat something, but everything she touched came right back up. She could do nothing but lie in bed and wait for Roy.

"Roy, something's wrong with me," Mattie said, as soon as he came through the door. "I've been sick all day. Everything I eat comes right back up."

"Let's go to my mama's house. She can fix you somethin' to make you feel better."

Mattie managed a fragile smile. She couldn't wait to get to someone—anyone—that could make her feel better.

As soon as they arrived at Roy's parents' place, he told his mother about Mattie's sickness. And after Mattie explained how she had spent her morning, Miss Esther exclaimed, "Oh, good God in heaven, she gon' have a baby. We gon' be grandparents!"

Mattie nearly fainted when she heard her mother-in-law say *baby*. "I can't be havin' a baby. We've only been married for a short while."

"Honey, you're so naïve," Mr. Marshall said.

Mattie ignored him and kept on talking. "We said we were going to wait till after I graduated before we start a family." She looked at Roy, wanting him to explain it all to her.

Roy's mother started talking up a blue streak about babies and the best names for her grandchild.

"Roy, we need to be gettin' home soon before it gets too late," Mattie said politely. She tired quickly of hearing her mother-in-law talk about baby names and such.

"Yeah, Mama, we got to be on our way," Roy said.

"Okay then. But you make sure you get plenty of rest, Mattie. You don't want to put too much strain on my grandbaby."

Mattie rolled her eyes.

"Can we stop by my mother's house for a minute? I need to talk to her," Mattie asked as soon as they got outside. She was anxious for her own mother to tell her what was really happening. Miss Esther had it all wrong.

As tired as he was, Roy agreed to stop by Eloise's house, where she confirmed what Roy's mother had told them. "Sweet Lord in heaven. You gon' give me a grandchild," she blurted, smiling.

Mattie started crying. "But I can't be havin' a baby. I'm supposed to graduate soon," she said, frowning. She turned to Roy, a desperate expression on her face.

"We're just gonna have to keep it a secret like we did with the marriage thing," Roy reasoned. "Nobody has to know. You can hide it until after the graduation."

Mattie sighed and wiped her tears. "You really think so?" Her eyes lit up with hope. "You really think they won't be able to tell and I'll get to graduate?"

"Yes," Roy replied. "How they gonna know if we don't tell them? And anyway, you'll be done graduated by the time you start to show."

Mattie thought about it some more. "I guess you're right. They don't have to know about our baby," she said softly. Then she smiled and reached down to touch her slightly swollen belly.

12

*M*attie hurled over the white porcelain toilet, releasing everything until her body went limp. After it felt like she had no more to give, she lifted herself from the floor and went back into the bedroom. Graduation day had finally come, and she was determined to walk down that aisle, sick or not. She pulled the white dress over her head and then sat on the edge of the bed, struggling to get her legs into the white pantyhose she'd purchased at the five and dime store. As soon as she'd managed that, she forced her swollen feet into a pair of white shoes that Roy had bought for her. She carefully combed her hair, put on red lipstick, and dabbed some pink rouge—which she'd borrowed from her mother— on her pale face. "I'm ready," she said weakly to Roy, as she walked into the living room holding onto the graduation cap. The ceremony was to start promptly at eleven a.m.

"It's time to line up, seniors," Mr. Jonathan, the principal, announced.

Mattie felt queasy—partly because of her morning sickness and partly because she was so nervous. She couldn't believe this day had finally come. It had been a strain on both her mind and body to be living a double life. Her pregnancy was starting to show, and she could no longer button the few pairs of slacks and skirts she owned.

After the students lined up and she heard the graduation theme song, she smiled and took a deep breath, proceeding down the aisle with her head held high.

As Mr. Jonathan handed Mattie her diploma, she peered out into the audience, looking for Roy and her mother. There were so many smiling faces looking up at her that she could not actually see them, but she could feel their eyes on her. She wondered what Isaac would think if he knew she had graduated. Perhaps her achievement would have changed the way he treated her. It was doubtful, she thought. So she shifted her mind back to the two people she knew were proud of her—Roy and her mother.

Mattie's High School Graduation Photo.

More than anything, she was relieved that she no longer had to hide her pregnancy. She and Roy could not afford new maternity clothes, but she was happy to accept the second-hand items Roy bought for her from the consignment store.

With each passing day,

Mattie's belly got bigger, and although she didn't know what to expect, she was open to the miracle growing inside her.

Mattie moved slowly as she cleaned the last of the morning dishes. Her belly ballooned out, wide and round, like a ripe watermelon. She scrubbed the last of the pots thoroughly with the steel scraper as she let her thoughts about Roy scrub against her mind in the same way. It seemed with each passing month, as her belly blossomed, Roy's appetite to run the streets grew in tandem. In the beginning, she didn't mind the periodic Friday nights that he'd arrive home late. She figured he deserved to get out and enjoy himself after working double shifts to afford what they and their new arrival would need. But before long, the occasional late Friday nights spilled into early Saturday mornings, and soon, on the weekends, Mattie saw Roy just for the amount of time it took him to change his clothes.

One Friday night, Mattie decided to try and put a stop to it. "You're not going anywhere tonight," she said, after thinking about it all day. As Roy changed from his blue uniform, she shut their bedroom door and stood in front of it like a doormat, her eight-month belly protruding.

"Yes I am, and you better move away from in front of that door," Roy said.

When she refused to move, Roy grabbed her, pulling her away. Mattie's mind conjured up thoughts of being left alone for yet another weekend. She felt her body tensing, and out of nowhere, she slapped him. Before she knew it, Roy slapped her back so hard that her head hit the side of the door, sending a fierce sting across her face. All the hurt and anger Isaac had caused her suddenly resurfaced. But this time it wasn't Isaac, it was Roy, her husband: the man she thought would make her feel safe, the one who was supposed to protect her. The surprised look on Mattie's face stunned Roy, and he knew he'd done something far worse than he could ever imagine. He had violated her in a way he couldn't understand. She had confided in him about how her father had treated her. But it didn't quite resonate until he saw the look of sheer hatred in her eyes. He knew instantly he had crossed a line—and not just any line—one that was much further-reaching. He had betrayed her.

Roy grabbed Mattie and held her, begging for forgiveness as she sobbed in his arms. "Why, Roy?" she cried. "How could you treat me like this?"

"I'm so sorry, Mattie," he said, looking contrite. "I will never lay another hand on you. I promise." Then he took her into his arms and they cried together, each apologizing for something neither of them was equipped to sort out.

Later in the month, on a hot muggy day, Mattie's thighs ached more than usual. The searing pain in her legs came in spurts. She had told Roy before he left that morning that she did not feel well. "But the baby's not due for another three weeks," he had told her. By late afternoon, when the spurts became more frequent and the pain more sharp, Mattie just couldn't wait for Roy any longer. She set out on the long walk to her mother's house. By the time she reached the front door, her whole body was stitched with pain. She hurried inside to find Eloise.

"Mama, I don't feel good. I'm in a lot of pain," Mattie said as soon as she saw her mother.

"You must be in labor. We gon' have to get you to the hospital. Gon' and sit down in the living room. I'ma run down the street and see if I can get Lill to give us a ride."

Mattie was buckled over in the chair by the time Eloise and Lill returned.

"Come on now, you gon' be all right," Eloise said as she helped Mattie to the car. Lill drove at top speed to the hospital. An EMT met them with a wheelchair and wheeled Mattie inside. A nurse signed Mattie in.

"We are ready to take her to the maternity ward. Did she bring anything with her?" the nurse asked.

"No, ma'am. Just what she got on is all she brought with her," said Eloise.

"Are you gonna go with me, Mama?" Mattie asked. She seemed as helpless as a child.

"No, there's no family allowed in the maternity ward. They'll be able to visit when it's time for you to leave in five days," the nurse answered.

Mattie became frightened when she learned that her family, not even her husband, was allowed to accompany her to the maternity ward. "Mama, you're gonna have to go to the apartment and tell Roy," she said.

"I will. You just keep your mind on bringing that young'un here."

The nurse wheeled Mattie to the maternity ward. There were rows and rows of beds with colored women, all moaning in pain. Mattie felt her temperature rise. She thought she'd already been through the worst of the pain, but apparently not. She became doubly alarmed when she found out that many of the women had been in labor since the previous day, and the only thing they'd been given to help with the pain were ice chips and a wet towel.

As soon as Mattie settled into the skinny hospital bed, the doctor came in to examine her. "Your contractions are only ten minutes apart," he told her. "We are going to have to wait until they get at least two minutes apart before we can take you into the delivery room."

"How long will it take for the contractions to get to two minutes?" Mattie asked eagerly.

The doctor looked down at his notepad and then smiled at her. "It really depends on how quickly the baby wants to come out," he said, chuckling. But Mattie was in no mood for jokes.

As the contractions started to accelerate, time no longer mattered to her. She just wanted the baby to hurry up. The nurse checked on her throughout the evening and encouraged her to take deep breaths. Mattie cried and screamed and pleaded for them to give her something, anything.

"There's nothing we can give you. It'll all be over soon," the nurse encouraged.

Twenty-two hours later, a tannish coffee-colored baby boy emerged with a scream that pierced the delivery room. After the doctor cut the umbilical cord, the nurse wrapped him in a white blanket and handed him to Mattie.

"Have you decided on a name?" the nurse asked.

"We're going to name him after his daddy," Mattie said proudly.

As the small baby lay cuddled in her arms, Mattie buried

her face in the newborn's skin and thought of how happy Roy would be when he finally met his firstborn son.

• ◆ •

One afternoon, about a month after Mattie brought Roy Jr. home from the hospital, she met Alifa, a young woman who had recently moved into the second floor apartment with her two small children. Alifa, a frail woman with auburn-colored skin and sandy red hair, was not much older than Mattie.

"Hi," Alifa said. "I been meanin' to stop over and introduce myself to you. I met your husband, and he told me that you just had a baby boy. Congratulations."

Mattie didn't quite know how to answer. She was still very shy and hadn't had a close girlfriend since Ruth moved away. She stood silent, clutching a brown paper bag from the grocery store. It nearly covered her face. "Well, I better be gettin' back inside. The baby's gonna wake up soon," was all she could think to say.

"I'm home every day if you ever want to come up sometime for a visit," Alifa called out after her.

Soon afterward, Mattie took Alifa up on her offer. She dressed baby Roy and they went upstairs to pay her a visit. Mattie and Alifa talked for hours. Mattie confided in Alifa about everything, telling her about her family and about Ruth. She told her about how she and Roy had met, how nice he treated her in the beginning, and how he had changed. She even told Alifa about how Roy had hit her.

Mattie liked Alifa because they had a lot in common, even though Alifa had spunk and lots of friends. Alifa told

Mattie about how she liked to cook and invite her friends over to play cards. "Why don't you and Roy come to the card game sometime? That way maybe he'll spend less time out in the streets and more time with you," Alifa suggested.

At first, Roy was glad to accompany Mattie to Alifa's card games, but the novelty of it wore off after a short while. Pretty soon, he stopped going and wouldn't come home at all on Fridays.

One night, Mattie dressed the baby, and they went upstairs to Alifa's. She could smell fried chicken as soon as she knocked on Alifa's door.

"I'm so glad you came by," Alifa said. "You shouldn't be sitting in that apartment all by yourself while Roy runs the streets."

"You havin' another game tonight?" Mattie asked.

"Yeah, a few friends are planning to stop by for a while. You're welcome to stay."

"I'll stay for a little while and help you cook," Mattie said.

Alifa and Mattie sat at the table. Every once in a while, they'd look out through the open door to check on Alifa's children, who were playing in the hallway.

"I think I just heard Roy," Mattie suddenly announced, peering into the hallway.

"Yeah, I did hear a man's voice," said Alifa.

As the voices got closer, Mattie raised her hand to silence Alifa.

"Go back down," Roy whispered to the woman behind him as soon as he reached the top step and saw Mattie sitting in Alifa's kitchen.

Before he and the woman could turn around, Mattie

rushed into the hallway. "There's no need to tell her to go back down. I see what's going on. You might as well stay, cause I'm goin' downstairs to pack my things." She turned and rushed inside Alifa's apartment, grabbed baby Roy, and ran downstairs to their apartment. Roy followed.

"Where do you think you're going?" Roy asked as Mattie rushed past him, pulling clothes from the dresser drawer and shoving them into a bag.

"I'm going to stay with my mother," she said.

"That woman wasn't with me. She was on her way to Alifa's card game when I ran into her."

"If she wasn't with you, then why did you tell her to turn around and go back down the stairs?"

The more Roy tried to explain, the more ridiculous he sounded to Mattie. Finally, he said, "You had no right to speak to me like that in front of Alifa."

"How dare you tell me about what right I have when I caught you with another woman. I've had enough. I'm leaving!"

"Come on, Mattie." He reached for her.

"No, Roy!"

Roy's patience was wearing thin. His eyes burned into hers as she struggled to release herself from his grip. He grabbed her harder. "I said you ain't leaving me. You ain't taking my son, either."

"Roy, please . . ." Mattie's voice became thin, the same way it had when her father grabbed her like that. "Please, Roy, don't do this . . ." She could feel her breath tighten inside her chest as she braced herself.

"You ain't going no damn where," Roy said, as his fist came crashing into her. The fierce blow sent a familiar pain through Mattie's body, the kind she thought she would never feel again. As she fell to the floor, Roy stood over her, punching and kicking her as though she meant nothing to him. For a moment, she thought he would kill her. And when she had no more strength to defend herself, he stopped beating her.

"See what you made me do?" He stood looking at Mattie lying curled on the floor. He reached down to help her, but she shoved his hand away. And then he grabbed his keys and left.

Eloise took one look at her daughter, and memories of her life with Isaac flooded back. Mattie handed Roy Jr. to her mother and collapsed on the living room sofa, burying her face in her hands as she wept. She thought about the time she had told Roy stories of her father and the way Roy had cursed Isaac. Now she sat with one eye swollen shut, her lip busted, her ribs bruised. A rage festered inside of her. "I'm gonna kill him," she suddenly announced. She rushed into the kitchen. Her eyes darted around the room, looking for what she needed—a butcher's knife.

"Mattie, don't do this," Eloise begged. "What good is that gon' do?"

Mattie turned and stared blankly at her mother. She could see her mother's lips moving, but the words landed on deaf ears. She tucked the knife inside her coat pocket, moved quickly past her mother, and stormed out the front door.

She walked with purpose in the cold night, counting each city block. Her first stop was Alifa's apartment. "Is Roy here?" she snapped at Alifa.

"No, he's not here, Mattie. But you come on inside. Let's talk," Alifa coaxed.

"There's no need to talk. I just need to find Roy."

"Mattie, come on inside. It's cold out there. I know you're angry, but let's talk about this."

A sudden spurt of blood trickled down Mattie's nose. She wiped it away with the back of her hand. Then she turned and walked away.

She made her way to the corner bar, went inside, and looked around. Roy was not there either.

She walked aimlessly for hours, stopping at every corner bar, every friend's house. And when it became clear that she was not going to find him, she reluctantly returned to her mother's house. Eloise was relieved to see her.

"Gon' an' lay down on the sofa while I get somethin' to take the swellin' down," Eloise told her.

The next morning, Mattie's body ached so much it was hard for her to swallow the grits Eloise had made. She ignored the familiar stares that she received from her sisters and brothers.

After breakfast, while Mattie was upstairs changing the baby's diaper, Eloise came upstairs. "Roy's here," she said.

Mattie froze.

"He jus' want to talk to you."

"Tell him to get out. I don't want to see him."

"Mattie, he's your husban'. Just talk to him for a while. See if y'all can work this thing out."

"Mama, I said I don't want to see him. Please make him leave!"

"Jus' listen to what he has to say," Eloise went on. "He still your husban'."

Realizing that her mother wasn't going to back down, Mattie went downstairs.

Roy sat on the sofa, a pitiful sight. As soon as he saw the bruises and how stiff Mattie walked, he began to cry. "I'm so sorry, Mattie. I didn't mean to do this. You gotta believe me. Please, Mattie."

Mattie gave him an evil look. "I don't want nothin' to do with you," she said. "I just want you to leave."

"Please, Mattie. I promise I'll never lay another hand on you again."

She turned away. "Just leave," she said. Then she walked back up the stairs.

Roy returned to the small apartment feeling so alone without his wife and son. He wanted nothing more than to make it right again. He vowed to get Mattie back, to bring his family home.

He returned to his mother-in-law's house every day for a week. And finally after the cries, pleas, and promises, Mattie agreed to return home with him. "If you ever lay another hand on me, I'm gone for good," she told him.

Roy nodded and smiled a sigh of relief. Soon his wife and son would be home again.

13

$\mathcal{M}$attie decided not to fret over Roy's missteps
and just went on tending to her daily chores—cooking, cleaning, taking care of the baby, and trying to put her family back
together. She cleared her heart of anything that remotely
resembled disdain for her husband. She had made up her
mind that she was going to forgive Roy, but she knew it
would be difficult to forget. She would never forget how Roy
had savagely beat her and how he brought to the surface so
many unwanted memories. She tucked that night away like it
never happened. But something more profound wrenched her
soul—the thought that Roy had revealed a side of himself
that she never wanted to know.

She had witnessed the same look in her father's eyes when
he had beaten her mother. The beatings were more about
who was in control: who would call the shots and who would

suffer the consequences should you blatantly disregard him. Consequences so brutal you imagined you deserved such afflictions. The moment she reminded herself of that perilous look, she immediately dismissed it from her mind for fear that she would become as paralyzed in her marriage as she had been in her life with Isaac.

Just when Mattie thought things were looking up, Roy reverted to his old ways; he started disappearing again on the weekends and returning home with barely enough money to buy milk for the baby. Mattie would have to go to the corner store and beg Mr. Jimmy, the owner, for credit to buy food. "I promise to pay you back as soon as my husband gets paid next week," she would tell him.

Mattie stood up to Roy when it came to things that really mattered, like the need to have shelter and food for the baby. "I don't care what you do with your money, but you better have enough leftover to pay back Mr. Jimmy," she would say with clenched jaws and teeth. He would threaten her when she confronted him, but his threats were nothing compared to the look she saw in her baby's eyes when he cried from hunger. So words were exchanged, threats were lodged, and love was lost.

As if things weren't bad enough, they got worse.

One afternoon, the landlord came knocking at their door to collect the rent. He didn't look much like a landlord, someone Mattie imagined would pound the door and threaten eviction. He looked more like a broken old man with eyes set so far in his face they seemed like a dated fixture. "Young lady, I'm here to collect the rent," he said, not caring if he delivered bad news. "Haven't seen much of your husbin' lately. Is he home?"

If sadness was evident on Mattie's face, the man ignored it. "No, sir," she replied. "He ain't here right now, but I have a little something I can give you till he gets paid next week." She gave him whatever she had managed to confiscate from Roy during the times he returned home in a drunken stupor and she had the opportunity to raid his pockets.

"If y'all can't pay the rest by next week, I'm gonna have to evict y'all," the landlord said, half feeling sorry for her.

Mattie was in tears when Roy came home that evening. "I don't care how you get the money, but you better find enough of it by the time he returns for the rent," she told him, ignoring her fears. And despite Roy's attempt to intimidate her, when the landlord banged on their door that following weekend, Roy paid him. Mattie didn't know where he had gotten the money, and she didn't care. This went on for several more months until one day Roy came home and announced he'd lost his job.

"How could you lose your job?" Mattie snapped.

"The boss man just didn't like me," Roy told her. But Mattie knew better than that. She knew he had lost his job for being late or not showing up at all.

The next time the landlord turned up, Mattie knew they would be evicted. "Y'all gonna have to be out by next week," he told her.

With no money and no place to go, their only choice was to move in with Roy's parents, who had moved into a two-bedroom apartment not far from where they lived.

Roy and Mattie argued daily for two months straight, until Roy managed to find another job and a small apartment.

"We're gonna be moving soon," he told Mattie.

Mattie wasn't moved by the news. The silence between them hung in the air like mildew clinging to moisture. "Where are we gonna live now?" she asked, looking down at a sink full of soapy water, as if it held more promise than Roy.

"I found us a place on Broad and Cumberland Streets. Janet says we can move in right away. One of my friends is comin' tomorrow to help us move," he said.

Janet was a stout, sassy, business-minded woman who didn't take anyone's crap. She owned a three-story building with four apartments and a restaurant. The restaurant inhabited the entire first floor, and there were two apartments on the second floor and two on the third. When Roy told her that he and his wife and child needed a place to live, she agreed to rent the vacant apartment on the third floor to him. She was familiar with Roy's reputation—that he liked to drink and waste money on the ladies. "I expect my money on time, every Friday," she had told him, not mincing words. "If you don't pay me, I'ma throw you and your family back out on the streets."

The new apartment was not much larger than the first one they'd rented. A small living room was adjacent to a kitchen, the size of a closet. The bedroom was fitted with a small bed and a dresser; a small bath was off to the side. The apartment needed plenty of cleaning and some tender loving care, but Mattie was pleased they had their own place again.

Mattie immediately got down to the task of fixing it up. First, she got on her knees to scrub the tiled kitchen floor. Cooking grease lay on its surface like it hadn't been cleaned in ages. She refused to cook in that kitchen until every nook and cranny had been scrubbed. Vigorously, she wrung the rag in a bucket, scrubbing each area until it was spotless. After a while, she wiped the sweat from her brow. Her hair was covered in an old scarf that her mother had given to her, and a housedress hung loosely on her lithe figure. When she lifted herself from the floor, she suddenly felt ill. At first, she thought it was because she hadn't eaten all morning. But when she felt the urge to vomit, she sensed right away that she was pregnant. This time, she didn't need to run home to her mother.

It was well past midnight when Roy came tumbling through the door. Mattie lay on the sofa, not stirring much when the hall light shined through. She wanted to give Roy the news the moment he set foot in the apartment. She had thought it through all day—things had to change; he had to change.

"What are you doin' up so late?" Roy asked, surprised to see her lying there. Mattie hardly ever waited up for him.

"We need to talk, that's why," she said. The tone of her voice was different than usual.

"Talk about what? Can't it wait till mornin'?"

"I'm pregnant." Her face showed no emotion.

Roy accepted the news like it was a time for celebration, as if he had not been sacrificing his family with his two-timing.

"Roy, if we're expecting another child, then you're gonna have to shape up," Mattie said. She got up and left the room to check on the baby. By the time she returned to the living room, Roy was sprawled out on the floor, snoring. She was too fed up to wake him, too tired to argue. Nothing seemed to register with Roy.

Mattie continued to raid Roy's pockets for leftover cash, but there were times her raids proved fruitless. Often, she would cry because she didn't know where their next meal was coming from. And with the pregnancy, it got worse. It didn't seem to affect Roy one bit when he'd come home to find Mattie and the baby crying from hunger, or when she would plead with him for money so that she could buy food and necessities for the baby. Sometimes, when Roy was in good spirits, he would come home and hand her a few dollars before leaving on another of his escapades. But those times were rare.

•◆•

The walls were beginning to close in on Mattie. The scents in the air from Janet's kitchen helped Mattie tell the time of day—especially noon, when the lunch crowd flowed into Janet's tiny restaurant. Mattie would lie on the sofa, imagining the taste of the meat, the sweetness of the pies. But more often than not, the spell was broken when she heard baby Roy crying, waking up from his nap. She went to him and held him in her arms while he rested his head on her shoulder. There was no more milk, nothing left in the refrigerator. She had fed him the last of the milk when he awoke that morning. All she could do to comfort Roy Jr. was to bounce him while she paced the floor. But her holding him could not quiet the hunger pains in his little stomach. Mattie had gone to her mother's house a few days before to ask for food, but her pride kept her from going again.

One afternoon, Mattie was startled by a sudden knock on the door. Janet's stout figure stood in the doorway, her presence taking up the space in the hall, the air in the room. "Is Roy home?" she asked tautly. She stood there with her hands on her hips, her lips pursed.

Mattie was silent: too tired to defend Roy, too weak to speak. "No, he ain't here right now," she finally said, barely audible.

"Well, he ain't paid the rent in weeks, and I'm going to have to evict y'all soon."

Mattie stood staring at Janet, not responding.

"Is everything all right?" Janet asked.

"I . . . I . . . we're hungry. We haven't had anything to eat all day, and Roy may not come home anytime soon." Mattie was barely able to get out the words.

"You don't have anything in the apartment to eat or feed that baby?" Janet asked, incredulously.

Mattie shook her head from side to side.

"Is Roy gonna be home soon?"

This time when Mattie raised her eyes to Janet's, her answer was totally honest. "No, he doesn't come home sometimes."

Janet was moved to tears, seeing that Mattie was at least six months pregnant and hearing Roy Jr. crying in the background. "I'm gonna feed y'all," she said. "As soon as I get back down to my kitchen, I'm gonna send y'all up some food. Don't you worry, baby."

Mattie was too hungry to feel ashamed. "Thank you, Janet," she whispered. She just stood with her head hung low, looking like a lost child.

"You tell Roy I want to see him as soon as he gets home, you hear?"

Mattie just nodded.

As soon as Janet returned to her kitchen, she put together two large plates of food and asked one of her hired hands to take it up to Mattie.

Mattie told Roy about Janet's visit as soon as he came home. She could tell by his reaction that he didn't have the money to pay Janet and that they would have to move again.

The following weekend, they packed their belongings and moved back in with Roy's mother and Mr. Marshall.

·—◆—·

That fall, Eileen was born.

Mattie awoke in her hospital room to the nurse standing over the baby's bassinet. The nurse's eyes were moist.

"Is everything all right?" Mattie asked, alarmed.

The nurse handed Mattie her new baby girl then walked over to the large picture window, looking out as she sobbed. "Somebody shot the president," the nurse finally replied. "President Kennedy is dead."

Mattie's memory fell back to the day when the young president was sworn into office. She and Roy had gone to her mother's house and watched it on the small black-and-white television. And she remembered how the young president had talked about change—a change for peace, a change for humanity. As they listened to his words, they all knew it was the start of something a long time coming.

Now, as she lay in the bed at Jefferson Hospital, her daughter snuggled in her arms, she couldn't help but wonder how change would ever come. She couldn't help but cry.

For the time being, they had two mouths to feed, no money, no job, and no place of their own. For the next few months, Mattie absorbed herself in mindless tasks. She cooked, cleaned, did the wash, fed the babies, and cried. Crying became a natural part of her day. Nothing much had changed. Roy was like night and day. In one way, he was like the noonday sun—loving and contrite, showering her with cool breezes, doing what he could to make up for his transgressions. On the other hand, he was like the winter night, disappearing with the sun, bitter and cold, leaving her stranded.

Once again, Mattie felt trapped, until one day when Roy came home and announced he'd found another job and a place for them to live. He had rented the entire third floor of a private home on 16th and Dauphin Streets. It had three rooms that could be converted to a living area and two bedrooms. They would be sharing a bathroom and kitchen.

Before long, a third child was born and then a fourth—a boy they named Anthony and a baby girl they called Lydia.

14

"Mattie Madison?" a voice summoned. Mattie had been waiting in the government building for at least three hours, and she was pleased to hear her name called. More than a year before Lydia turned up, she had put in an application with the Department of Housing for low-income families. The beatings from Roy had not stopped, and she was desperately seeking a way out.

A young man escorted her to a small office, where she was given additional forms to complete and barely any instructions on how to fill them out. He only said that someone would be in to discuss her application with her. She sat there in silence, hoping for the news she had so often prayed for. A short while later, the door opened and a middle-aged white woman walked in. Looking over the paperwork for a long while, she hardly acknowledged Mattie. Then she said,

"I'm Mrs. York, and I'm going to help you get acquainted with the guidelines of the Fairview Park Housing Projects. You've been approved for a three-bedroom apartment, and you can move in within thirty days."

Mattie's eyes got wide. "You mean I've been approved?" she asked, stunned.

"Yes. We have just a few more items to review before we finalize your application."

Mattie felt her heart beating so wildly inside her chest she thought it would explode. She had figured they were going to have her fill out more unnecessary paperwork and tell her the same *We'll keep your application on file* story. But to her surprise, she'd been approved for a three-bedroom apartment, where the rent would be a fraction of what they were paying now.

Mattie was so excited about the news she'd forgotten about the bruises Roy had given her that day; she forgot about the purple circle that shadowed her left eye and the split on her bottom lip. She was startled when Mrs. York asked, "Mrs. Madison, is everything all right at home?"

Mattie looked away and said nothing.

"Do you need to talk to somebody? Are you in any trouble?"

"No, everything's fine. It was all a misunderstanding. I'm fine now." Mattie seemed fragile and innocent as she spoke. She really wanted to talk to someone but was too afraid, and Mrs. York sensed it.

"Well, if you ever need to talk to someone, I would be happy to refer you to Social Services."

Mattie nodded and smiled briefly. She looked sad and tired, certainly much older than her twenty-two years. Maybe she should have taken the woman up on her offer to help, but that would only bring more grief and pain. In her own sad way, she loved her husband. He was the father of their four children, and at times, he made her feel special. Strangely enough, she understood his plight, even if it was at the risk of her suffering. But she could no longer take his beatings. She despised him for making her feel like she was to blame for his shortcomings and failures. She had made up her mind a year ago to leave him if she could only get approved for the low-income government housing. And her prayers had been answered. But now with a new home, maybe a new start was just what she and Roy needed to mend their differences, she thought. And now, she was looking forward to her, Roy, and the children moving into their new home.

· ✦ ·

They moved into the Fairview Park Housing Projects just before Christmas. It was one of the most memorable Christmases that Mattie and Roy ever shared. With subsidized housing, they could afford the rent and food. They had enough money to buy the children toys and clothes, and Mattie decorated the apartment and a small tree. She made cakes, pies, and a turkey with all the fixings and invited their families over for Christmas dinner. It was the first time they'd ever had Christmas in their home.

From that day on, things changed. Roy worked and cared for his family, while Mattie took care of the children. The beatings stopped, and Mattie began to piece their marriage back together yet another time. She loved living in Fairview Park. The community was peaceful and clean. The superintendent came around occasionally to inspect the inside of the apartments to ensure they were well kept by the tenants.

Roy and Mattie joined a church, and when Easter came, they bought outfits for the children. The boys got dressed in three-piece suits with little brim hats, and the girls wore white dresses and tights with lavender ribbons in their hair. Mattie borrowed a camera from one of the neighbors and took pictures. It was hard to believe this was the same family.

Mattie's Children on Easter

They had been living in Fairview for close to a year when Roy convinced Mattie to let him throw a birthday party. It was his twenty-fifth birthday, and he wanted to celebrate it in a big way. "All right," Mattie said reluctantly. She didn't think it was a good idea now that they were finally getting back on the right track, but she didn't want to disappoint him. Besides, he had been on good behavior for almost a year.

Mattie helped Roy plan the party and even cooked for the occasion. All of Roy's friends and family attended, as well as Alifa, the only friend Mattie had. They danced to the tunes of Smokey Robinson, the Temptations, Gladys Knight and the Pips, the Isley Brothers, and the O'Jays. Everyone was having a good time until a fight broke out. One of the neighbors called the police, and they were forced to shut down the party.

On Monday morning, the superintendent showed up at their apartment and posted a notice on the door. **Eviction Notice for Misconduct and Disturbing the Community**, it read. They had fourteen days to vacate.

Mattie blamed Roy for losing the only real home she and her children had ever known.

"We're gonna have to move back in with my parents until we can find somethin' else," Roy told her.

"I'm not movin' back in with your parents. I'm takin' the children, and we're gonna go stay with my mother. I'm tired of runnin' back to your parents every time you mess up."

They packed their belongings, and Mattie went to stay with her mother, while Roy moved back in with Miss Esther and Mr. Marshall. Mattie was so angry with Roy that whenever he came to visit, she barely spoke to him.

"I'm gonna fix it," Roy said every time he came to visit. But Mattie let his promises go. She didn't have a morsel of faith left in him.

After Mattie spent three months living with her mother, Roy showed up one evening and handed her the keys to an apartment he'd rented on 17th and Francis. It was a three-room apartment with barely enough space for two people, let alone six, but she would have to make do like she'd become accustomed to doing. It was no Fairview, but it would have to be home.

• ◆ •

On a cool, early April evening, the thick smell of gin hung in the air. Roy's breath was heavy as he stumbled around in the dark living room. The alcohol had soaked up all reason, making him almost forget where he was, where he belonged. He had been out since noon the previous day, drinking as much as his body could hold, and had returned home eighteen hours later. A small voice, the one that often played tricks on his mind, told him that his wife was seeing another man.

Mattie lay in bed motionless. She could tell by the clumsiness of Roy's footsteps that he was drunk again. Fear swallowed her as she braced herself for what might come.

"I know wha' you been doin' behind my back," Roy slurred. The silhouette of his frame standing in the bedroom doorway was illuminated by the light behind him. He shuffled toward her, his feet dragging. Then he stopped and stood over her. Mattie lay with her back to him, her eyes shut tight, a silent prayer parting her lips.

"You bitch, I know wha' you been doin'."

Mattie felt his cold hands gripping at her nightdress. Then he dragged her out of the bed and onto the floor.

"Please, Roy. Don't do this. Please . . ." He ignored her pleas and cries. He stood atop her, hammering at her again and again with his fist and foot, until she seemed to drift into an unconscious state, wishing that finally, mercifully, he would kill her. "You ain't never gonna cheat on me again," he said, then stumbled into the living room and passed out on the sofa.

Mattie pulled herself up from the floor and lay down on the bed. She heard voices coming from the small television, and she could hear Roy snoring above it. As she felt the swelling on her body, she buried her tears into the pillow and sobbed herself into a fitful sleep.

A few hours later, the blaring voices coming from the television awakened her. Mattie tried to force her eyes open, but the bruises had already set in, shutting one eye closed. She tried to move her body gently, but a fierce pain shot through her legs and up to her chest. She struggled to sit up. She wanted to check on the children.

She went inside the children's room, and they were sleeping, all four of them. She walked over to the bed and pulled the blanket over the children, whose limbs lay sprawled across each other. She bent slowly and kissed each child before she turned the lights out and left.

She quietly moved past the sofa, where Roy still lay snoring, one leg on the sofa, the other stretched across to the floor. She concealed a painful sigh as she hobbled by him. Just as she was about to turn into her bedroom, an urgent voice caught her attention.

"We are saddened to bring you the message," the news anchor said, "that Dr. Martin Luther King Jr. died this evening from a single gunshot wound to the neck."

The news shattered Mattie's heart.

She returned to her bedroom and gently lay down. She made herself still as she cried for herself, as she cried for Dr. King.

15

The fear of death came lurking for her one dismal morning in September 1968. Sheets of rain poured from the sky, slamming against the windows, while dark clouds fogged the streets. Sharp pains in her chest suddenly awakened Mattie, and she rushed into the bathroom to relieve the mucus. She was alarmed when blood came up. She washed her face and then went into the kitchen to prepare breakfast for the children. Mattie moved around slowly, the pain in her chest nearly crippling her. Finally, she went into the bedroom to awaken Roy.

"Something's wrong with me. I've been spittin' up blood all morning," she told him when he finally stirred awake.

"You're probably just comin' down with a cold or something. Ain't nothin' wrong with you."

"There is something wrong. I'm spittin' blood. No cold

makes you cough up blood. You need to get up and take me to the hospital."

Nearly an hour passed before Roy finally got up and dressed. "I'm going to put some gas in the car. Be ready by the time I get back."

Mattie went into the children's room. "Little Roy, I want you to keep an eye on the other children while Daddy takes me to see the doctor," she told him.

Little Roy nodded his small head and smiled at his mother, happy that she considered him a big boy now that he was six.

Mattie went into her room to change out of her house-dress and returned to the living room. She sat on the sofa with her jacket on, waiting for Roy. With each passing minute, the pain in her chest worsened, and blood kept coming. When the first hour passed and Roy had not returned, she watched the door, willing him to come through it. But then another hour passed, and another, and it dawned on her that Roy had probably stopped at the corner bar.

Just as she was about to leave and take the children to her mother's house, Roy showed up. "I gotta go to the hospital now," Mattie said, clutching her chest, barely able to stand. Roy reeked of alcohol.

"I can take you now," he slurred. He helped her to the car and drove her to Hahneman Hospital.

As soon as the attendant saw traces of blood in the corner of Mattie's mouth, she called a nurse, and they took Mattie to the back. The doctors were called in immediately to examine her, and they administered antibiotics to relieve her pain and suppress the bleeding. They ordered a litany of tests, and by the time the results came back, Mattie lay in a daze.

"Mrs. Madison," the doctor said, looking worried. "You have a blood clot in your lungs. This is a very serious condition. We are going to have to prescribe a blood thinner to clear the clot. Are you taking any medications?"

"Just birth control pills," Mattie said, looking like a small, confused child.

"Is anyone here with you?"

"Yes, my husband is outside in the waiting area."

"I'll send a nurse out to bring him in. We're going to have to admit you for a few days until we're able to get the clot under control."

Mattie didn't ask how long she would have to stay in the hospital. She didn't ask anything. She just lay there, staring up at the white speckled ceiling, her eyes clouded with tears. She knew what had caused the clot, but she didn't dare contradict their diagnosis that the birth control pills were at fault. She lay silent, mulling over the fact that if they'd prodded, taken a closer look, they might realize the culprit responsible for her condition sat ten feet away in a corner, intoxicated.

For a week straight, they administered the blood thinner and other antibiotics. When the doctor came to see her on Sunday morning, she told him she still felt the same pains in her chest. He requested another ultrasound.

"Mrs. Madison," the doctor said when he returned to her room after receiving the ultrasound results. "Your condition has worsened. We need your permission to perform surgery."

"Why do you have to operate on me?" Mattie asked, alarmed.

The doctor looked at his chart, then back up at her. "Well,

the clot in your chest has thickened. If we don't operate, you could die."

Mattie stared at the doctor. He looked like a ghost delivering bad news. She couldn't believe what he'd just said. She must live, she must go on. She had four small children at home waiting for her. "How soon can I have this operation?" she choked.

"Immediately. As soon as you sign the consent forms, I will schedule the surgery for this afternoon."

She signed the forms then said, "Y'all are gonna let my husband know, right?"

"Yes. We have already contacted him at the number he left with us."

The nurses came to Mattie's room that afternoon to wheel her away to the operating room. She looked like a small, fragile child in the big white hospital gown and light blue hair cap. She barely moved, just holding onto the sheets beneath the blanket and counting the passing fluorescent lights.

"How are you feeling?" the doctor asked. His body was shrouded in scrubs, and a head cap and mask protected his face. She recognized his eyes, the same eyes that bore into hers when he told her she may have only a short while to live. She nodded, a faint respectable gesture. Everything faded when she got to the '*Lead us not into temptation*' part of the Lord's prayer.

Nineteen hours later, Mattie awakened to the doctor standing at her bedside. "Mrs. Madison, the operation went well. We have done all we can for you. It's now up to you."

She was in intensive care, with forty-eight stitches that sealed an incision from the top of her chest down to her navel. An intravenous line hung from both arms. She lay quiet, barely able to move. And though she was still somewhat incoherent, she knew something phenomenal had occurred. The words *Put your trust in Him and don't let no one touch you* were etched in her mind. She was resolved in that conviction.

An hour had passed when two nurses came to her bed. "Mrs. Madison, we are going to have to move you onto another bed."

Mattie panicked. "No. No, y'all can't touch me. I'll move myself. Please just don't touch me," she told them.

They were surprised by her behavior. "You have a lot of stitches, ma'am. We need to help you."

"No. Please. Please, just don't touch me. I can do it."

The nurses stood there baffled. Before they could say anything further, Mattie held onto the bedside bar, delicately pulling herself up. She stood finally, stooping as she took a few steps and hoisted herself onto the other bed. The nurses were dumbfounded. She must have gone mad, they thought. But there was nothing mad at all about her. She believed in the conviction that was planted at the center of her heart, at the gut of her soul. And though she was incapacitated for four weeks straight, she allowed no one to touch her: not her husband, not her mother, not even her own children. It was the first time ever that her faith had been challenged, and she knew that the only way she would survive was if she put her life in the Lord's hands.

16

Winter and spring had come and gone, and Mattie had long moved on from her brush with death. Her ten-inch scar was the only reminder. The incident didn't change Roy. Still, he barely saw to it that his family had a decent home and food on the table. Mattie could no longer stand to watch her children go hungry, so she made up her mind that as soon as she was able, she was going to find a job.

Soon, Mattie found work at a factory that cleaned uniforms for large hotel chains. The pay wasn't much, but it was enough to cover the rent and food. She worked the four p.m. to twelve a.m. shift, the kind of schedule she needed in order to be at home when Roy Jr. and Eileen came home from school. It also allowed her to prepare dinner and feed the children, help Roy Jr. and Eileen with their homework, and get them ready for bed by the time Mattie's sister Leona arrived to help out. She had asked Leona to look after the children for a few hours every day until Roy came home from work.

Mattie had managed to work for two months. Then one day, she came home to find the children alone playing in the hallway. They had been running up and down the stairs since eight that evening, according to Mrs. Hanks, who lived on the first floor. Leona was nowhere in sight, and nor was Roy. He didn't show up until three a.m., well past the time Mattie had gotten home. He had never come home that evening to relieve Leona. When he didn't show by seven, Leona put the children to bed, locked the door, and left. She needed to get home to prepare for school the next day.

Mattie confronted Roy as soon as he came home, but he blamed her. "It's your fault these children got out. You should have been home like you're supposed to be, instead of runnin' the streets with those men at that job."

Mattie decided to quit her job—not because of Roy's ranting, but because nothing was worth putting her children in harm's way.

• ◆ •

The summer of 1969 brought unsettling news. With the doctors forbidding Mattie to take birth control pills, and her having no way to avoid Roy's advancements, she found herself pregnant with her fifth child. This time, she wouldn't tell Roy. He would learn about it in time, when it would become nearly impossible to keep it from him. That time had come when she said the only words that would make him stop beating her. "You're gonna hurt the baby," she told him one day when he came home and jumped on her for no reason.

When Roy left for work the next morning, Mattie locked the children in a room and walked briskly, nearly running, the fifteen blocks to her Aunt Alma's house.

Aunt Alma, one of Eloise's sisters, had recently moved to Philadelphia from Kingstree. She and Uncle Otis shared a two-bedroom apartment not far from Eloise.

"Aunt Alma," Mattie said when her aunt opened the door. "Can me and the kids come and stay with you for a while till I find us another place?" Mattie stood there, breathless, tears burning behind her eyes.

Aunt Alma was moved to tears when she saw the bruises on Mattie's face and the way she stood, almost sideways. "Come on in here," she said. She grabbed Mattie and held her for a long while, then she ran to get some ice for her bruised face. "Lawdy, Lawdy. No man should beat no woman the way he beatin' on you Mattie. Where he at? I'ma send Otis afta' him."

Mattie stood there, her bottom lip quivering, embarrassed that her aunt had to see her this way. "He left for work, ma'am. The kids are at home alone."

Uncle Otis and Aunt Alma went back to Mattie's apartment and helped her move her things. They took everything that could fit into Uncle Otis' old Buick.

"I dare him to come 'round here and try to put his hands on you," Uncle Otis said, clutching his thick hands together as he released the air from his wide frame. "He got no right to beat you. You deserve better."

Mattie's head hung low. Everything felt clouded to her, like she was living a bad script. She reminded herself of the time she wished for death, the time that death had come for her but, through God's grace, she'd managed to break loose.

She knew her life was meant for something more, and she was grateful to Aunt Alma and Uncle Otis for helping her.

It wasn't two days later until Roy came for her. This time, he couldn't come for her with his pitiful excuses—not without confronting another man.

"You gon' away from here," Uncle Otis told him. "You got no right to beat on that girl that way. What kinda' man are you, anyway?"

Roy stood there, unable to look Uncle Otis in the eyes. "Sir, I didn't mean to hurt her. We sometimes go through things. Mattie knows I love her."

Uncle Otis wasn't hearing any of it. He'd seen the bruises on Mattie's body, and in the two days she had been with them, he saw how fragile she was. The only time Mattie's eyes ever lit up was when she was taking care of her children. Other than that, all he saw was a broken young woman.

"The way I see it," Uncle Otis said, "ain't no need for you to come 'round here. You ain't welcome in our home. Now, if Mattie wants to leave here with you, I can't stop her. But you ain't comin' in my house."

Roy's pity was no match for Uncle Otis. And when Mattie refused to come to the door, he left without her.

It was a blessing that, this time, Mattie had let go of her shame and turned to her family. Aunt Alma gave her strength with her dreamy stories. She told Mattie about the times when she and Eloise and their other siblings lived on the farm with their parents, and no matter how hard times had gotten, they managed to pull through because of their mother's love.

"You have to be strong for your chi'ren," Aunt Alma chatted on one day. "Those chi'ren is dependin' on you. Roy gon' do

Aunt Alma

his dirt. He gon' beat you down till you feel like you ain't worth nothin'. But those chi'ren always gon' look up to you like you a mountain." Aunt Alma took Mattie's hand and let her soft, gray eyes comfort her. "Don't let Roy take that from you; don't let him rob you of your worth to those chi'ren. You still young, Mattie, and you got to figure a way to move on, get past this."

Tears rolled down Mattie's face as Aunt Alma took her in her arms. "I'ma pray for you," Aunt Alma said, as she stroked Mattie's back. "I'ma pray for you, chile."

Mattie listened to Aunt Alma, took strength from her. The time away from Roy gave her hope again. She took her aunt and uncle's love and stored it in a place where she could quickly retrieve it whenever she felt empty, lonely. Spirits that lifted her surrounded her and made her believe that she could make it without Roy. Her body healed, and her heart healed along with it.

A mere two months had passed when Uncle Otis came home one day and told Mattie he had found a place for her right across the street from them. With the public assistance that she had recently been approved for, she could afford the small apartment.

For the first time ever, Mattie and the children would be living on their own, without Roy.

17

Roy had come for her a week before Christmas. It was a Saturday evening, a foot of snow covered Philadelphia, and Christmas décor laced the neighborhoods. Mattie had even decorated a small, old artificial tree that Uncle Otis had given her. She sat in the kitchen, watching the children play, when she heard a knock at the door.

"Mattie, it's me. Can I please talk to you?" Roy stood there covered in snow and contrition.

Mattie stood on the other side of the door holding her breath.

"Mattie, I know you're in there. Please, I just want to talk to you."

Mattie stood still, the roundness of her belly protruding, the baby kicking inside as though it felt the rise of her heart-beat. She looked beautiful, the way pregnancy had a way of making a woman's skin glow. The children paused when they heard the sound of their father's voice.

"Mattie, I know I hurt you, and I'm sorry," Roy said, as soon as Mattie cracked open the door. "I've cut down on the drinkin', and I've been workin' every day so that I can take care of y'all."

Mattie half listened, careful not to fall too easily. Three hours later, Roy finally left. He made promises, pleaded, and even cried, but Mattie wasn't moved. She no longer trusted him. Still, she feared him. Every day for an entire month, he came to be with his family, begging her to take him back. She felt silly denying him, especially now that she was less than two months away from delivering their fifth child. She couldn't stand the way the children cried every time Roy left them. She cried, too. She wanted her family back together, had prayed for her marriage to work. But she just couldn't go back to a life of fear, a life where she didn't know where their next meal would come from. She'd been there before—been where Roy's promises were as fragile as her heart.

• ◆ •

Roy smiled to himself, the sweet melodic sounds of a Smokey Robinson tune rolling off his tongue. He paused the car at the stop sign, making his way to the hospital, recognizing the bars and houses he used to frequent. It had been a while since he had gone to those places; they no longer interested him, especially when he thought about the time he'd spent away from his family.

Mattie had been able to fend him off until someone stole the water heater and pipes from the basement of the building.

When Roy showed up at his usual time one day and learned that Mattie didn't have water, he returned to his apartment and filled buckets with water and brought them to her. Every day, he managed to chisel away at the protective surface of her heart. He'd play with the children, eat dinner with them, and rub Mattie's belly until she would tell him it was time for him to go. Then one night, as Roy rubbed her belly, Mattie fell asleep. When she awoke the next morning, he was still lying next to her. Before long, Roy had managed to place himself back in their lives again.

"I'm here to pick up my wife and daughter," Roy told the nurse when he arrived at the maternity ward. The nurse escorted him to Mattie's room, where she and the baby were dressed and waiting. The baby slept in Mattie's arms. She weighed in at six pounds, three ounces; her smooth, oatmeal skin and big dark eyes favored Roy. She looked like an angel to him, similar to the name they'd chosen for her: Angelica.

The nurse wheeled Mattie down the hall as she held the baby in her arms. Roy walked close by, carrying all their personal belongings. "Thank you, miss," he told the nurse, after she helped put Mattie comfortably in the car. Roy ran around the other side and hopped in. He was so happy to be taking his wife and fifth child home.

With the hot, sticky August sun beaming down Mattie's neck, she welcomed the cold water Eileen had brought to her. She stood on the steps, waiting for Roy to return with the truck to move their first load of things. Today, they were moving to South Philadelphia into a large, three-bedroom apartment in the Eight Building, one of four new high risers in the Wilson Park Housing Projects.

"Are you ready?" Roy asked, jumping out of the old pick-up truck he had borrowed from a friend.

Mattie nodded. "Yes, I think everything is ready," she answered, looking around.

Roy smiled as he trotted up the stairs. He knew that today was a fresh start for them, that he finally had his family back. It would take time to fully gain Mattie's trust, and he was determined as ever to do that.

The words Aunt Alma had imparted to her almost a year ago suddenly came back to Mattie. She smiled gently as she followed Roy up the stairs. She had put her faith in the Lord, and now she was going to put her faith back in her marriage and family one last time.

18

$\mathcal{R}$oy rose just before daybreak to head off to his job as a maintenance worker with the City Housing Authority. He'd been working there for close to a year and was assigned to Tasker Homes, a housing development not far from Wilson Park. He always walked the twenty-two blocks, a brown bag with lunch shoved under his arm, a cigarette dangling from his lips, the hope that the time would pass quickly lingering on his mind.

As soon as he arrived, his supervisor gave him his maintenance schedule for the day. His first assignment was to repair the faucet at old lady Lola's house.

Mrs. Lola had been one of the first tenants to move into Tasker Homes. She was a handsome woman with a perfectly round face, gray hair pulled back into a braided bun, and weight that looked good on her. Her voice had a pitch that commanded respect, and though she moved around slowly with her cane, she was quick on her feet and tongue. She lived alone in her two-bedroom townhouse, which was laced with old furniture and family photographs. She was the epitome of grace and wisdom, the kind that made Roy immediately respect her the moment he set foot in her home.

"Ma'am, I'm here to fix your faucet," he told Mrs. Lola when she came to the door, slightly leaning on her cane.

"I kno' who you are. I done seen you round here befo'. Come on in."

Roy followed her into the kitchen, paying close attention to the cleanliness of her home. He wondered how an old woman could keep up with such chores, but Mrs. Lola was much stronger than she appeared. She had worked for fifty-five years, and she and her husband had raised ten children.

While Roy went about fixing the faucet, Mrs. Lola sat in the kitchen watching him intently. Roy reminded her of her youngest son, the one who had recently died, the one who had called her every day and told her how much he loved her. She missed him deeply. His loss was still set in her eyes.

Mrs. Lola made Roy uncomfortable with the way she peered at him. He felt ashamed, like he had something to hide. Like she knew all his secrets and inferiorities. It hurt him to live with the shame of how he treated his family, the way he beat his wife. He worked hard to keep his anger at bay and protect his feelings of defeat. Mattie was good to him, even when he managed to break her. He didn't understand where the urge to hurt her came from. Most times, he could control his anger and would walk away before it elevated to a point of no return. But other times, he couldn't help but take his frustrations out on her. He loved his wife, the way the bible speaks of loving your family, and he would do anything in his power to protect them.

Roy was taken aback when Mrs. Lola started asking him all kinds of questions. He was spooked by her questions and even more perplexed that she seemed to know the answers. It was as though she already knew him, could see right through him. He wondered how it was that she knew he struggled every day with grief. She seemed to see through his tough exterior and could comfort the wounds that even the vodka couldn't mask.

Mrs. Lola was sad to see Roy go. "You welcome to come back anytime," she told him. There was something special about Roy, she thought.

"Thank you, ma'am. I'll try." He didn't know how to respond to her and didn't understand her obvious interest in him. He did know that he had no intention of ever going back to see the old woman.

Two weeks went by, and Roy received another maintenance order for Mrs. Lola.

"Old lady Lola called and said the faucet actin' up again. Go on by there first thing this mornin' to check on it," the supervisor told him. Roy paused, then picked up the maintenance slip. He was puzzled, because he had made sure the faucet was in working order when he repaired it the first time.

Roy gently knocked on Mrs. Lola's door.

"The doh' is open. Come on in."

Roy pushed the door ajar and walked into the kitchen, where Mrs. Lola was having her morning coffee. "I got another order to check on that faucet again," he said.

"I kno' why you here, boy. No need to explain. Come on over here and have a seat." She patted the seat of the chair next to her. "Have a seat and stop rushin' through the day so much. You have any breakfast yet?"

"No, ma'am. I don't eat much in the mornin'."

"Well, you need to put somethin' on your stomach fo' you go rushin' out the house in the mornin'. I just made a pot of grits. Let me get you some."

"No thank you, ma'am. I just need to check on that faucet and be on my way." Roy shifted his eyes toward the sink.

"It ain't gonna hurt you to sit for a minute and eat somethin', boy. B'sides, I already done cooked the grits anyway."

No matter how hard Roy tried to escape, Mrs. Lola wouldn't let him. And when she refused to take 'no' for an answer, he sat tentatively.

Mrs. Lola moved around the kitchen without reserve, talking while she fixed his plate. She loaded the plate with grits and fresh eggs that she had just fried. Then she sat across from him.

"You remind me of my youngest boy," she said, staring at him, an awkward smile on her face. "How old are you?"

"I'll be twenty-nine in November."

"He was a bit older than you. He would have turned thirty-two on his next birthday. You favor him a lot. He was 'bout your size, and he had the same eyes as you. His name was Thomas."

Roy looked away. "Well, maybe I'll get to meet him someday," he said clumsily.

"No, I'm afraid you won't be able to do that." She looked

away, grief covering her face. "He done gone on home to the Glory of the Lord," she said.

Something unsettling tugged at Roy's heart. He didn't know what to say to the old woman. He just sat there, staring out the back door.

"You want anymore?" Mrs. Lola finally asked.

"No, ma'am, I've had enough. It was very good."

Mrs. Lola stood to get another cup of coffee, and when she returned, she told him all about her Thomas: how he was her greatest joy and how he died tragically in a car accident. Before long, she told him about each of her children and about how she had grown up in the South, not far from where Roy was born. She told him stories of how she and her husband had saved enough money to move their family north so that their children could have a better chance at a decent education and raising their own families. She told him how she'd lost the feeling in her right leg after surviving a horrific accident on the farm and how much she loved her husband, who had passed away four years ago, after forty-nine years of marriage. "He sho' was a good man," she said, smiling like it was only yesterday that they had seen each other.

"You got any young'uns?" she finally asked, realizing that she hadn't given Roy much of a chance to talk.

"Yes, ma'am. I got five. Two boys and three girls."

"I bet they some handsome little devils. What's they names?"

"Well, my oldest boy is named afta' me. And the other boy is named Anthony. My girls are Eileen, Lydia, and Angelica."

"How old are they?"

Roy looked at her and smiled. "They're ages five through eight, except for my youngest. She'll be three in March."

"You married, ain't ya?"

Roy Jr. Age 8

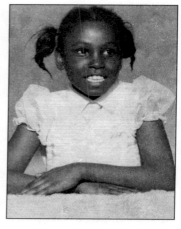

Eileen Age 7

Anthony Age 6

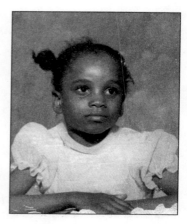

Lydia Age 5

"Yes, ma'am."

"What's your wife name?"

"Mattie."

"She named the same as one of my sisters. Ain't that somethin'!" Mrs. Lola said, smiling, her head moving from side to side, like it was no coincidence.

"I betta' hurry and check on that faucet and be on my way," Roy finally said. "I've got six more jobs to finish before my schedule ends."

Angie Age 3

"Well, you can cross one of those jobs offa' your list. My faucet workin' just fine."

Roy smiled and stood up to leave. In that moment, he knew the old woman was special. He thanked Mrs. Lola for the food and hospitality. And when he said goodbye, he knew that it would not be the last time he would see her.

"You welcome to come back anytime you like," she said.

"Yes, ma'am. Next time, I'll bring the food so you don't have to cook."

Roy went home and told Mattie all about Mrs. Lola. "She's very special," he told her. "She told me about her family and about the son that she recently lost. She says I remind her of him."

For the first time in her life, Mattie saw a calm in Roy. It were as if the old woman had a way of quieting the strife simmering in his soul. She was glad to see her husband so enamored with Mrs. Lola. Roy had never spoken of anyone the way he spoke of her.

"Can you make somethin' for me to take to her?" he asked Mattie. "I'd like to pay her back for the breakfast she fixed for me."

A few days later, Roy took a dish of smothered pork chops and rice that Mattie had fixed.

"Boy, you didn't have to put your wife through all this trouble," Mrs. Lola said when she saw the meal he had carried to her.

Mrs. Lola heated the dish, and they had lunch together. This time, Roy told her about his family and work. When he talked about his kids, his eyes lit up, but Mrs. Lola could see a hidden sadness. His voice lowered when he spoke about Mattie.

"Is everything okay between you and Mattie?" she asked him.

"We sometimes go through things," he finally said, when she reached for his hand.

"You know you can talk to me 'bout anything."

But Roy was ashamed. He was too ashamed to tell her about his anger and how he sometimes took it out on his wife. Or about how he felt like he was less than a man because he was sometimes unable to properly care for his family—and how he found solace in a bottle. It was too hard for him to look Mrs. Lola in the eyes and talk about those things.

"I better be goin' soon. I need to get back to work."

This time, Mrs. Lola didn't pressure him to stay. She knew he was hurting and that, in time and in his own way, he would open up to her.

"You know you always welcome to stop by."

Roy nodded and left.

He stayed away for weeks, unable to bring himself to open up to Mrs. Lola, to tell her he was not befitting of her son's memory. He missed her while he was away. And when he felt restless and tired, he finally went back to see her. This time, he didn't clam up when she asked him if everything was okay.

"No, ma'am," he told her. And then the floodgates opened.

Mrs. Lola just nodded with understanding. She could see the good in Roy. "It's gonna be all right, baby," she told him. "It's gonna be all right."

Before long, Roy was visiting Mrs. Lola at least three times a week. He no longer hid anything from her. He trusted her. Felt like he could tell her anything. She made him believe he could be a better man. And as strange as it was, he was beginning to feel the same way.

"Earl always made me feel special, no matter how angry he got. Marriage is hard, Roy, but you gotta work at it. Earl and I stayed married for so long because we respected each other, we loved each other no matter what. We had hard times, times when we didn't know where our next meal was comin' from, but we got through it. You gotta learn to do the same," Mrs. Lola encouraged.

Whenever Roy spent time with Mrs. Lola and then went home to his family, he saw past the shame and the bottle. He saw how much he loved his family. With Mattie's love and Mrs. Lola's support, he slowly began to change. Each day became a little bit easier.

As the months went on, Roy continued to do right by his family. He went to work every day, he visited with Mrs. Lola whenever he could, and he did what he had to do to keep his family together.

19

$\mathcal{M}$attie prepared dinner, while the children sat at the kitchen table completing their homework. Angelica sat in the corner with a coloring book, mimicking them. Mattie moved around the kitchen, humming to herself. Despite the strange dream she'd had of a robin pecking at her window, she was in a good mood.

She had just finished clearing the children's dishes when Roy came into the kitchen. "That fish sure smells good," he said.

"You ready to eat?" She could smell the vodka on his breath.

"Yeah. I saw Grant on my way up. He said he and Pauline are gonna stop by. He wanna play some poker."

Pauline, one of Mattie's youngest sisters, and her husband, Grant, had recently moved into an apartment in the same building.

The evening passed quickly, and the vodka was gone by the

time Roy and Grant started on their fourth round of poker.

"Grant, come on and let's run to the bar to get a six pack," Roy said.

Mattie rushed in from the kitchen when she overheard him. "Roy, you promised me that you were gonna stay in tonight. Why do you wanna go out this late? Ain't you had enough to drink?"

"We're only going to get a six pack. We're comin' right back. It shouldn't take that long."

"Well, we're gonna go with y'all," Mattie said.

The temperature had dropped thirty degrees, and the night air had a bite to it. They walked the twelve blocks to YoYo's Bar, and when they arrived, Roy ordered a round of drinks. "Give me a six pack to go, too," he told the bartender.

An hour had passed before they finally got up to leave.

"I wanna make a quick stop to see Mrs. Lola," Roy announced.

"Let's just go home, Roy," Mattie pushed. "You can see Mrs. Lola tomorrow."

"No, I need to see her tonight. I ain't been there in a few days to check on her."

"Well, can't it wait till tomorrow? I'm sure she's okay."

Despite Mattie's protests, Roy took a left turn in the direction of Tasker Homes.

They walked down 29th Street and turned onto Snyder. The short distance immediately gave way to the invisible dividing line between the black and white neighborhoods. Many Italian and Irish owned the beautiful brick homes that occupied the fifteen blocks between Wilson Park and Tasker Homes.

"I gotta go to the bathroom," Pauline said, as soon as they turned onto Snyder.

"Well, can't you hold it till we get to Mrs. Lola's?" Mattie asked, her pace quickening.

"I ain't gonna be able to hold it much longer," Pauline answered.

Grant pointed to a small space between an old Cadillac and a Buick. "Here, you can go right there."

Pauline stared at the space and rolled her eyes, offended that he would even suggest she pee in the street.

"There's a bar on the corner up ahead," Roy said. "Run in there and go."

They walked the two blocks to the bar.

A room full of pale faces gawked at them when Grant opened the bar door, daring them to come inside.

Pauline panicked. "I ain't going in there with all those white people."

"Well you're gonna have to either go inside or hold it till we get to Mrs. Lola's," Mattie said.

As they stood in front of the bar trying to convince Pauline to go inside, the door pushed open and two men came out. One walked with a swagger, the other with contempt. They spelled nothing but trouble. One of them, obviously drunk, bumped into Roy.

Mattie heard Roy say, "Man, say excuse me."

"Nigger, what did you say to me?"

Mattie barely heard the man's words and didn't even see the knife. Then everything became a blur.

"Run, Mattie," she finally heard Roy say after her mind came back to her. But she couldn't move. Her legs were heavy, and she felt frozen. All hell broke loose. Then she saw blood.

"Mattie run," Roy shouted again. When he saw that she was paralyzed with fear, he ran and grabbed her hand, pulling her down the street with him. Pauline and Grant followed.

The men chased them until they saw a police car coming around a corner, and then they ran the other way.

"Did he stab you?" Mattie asked Roy urgently.

"Yeah," Roy said, his hand shrouding the blood that poured from his neck.

They flagged down the police car.

"Sir, a man just stabbed my husband, and he's bleedin' real bad," Mattie said to the officer, her voice filled with fear.

"Which one is your husband?"

Mattie pointed to Roy, who stood behind her, his hands and jacket covered in blood.

"Do you know who stabbed you?"

Roy shook his head no.

"What are y'all doing around here anyway?"

"We were on our way to visit a friend in Tasker," Mattie explained.

"Where do y'all live?"

"Wilson Park," Mattie answered impatiently.

"Get in," one of the officers finally said.

More than twenty minutes later, they arrived at the emergency room. Roy handed Mattie a large knife that he carried in his coat pocket. "You hold onto this," he told her.

Mattie took the knife, which was soaked in his blood, and shoved it in her pants.

They immediately took Roy to the back and left Mattie, Pauline, and Grant standing in the waiting area. Two hours later, the doctor came out to see them.

"Mrs. Madison," the doctor said anxiously, "your husband has lost a lot of blood, and his injury requires surgery. We would like to prep him immediately, and I need your permission to operate."

Mattie stared at him blankly, then nodded her consent.

"Why don't y'all go on home and check on the children," Mattie suggested to Pauline and Grant. "I'm gonna stay here and wait till Roy gets out of surgery."

Four hours later, the doctor came out to see Mattie again. He sat next to her, the smell of antibacterial soap seeping from his pores. His eyes squinted in an uncomfortable way, as he brought his face closer to hers. "Your husband has lost too much blood, and he went into shock while we were operating. He's in a coma, and it's not likely he'll wake up. If he does, it's likely he will have lost some of his physical and mental capacities."

The smell in the waiting room suffocated Mattie. She looked toward the door that led to her husband. "Can I see him?" Her voice sounded small and far away from her, like it was devoid of oxygen.

"Yes, he's been moved to intensive care. I'll take you there."

Mattie followed closely behind.

Roy lay still in the bed, an intravenous line running from his left arm and white gauze with a clear tube at its center covering his neck. His arms were at his sides, and white patches covered his eyes.

Mattie noticed the white sheet that neatly covered his body, with a crease that folded at his chest. He looked like he was asleep, and the slow rise and fall of his chest was the only indication he was still alive.

Over the next few days while she sat at Roy's bedside, Mattie thought hard about the past ten years she and Roy had shared, about the good and bad times. No matter what had happened in the past, she still loved her husband deeply. Seeing him so fragile haunted her day and night. Every evening, before bed, she got down on her knees and said the same prayer over and over again. She asked the Lord to bring her husband back to her.

One evening, not even a week later, Mattie lifted herself from the tub, dried off, and put on her night dress. She was tired from the long days and nights spent at the hospital. She went to check on the children, who were all asleep, still unaware of the seriousness of their father's condition. After she pulled the covers over them, she returned to her bedroom, said the same prayer she'd said every night, and then lay down.

She had not even shut her eyes when she looked at the foot of the bed and saw Roy standing there, the same patches covering his eyes. When she shifted her body and mind to be sure it was him, he slowly removed the patches and looked at her. Their eyes met, and then he disappeared.

As miraculous as the moment was, she was not afraid; a single thought gave her peace—*Roy must have awakened from the coma. He'll know me when I visit him tomorrow.* Then she turned and slept.

Mattie awoke to a loud knock on the door. She put on her robe and rushed to the door. "Who is it?" she shouted.

"Ma'am, it's the police," a deep voice replied.

Mattie opened the door.

Two uniformed policemen stood there. One of them spoke up, "Ma'am, I'm sorry to tell you that your husband passed away last night. You need to call the hospital immediately."

Mattie stood dazed and confused, empty. "No. No, he ain't gone," she screamed as she broke down in tears. Roy was just at her bedside only hours ago, gazing at her, giving her hope. The children heard her cries and got up from their beds. Mattie shooed them back inside. It took the police officers twenty minutes to convince her that he was gone.

She had no more strength to give.

During the days that followed, Mattie moved around in a trance. Roy had not reached his thirtieth birthday, and she missed him terribly. Grief engulfed her, but it would have to wait. She needed to be there for her children, to prepare them for the news and then, ultimately, the funeral. She and Miss Esther made the arrangements. A viewing would be held in Philadelphia, and then Roy would be returned to Ash, North Carolina, for the funeral and burial. There, he would lay in rest with his ancestors.

On the morning of the funeral, a black limousine came for them at exactly ten thirty a.m. The funeral was to start at eleven. Mattie had already seen her husband since his passing. She had viewed his body at the coroner's office and then later at the funeral home, when she took the dark blue suit, light blue shirt, and black shoes he was to be buried in.

Mattie slowly walked down the church aisle, a black veil covering her face. Her five brave children surrounded her. When she got close enough to see Roy lying in the casket, she fainted. Roy Jr. and Eileen walked up to the casket on their own. Anthony, Lydia, and Angie followed.

"Do you want to see your daddy," a strange voice asked Lydia and Anthony, as they stood on their toes trying to peep inside the casket.

Anthony nodded, and Lydia mimicked him.

The man picked them up, holding one on each side of him. They stared into the casket, and for the first time, they understood. Tears gathered in their eyes, as they looked down at their father, who lay in his dark blue suit, resting peacefully.

Roy Age 29

PART TWO

Lydia

20

*L*ydia was roused by the smell of sizzling bacon and homemade biscuits swirling its way from the kitchen to her nostrils. She shifted the pillow away from her nose so she could more fully take in the pleasant aroma. Never an early riser, her consciousness continued to float between her dream and her mother's blaring voice. "You girls get on up and get ready for school." Today, Lydia would be starting third grade. The excitement of it hadn't yet filtered into her awareness.

As Lydia listened to her mother's footsteps make their way down the hall toward her brothers' room, she slowly began to awaken. She could hear the even breathing of her little sister Angie, who lay tangled in a blanket in the bunk beneath her. Across the room, she could hear the grunts of her eldest sister, Eileen.

Lydia pushed herself up from the comfort of her light

blue cotton blanket and squinted as the sunlight crept through the sheer curtain, its rays temporarily blinding her. She jumped down from her bunk and swaggered toward the dresser the three girls shared, taking care not to bump the drawer against Eileen's bed, as she usually did. She was in no mood for another scolding from her older sister, the kind she always got when she challenged Eileen. Though she was eight years old—*No, eight and a half,* which was what she told her sisters and brothers when they treated her as a child—she still felt like she and Angie got the short end of the stick no matter what.

Quietly, she pulled out the new polyester blue pants and pink pullover top that her mother had bought for the new school year. Just when she thought she had avoided a confrontation, Eileen stirred and gave her a look of warning as she turned and pulled the covers over her head. *That was close,* Lydia thought. Eileen's breathing was still choppy when Lydia slipped out of the room and across the hall to join Angie in the bathroom.

The children moved the morning along like clockwork. Lydia and Angie usually shared the bathroom for the first few minutes until Eileen shuffled in and joined them. Then, muffled thumps and slow movement barged from the back bedroom, where Roy Jr. and Anthony came to life.

Within half an hour, they were all gathered around the table for a hot breakfast.

It had been a memorable summer.

The summer Lydia had been caught stealing a Tastykake from the Pantry Pride grocery store. The security guard, Mr.

Robinson, told her brother Roy Jr. and made him promise to tell their mother. Instead, he made Lydia do all his chores, with no lip, in exchange for his silence. The summer Lydia and Eileen had their biggest rivalries, ones that often ended in a brawl that Eileen usually won because she was so much bigger than Lydia. The summer that Lydia and Anthony became very close and began to share everything, including their secrets and friends—and the summer that Roy Jr. made Lydia realize for the first time how different she was from the rest of them. She was the only one of the bunch that had lighter skin and red hair. She was unlike the rest of her siblings, who were dark skinned with coarse hair and dark eyes. But most of all, it was the summer that Lydia understood just how tired and sad her mother was. When she looked at her mother really closely, she could still see that look in her eyes, the same look she had the day of their father's funeral.

More than two years had passed since Roy's death. The children watched their mother grieve silently for their daddy and then, somehow, she found the strength to push on, for their sake.

During the day, Mattie moped around most of the time. At night in her bed, she would reminisce about the last time she saw Roy, then she'd cry herself to sleep. And when she had no more tears to give, she relinquished her grief. Each day became a little easier for her, with the support of Eloise. When life seemed darkest, Eloise would urge her to hold on. "You got to be strong for those chi'ren. Roy gone. But you got to hold on Mattie." And Mattie did just that. Every day, she prayed harder. Before long, it was as if a dark cloud was beginning to lift.

Lydia looked over at her mother as she piled a plate with grits, eggs, biscuits, and bacon and sat it next to the fresh pitcher of grape Kool Aid drenched in sugar, the way Eileen liked to make it. A slow hum came from Mattie as she moved between the stove and the table.

Chomping down on the soft eggs and staring at her mother, Lydia was trying to decide if now was a good time to ask her if she really belonged to her or someone else. The *someone else* is what Roy Jr. tried hard to make her believe. "She's not related to us. Look at her," he'd told Eileen one day in front of Lydia. "She belongs to a white family." When Lydia was about to confront their mother, Roy Jr. threatened to tell her all about the Chocolate Junior Tastykake that Lydia had *borrowed* from Pantry Pride. "That's right, I borrowed it," Lydia had told him. "I plan to pay them back when Ma gives us some money for school." Now Lydia looked over at her mother, then back at Roy Jr., whose eyes locked on hers. She could have sworn they said: *If you say anything, I'll tell Ma about the Tastykake.* Lydia swallowed the eggs down so hard you could hear her gulp. It brought strange looks from her siblings.

Lydia had tried for a long time to ignore it, but there had to be some truth in what her brother was telling her. After all, she was the only one with light skin and reddish hair. And when Roy Jr., Eileen, Anthony, and even Angie—who was clueless about everything—stood around staring and pointing at her, she knew it had to be true. And then Eileen added her two cents: "Mommy found you on the doorstep," she sang out loud one day.

Lydia often dreamed about what her real family was like,

hoping for the day they would come for her. *You come from a white family*, she repeated over and over in her head. She thought about what it would be like to live with a white family. Maybe then she wouldn't have to live in Wilson Park or share a room with two people she really didn't like. She would wear finer clothes and have all new friends. She'd even get to have a father again, a father who didn't suddenly get sick and die.

In the months that followed, Lydia wished her mother would come clean with the truth. But she simply looked puzzled whenever Lydia walked around with a white towel on her head, mimicking Jan Brady.

Anthony tried to reason with his sister. "Well, maybe they're just making it all up. Don't you think Mommy would have told you by now?" His reasoning didn't help her one bit. In her mind, she finally understood why she looked so different. Trying to convince her otherwise just worsened the stress she was already feeling.

The day after Mayor Rizzo came to Wilson Park was the day Lydia decided to confront her mother.

Mayor Rizzo had paid a visit to Wilson Park the night a police officer was shot. The shooting occurred right in front of Lydia's building, less than two hours before Mattie and Eileen were returning home from work. Eileen helped her mother clean office buildings once in a while. When they arrived home, Wilson Park was crawling with police officers.

Wilson Park's climate had changed as soon as the Youngston family moved in. The Youngstons had eight menacing boys and three girls who would cut you down the middle if you even looked at them the wrong way. Their mother, whom everyone called Ms. Gladys, knew that her family had clout, and she didn't spare the intimidation. Roy used to hang out with the Youngstons' father, and when Roy passed away less than a year after Mr. Youngston, Ms. Gladys told Mattie she and her family were going to look out for her and her children. They were given asylum.

Drugs and gangs followed the Youngston family. Before long, Wilson Park was no longer the clean and orderly public housing that Mattie was proud to call home. It was now infested with gangs, drugs, and shootings.

"You can't go this way," a police officer standing next to a barricade told Mattie. Police surrounded their building, and she saw a chalk marking where one of the bodies had fallen— the same spot where Eileen, Lydia, and Angie jumped rope.

"What happened?" Mattie asked, confused by all the ruckus. As soon as Mayor Rizzo appeared out of nowhere surrounded by the media, Mattie knew that whatever had happened was serious.

"A police officer and two suspects have been shot," the officer answered.

Mattie gasped and covered her mouth with her hand.

"Do you live near here?" he asked.

"Yes, we live in the Eight Building."

"Then you'll have to wait a while before we can let you through. Another suspect is at large, and we believe he's in your building."

Mattie looked up toward her window. She could see the children's rooms from where she stood. She had spoken to Roy Jr. just before she left work, less than thirty minutes ago.

Everyone stood around in clusters, chaos surrounding them. Mayor Rizzo stood nearby, promising to bring everyone involved to justice. "We have to take back our communities," he announced. "One of our finest officers is a victim of this catastrophe, and I am committing to crack down on crime." Bright lights from the media cameras flashed. Mattie and the other bystanders were so close they could see the political propaganda pouring from his lips.

Mayor Rizzo signs autographs for Mattie (left) and Eileen (center).

An hour later, the police officer told Mattie and the others their building was safe and they could return home. Mattie held Eileen's hand as they walked through the barricades, passing by the blood-stained courtyard. They were escorted to their apartment by uniformed police officers. The boys ran up to Mattie as soon as she came through the door.

"Ma, did you hear? Somebody got shot. The police officers knocked on our door to make sure we were okay," Anthony said.

"Yes, I know. Y'all go on back to bed. Eileen you go and get ready for bed, too."

Lydia lay on her back staring at the ceiling, waiting for morning to come.

"You sleep?" Eileen asked, when she came into the bedroom.

"No," Lydia answered. Angie slept through everything.

"Did you hear what happened?"

"Yeah, Anthony told me."

"You scared?"

"No."

"I am," Eileen said. "I saw the blood in the courtyard. I don't think Mommy's gonna let us play out there anymore."

Lydia turned and faced the wall, her back to Eileen. She didn't want to think about it anymore. She had more important things to think about. Getting out of Wilson was no longer just an option—it was crucial. She slid under the covers and buried her head in her pillow, thinking about how white people didn't have to live in places like this. They lived in nice neighborhoods with beautiful houses and fancy cars. She closed her eyes tightly and whispered to God to help her find her real family. The room stood in perfect stillness as she drifted off to sleep, the words she planned to say to her mother drifting along with her.

Roy Jr., Eileen, Anthony, and Angie spent a lazy Saturday morning slouching around in their pajamas, watching cartoons

and eating Cocoa Cocoa Puffs, clueless that they were about
to lose a sister. Lydia was in the bedroom, pacing the floor,
trying to figure out how she would confront her mother.
There was only one way—to say it, and say it fast.

She reached for the door. The doorknob felt sticky, like
someone had sabotaged it with Elmer's glue. She wiped her
hands against her pajama pants. Her tongue felt thick, and
her little body smelled musky.

She walked into the kitchen. From where she stood, she
could see her sisters and brothers sitting around the television, chomping on cereal and watching Popeye. Her mother
stood on a chair, reaching up into the kitchen cabinets, holding a bottle of ammonia like arsenal. Mattie's hair was pulled
back into a ponytail. The pink and white floral housedress
she wore had seen better days.

"Well, look who finally came to life," Mattie said. "You
want some cereal?"

Lydia stood looking up at her mother, everything starting
to blur in her mind. She pursed her lips to say something,
but nothing came out.

"Girl, what's ailing you? You sick or something?"

The room closed in on Lydia. The fumes from the
ammonia sucked the air from her lungs. She choked a dry
cough.

"Why are you standin' there looking crazy? What's ailing
you?"

Lydia stretched her lips, and the words came tumbling
out. "I'm white, and I wanna go live with my real family!"

Either gravity or Lydia's words shifted the chair that
Mattie stood on. She came tumbling to the floor, ammonia

splashing everywhere. "Girl, see what you made me do with your crazy talk," she said.

Lydia stood stiff, scared wimpy, as she watched her mother fumble to stand upright.

Eileen, Roy Jr., and Anthony came running into the kitchen. Angie stayed in the living room, still mesmerized by Popeye.

Lydia pointed her finger at Roy Jr. and Eileen, "They say I'm white. And I wanna leave," she blurted.

Fear smacked Roy Jr. in the chest. Eileen let out a snort so loud it sounded like a belch. Sorrow gripped Anthony's heart so hard he fluttered. Mattie looked confused.

"What are you talkin' about?" Mattie snapped. "Why are you talkin' crazy?"

Roy Jr. glared at Lydia. For a long moment, there was nothing but the sound of Popeye's voice in the background, and Angie's giggles.

"They keep saying I'm white and that you found me on the doorstep." Lydia held out her arms to show her mother, as if she had not recognized her skin color all this time.

"I know y'all haven't been talkin' crazy in my house," Mattie said, her voice tight and deliberate. "You wait till I get back."

Mattie went into her bedroom and returned with the black leather belt, the one she'd kept from Roy. "I'm gonna teach y'all never to talk like that in my house again," she said.

They all ran, except for Lydia. She just stood there with willies in her stomach and her arms stuck out, like her mother had missed the whole point.

Lydia got it because she had no business talking crazy.

Anthony got it . . . well, they weren't sure why he got it. Eileen got it for being Roy Jr.'s accomplice. Angie was safe. And Roy Jr. got it for making his sister feel as humiliated and inferior as his father had felt the night his life was snatched away from him—for no reason other than the color of his skin.

21

$\mathcal{M}$attie placed two dresses side by side on her bed. The pale blue one made her caramel skin glow, but she liked the way the tan one made her appear not so plain. She had been going back and forth between the two dresses ever since her brother Walton called to invite her to his birthday party. "My friend John is gonna be here. Remember him?" Walton had mentioned. John was divorced and living in West Philadelphia. Mattie remembered how handsome and kind he was. But when Walton had introduced them at a holiday party the year before, she had pretty much ignored him. Her heart was still with Roy.

She grabbed a pair of black sandals from her closet and then quickly closed her eyes before reaching down to grab one of the dresses. *Whichever one I pick up is the one I'll wear,* she reasoned. When she opened her eyes and saw that she'd picked the tan one, she was pleased.

She went into the bathroom, turned on the faucet, and let the hot water fill the tub. Moments later, she returned and set a towel on the edge of the bathtub where she could reach it, then she stepped gingerly into the water and sunk down as she let the hot water soak away the aches from her tired body. A bath always seemed to calm her, and it was rare that she had this time for herself.

She soaked for a while longer, letting the warm water carry her mind and body to a soothing place. She thought about how blessed she was to be able to raise her children on her own and to keep a roof over their heads, food on the table, and the few clothes they had on their backs. She was grateful that she'd been able to find a way to supplement the small check she received every month from Social Security—and more grateful that the last job Roy held had been with the city, leaving her some benefits after his death, no matter how small.

Mattie was about to reach for the soap when she heard her girls' voices.

"Ma, we're home," Eileen called out.

Mattie quickly toweled off and put on her robe. "Have y'all seen those boys?" she asked, as she walked into the living room.

"Yes," Lydia responded. "They were on the other elevator. They should be here soon."

"All right then. Get on in here and eat. I'm gonna be leavin' soon."

"Okay, Ma," Eileen answered.

Mattie went into her room and slipped on the tan dress. She turned from side to side, looking into the oval-shaped mirror above her dresser as she smoothed out the creases. It fit her well, and she felt beautiful in it. She slipped on her black sandals and then returned to the mirror to dab on some makeup—just a touch of eye shadow, a bit of blush, and very little lipstick. A quick spray of Secret deodorant was the only fragrance she wore. Then she unraveled the pink sponge rollers from her hair and brushed the firm curls until they fell just right. She stepped back and examined herself.

As soon as she heard the boys come inside, Mattie grabbed her pocketbook and made her way into the kitchen. "Roy Jr., I expect you to lock this door after I'm gone, and don't you open it for nobody, you hear?"

"Yes, ma'am," he replied, eyeing his mother suspiciously.

"Now, y'all finish up your dinner. Eileen, you and Lydia need to get the kitchen cleaned, and make sure Angie gets a bath."

Eileen nodded, looking at her mother bemused.

"You hear me talkin' to you, girl?"

"Yes, ma'am," Eileen answered quickly.

"All right then," Mattie said, after looking around one last time and counting all five heads. "I'm going now. Y'all remember what I said about this door, and I shouldn't be too long."

Mattie put her keys in her pocketbook, turned, and looked at her children. "What's wrong? Y'all ain't never seen your Mama look like this before?" Then she shut the door, leaving them wondering what on earth might happen next.

The sun had just begun to set as Mattie made her way up Susquehanna Avenue. It looked so different to her now, with the large brick rowhouses and wide streets. It seemed a lifetime had passed since she and Roy shared their first apartment together not far from there.

The bus she had just gotten off drifted into the distance as she rounded the corner to her brother's house. There were some things that were unchanged—like Walton, Lionel, and Rollie's choice to remain in North Philadelphia, close to the home they had grown up in on Boston Street.

Mattie hadn't even raised her hand to knock before the door flung open.

"Mattie's here," Walton called out, holding the door open for her. "Mattie, I told you I could have come to pick you up," he reminded her.

"I know. But you got enough on your hands already. Anyhow, I like takin' the bus sometimes."

"Well, you ain't takin' the bus home late this evening. Me or Lionel will take you."

"All right then," Mattie said, making her way into the crowd that had already gathered.

John spotted her the moment she came into the room. He remembered the time he last saw her. She still looked like the same beautiful Mattie to him. He kept himself quietly tucked in corners, watching her every move, never taking his eyes off her. After guzzling down a couple of beers, he gained enough confidence to approach her. "Hello, Mattie. It's good to see you again," he said.

Mattie smiled and held out her hand. "Hi, John. It's good to see you again, too."

In her tan dress and black sandals—and just enough makeup to look natural—John marveled at the same wholesome woman he remembered.

John and Mattie sat themselves down in two chairs near a window and exchanged stories about their lives and her children. By the time Mattie took notice of the time, she realized just how long they'd been sitting in that corner, absorbed in each other. She quickly stood up.

"Are you okay?" John asked, thinking he might have said something out of place.

"I should be going now," Mattie said, straightening the creases in her dress.

John stood slowly. "I can take you home," he offered.

"That's okay. One of my brothers will take me. I had a good time though," she said, surprising herself.

"Me, too," John answered, hesitating before his next words. "Do you think we might get together again sometime?"

Her soft smile made Mattie look even more beautiful. "Maybe," she replied.

John had half expected she'd turn him down flat like she'd done the previous year. But this time, there was something subtly different about her. After Mattie finally turned and walked away, he recognized what it was. Her eyes. The grief in Mattie's eyes was gone.

• ◆ •

Over the next several months, John spent more time with Mattie and her children than he spent at his own place. At first, Mattie's children didn't know how to take him. But they could see how much he made their mother smile again, and in time, they warmed up to him.

John really liked Mattie. In fact, he'd started to believe that he loved her, but he wasn't sure he wanted to be with a woman who already had such a large family.

"Well, if you can't accept my chi'ren, then you can't accept me," Mattie told John. She made no qualms about speaking her mind when it came to her children.

"Mattie, I ain't saying that I won't accept the children. All I'm saying is that I ain't never been around so many."

From left to right: Deller, John, and Mattie.

"Well, then it seems to me like you ain't gonna be around me, either, if you think I'm gonna put my chi'ren aside for some man."

John hadn't meant it that way, but he couldn't seem to make himself heard. He tried not to take it personally, but Mattie's words had stung. One thing was clear by the time he left that evening—Mattie was definitely a different kind of woman, one that had found her place in life.

A few months went by, and John had not returned. The children wondered what had happened to the man who had made their mother smile again. After a while, they forgot about him. John, however, still thought about Mattie and the children. And one day when he ran into Walton in the hardware store and learned that Mattie had moved, he panicked. "Where did she move to?" he asked.

"Not far from where she was. She finally got approved for a three-story house. She still lives in Wilson Park."

"Do you have her address?" John asked impatiently.

"Not on me, but call me later and I can give it to you," Walton said.

The following day, with Mattie's address in hand and determination in his heart, John went straight to Mattie.

She was not all that surprised to see him. She figured he would come around when he'd sorted things out in his mind. She masked a smile as she ushered him into her new home.

John poured out his feelings, like they'd been stored up inside of him since the day he last saw her. "I'm sorry, Mattie. I don't know what came over me. I think I was afraid to get too close to you and your children. But I've had a lot of time to think things through."

Mattie stood, quietly taking in his every word.

"I guess what I'm trying to say is that I want you to give me another chance."

Mattie kept a straight face, but on the inside, she could feel her heart warm. After a short while, she wiped her hands on her apron and gave John a nod. And then she turned and walked into the kitchen, a subtle invitation for him to stay for dinner.

Before long, John was once again a permanent fixture in Mattie's life. When he told her that it didn't make much sense for him to keep the house in West Philadelphia because he was spending so much time with her and the children, she knew he wanted to live with her and make the commitment to her children.

"That's fine," she told him. "But I went through a lot with my first husband. So whatever you do, don't you ever put your hands on me. I can't go through that again. I'd rather be by myself and raise my chi'ren on my own before I ever let another man beat on me again."

John couldn't imagine treating Mattie or her children with anything but respect and kindness. Granted, he was no prince charming, but he knew his place. For now, at least, it was with Mattie and her five children.

22

L ydia moved around the room so quickly, preoccupied with her thoughts, that she didn't hear Eileen come up the stairs to the third story of their home on 25th Street.

"Duck, you done with this broom?" Eileen asked, grabbing it before Lydia could respond.

Eileen, Lydia, and the others no longer referred to each other by their proper names; they all had nicknames they had given each other.

Roy Jr. was called *Stick* because he was tall, lanky, and skinny; and if you looked at him really hard, he would break in two.

Eileen was called *Ox* because she was big and dark and shaped like one.

Anthony was called *Jug* because he had a big head and was so smart they thought that only a jughead could hold that much knowledge.

Lydia was called *Duck* because of her fair skin and the way she always pranced around like one.

And Angie . . . well, Angie was given the worst name of all—*Roach*. A slimy, brown, beady-eyed, mischievous, sneaky bug that makes your skin crawl and makes you want to squash it dead. She was given that name for no reason other than that it sounded and was disgusting.

The girls were expected to clean the entire house, from top to bottom. That's what their mother would tell them every Saturday morning, just before she left to clean the white folks' homes.

"Get up," Lydia yelled when she reached the boys' room. They didn't move.

Lydia twisted her lips, upset that the boys didn't have to do anything but take out the trash. No cleaning. No dishes. No laundry. No cooking. No nothing. They got to sleep late on Saturday and wallow in front of the television watching cartoons and eating cereal.

Lydia grabbed the blanket off Roy Jr. He stirred and pulled the blanket back over his head. Brazenly, she pulled the pillow from under him. He startled awake, jumped up, and balled his fist so tight she thought she heard his knuckles crack. Then he punched her.

"I told you not to come in our room, you stupid Duck!" he said.

Lydia screamed and lunged at him. She was tired of him hitting her like she was a boy, and a big one at that. Before she could even get a hold of him, he punched her again, this time in the chest. She fell to the floor and went for cover.

Anthony got up and jumped between them. "You can't

keep hitting on her like that. She's a girl," he said.

Anthony was much smaller than Roy Jr., and even though Roy Jr. was very skinny, Anthony looked puny up against him.

"Well, I told that Duck to stay out of my face," Roy Jr. said. "It's none of your *bizness* anyway."

Lydia squatted in the corner with her arms and hands covering her head, tears streaming down her cheeks.

"It is my *bizness,* and I'm not going to let you hit on her like that no more."

"Then you're gonna get it worse than her." Roy Jr.'s threats ricocheted around the room. The boys stood there in silence with their chests poked out.

"Why are you always treating her like this?" Anthony finally broke the silence.

Before Roy Jr. could reply, John came running up the steps. "What's all this noise I hear up here?"

Lydia stood up, holding her face and pointing at Roy Jr. "He won't get up so I can clean the room. Mommy told us to make sure the house is cleaned before she gets home." Lydia moved her hand from her face, the swelling rising beneath her eye.

"Boy, you can't be hitting on her like that. You should know better. She's a girl. Look what you done to her face," John said.

Roy Jr. just stood there, anger gripping him.

"Y'all get out of her way so she can clean. I'm gonna talk to Mattie about this when she gets home," John said before leaving the room.

"Are you okay?" Anthony asked Lydia.

"Yeah, I'm okay."

"I'll help you clean the room," he offered.

They cleaned in silence.

"Mattie, you need to talk to that boy about the way he's hitting those girls, especially Lydia. He hit her so hard this morning her eye swelled up," John said to Mattie as soon as she returned home from work well past six.

Mattie nodded. "I'm gonna straighten it out," she said. But the boys were nowhere to be found. Mattie went into the girls' room. Lydia lay across her bed, staring up at the ceiling.

"Get up and come on downstairs so I can put somethin' on that eye," Mattie said.

Lydia followed her mother downstairs, watching her as she fixed an ice rag.

"Hold this on your eye for a while," Mattie told her. Then she went upstairs, grabbed her belt, stuffed it in her pocketbook, and walked out the front door. She was on a rampage to find Roy Jr., and she knew just where he'd be.

Roy Jr. ran up and down the court with the other players. Just as he was about to shoot the ball, his mother's words resounded off the cement. "Roy Jr., come over here now!"

Embarrassed, he passed the ball to one of the other play-ers and sauntered over to his mother.

"You know why I'm here, don't you?" Mattie asked.

"No. What did I do?"

"I didn't raise you to beat on girls," Mattie said tightly. "There are two things I can't stand: a man who beats on women and a man who disrespects his mother."

"Ma, she's always in my face. She hit me, too," he complained.

Mattie put her hands up. The gesture—and the look on her face—brought his excuses to a halt. "You come home with me now! If I wasn't in my right mind, I would whoop you in front of all these boys out here."

Roy Jr. walked with his head down, too afraid to look at his mother for fear that she might change her mind.

When they arrived home, Mattie gave him a whooping he wouldn't forget. "And you ain't going out that door until I think you know what it means to hit on a girl. Now go to your room!"

Roy Jr. ran up to his room and cried like he was the one who'd gotten the eggplant eye.

In the weeks that followed, Lydia went out of her way to avoid her brother. She hated feeling like something was wrong with her because of something she could not change. She talked to no one about it, and although she often wondered how it was that she looked so different from her siblings, she dared not ask her mother any more questions. She just tucked those thoughts deep in the back of her mind and tried as hard as she might to ignore the one thing that she lived with every day: the fact that she was only eleven years old and was being terrorized by her brother because of the color of her skin.

•—•—•

It was a usual Sunday, the day Mattie always visited with her mother. She carefully scraped her shoes on the welcome mat to get the wet fall leaves off before walking into the house.

Eloise sat reading a letter, the look on her face revealing more than Mattie cared to know.

"Is everything all right?" she asked cautiously.

Eloise stared at her and said nothing for a long while. "This letter is from Isaac," she finally said, avoiding Mattie's eyes. "He been writin' me for years now. I write him sometimes, too. He done got out of prison and he livin' in Kingstree."

Mattie felt like she'd been kicked in the gut, the breath knocked out of her. She steadied herself.

"We been talkin' 'bout gettin' back together," Eloise went on, her voice sounding small and frail. "He want me to move to Kingstree with him."

In the silence that followed, Mattie did not recognize her own mother, the woman who had survived so much and was willing to give it all up.

"It's all right, Mattie. I knew you wouldn't understand," Eloise said.

"How can you even consider goin' back to him after all he's done to us? Why would you even want to go back to that?" Mattie choked. As soon as the words left her, she wished that she could take them all back. She had never spoken to her mother in that way before, and she didn't intend to start now, especially on account of Isaac.

"He still my husban'," Eloise said, as if that were excuse enough.

"What about the house? What about us?" Mattie asked desperately.

"Y'all grown, and I'm givin' the house to Lionel to look afta."

Mattie looked at her mother, searching for a hint of insanity. But Eloise looked as sane and emotionally intact as she had the Sunday before, and the Sunday before that.

"I've made up my mind. I don't spose you'll ever understand," Eloise said quietly. "I love Isaac. Always have and always
will. He a changed man. I know it in my heart. He went to
prison, and he got saved. He sorry for how he treated us."

Mattie sat uncomfortably on the edge of the kitchen
chair. The thought of their father being back in her life was
suffocating. "If that's what you want," she finally said. She
stood and looked directly at her mother. "I hope you know
what you're doing."

"Mattie, I really want y'all to come and see your father.
He really wants to see you," Eloise rushed to explain.

Mattie grew still. She looked her mother square in the
eyes, her words so sharp they severed the silence in the room.
"If you want to go back to him, that's your choice. But I
want nothin' to do with that man," she said, and then left.

Eloise didn't have the heart to be angry with Mattie. In a
way, she understood. It took her years to forgive Issac, and it
would take a lifetime to forget. But she believed he was a
changed man. She could feel it in her heart.

A month later, before the first snowfall, Eloise packed up
everything she could fit in her old suitcases, the same ones she
had brought to Philadelphia many, many years before. She took
her clothes, her pictures, her letters, and her memories. Mattie
and John drove her to the Greyhound bus station. The silence
between them filled the car with sadness. Eloise was sad to be
leaving her family. Mattie was sad because she never had imagined the day her mother would return to the man who had
caused them so much pain—the man who had abandoned
them, the man she no longer considered her father.

Return to Isaac!

23

The stifling August heat burned the grass, and the trees stood stiff and looked toward the sky for a sliver of rain. The heat wave had brought no moisture to South Philadelphia in over a month, and the sun poured down so intensely even the blacktop on the streets melted slightly.

Roy Jr. knelt behind the fire hydrant and wrapped his long arms around its snout to splash the neighborhood children. The cool water glistened like rainbows against their skin. On days like this, it was impossible to believe that Wilson Park was plagued with crime. The days were filled with kickball, dodgeball, hopscotch, and jump rope, as well as water ice and soft pretzels from the Jack and Jill ice cream truck. Other neighborhoods paled in comparison.

Mattie sat on the sofa, her eyes fixed on the window. She watched the children play outside, a copy of *True Story* magazine resting in her lap. She would read every page from front to back. Lydia couldn't wait till her mother was finished with it because afterwards, Mattie would retell the stories in a calm voice that always sounded like music to Lydia's ears.

Lydia loved the way her mother recreated the stories so poetically, the way her voice rose to emphasize a point and the way she sometimes fixed her face in an expression. Oftentimes, Lydia would return to her room and jot down words in a black-and-white composition book that she kept tucked under her mattress. Before long, she had written her first poem, and in no time at all, she was writing poems about everything—her mother, her father, John, Stick, Ox, Jug, and even Roach. They all magically found their way into the most private places in her mind, then on a dedicated page in her composition book. Next to listening to her mother recreate the stories from *True Story* magazine, poetry became Lydia's first love. She was proud of the way she could put words together so rhythmically and make them sing and dance on a page. She loved the stillness of the words and how they came alive. At thirteen, poetry gave her a way of being outside herself, an uncompromising freedom—a freedom to say and be whatever she wanted.

One quiet evening, Lydia ripped a page from her composition book, leaving a chiseled piece that hung from its spine. She had just written a poem about her first love, Darol.

Darol lived two doors away from her and was the only boy, so far, that had ever confessed his undying love for her.

"I think I love you," Darol told her one afternoon, as they sat on her porch.

"Are you sure?" Lydia whispered to him. She could hardly believe anyone had noticed her. Whenever she and her friends played catch a girl-kiss a girl, the boys always ran after the other girls. When, finally, Darol ran after her, she blushed—happy that someone was smitten with her. But after the initial excitement wore off and she really got a good look at him, she realized that Darol wasn't the best looking cookie in the batch. In fact, he was rather ugly with his ashy skin, beady eyes, and hair that always had pieces of lint stuck in it from his bedspread. All of that didn't seem to matter to her. At least Darol had given her a good chase.

One evening, he came over and joined Lydia on the porch. "Here," he said, handing her a small box wrapped in newspaper.

Lydia opened it to find a tiny heart that hung on a gold-plated chain. She gasped and dropped the box, spilling its contents on the step below them. "Darol, I can't take this from you," she whispered.

"But I want you to have it."

"Where did you get it from?"

"I found it."

He picked up the chain and fastened it around Lydia's neck. When she turned around, he bent toward her, his lips slightly puckered. Lydia looked around, and when she was certain nobody was looking—especially her mother—she leaned in and kissed him on the lips until she felt almost dizzy. She wasn't sure if it was the kiss that made her dizzy or the smell of corn chips that reeked on Darol's breath.

That night when Lydia went to her composition book, she closed her eyes and thought only of Darol. He had stirred up all kinds of things inside her chest and between her legs. For the first time, she noticed the two large, pink dots that sat on the flat surface of her chest, and the way her behind began to curve out from above her long, thin legs. Her hips were beginning to form the shapes of parentheses.

The poem she wrote that night was simply titled "Darol."

When he learned what it took to get a kiss from her, he showed up every week with something, anything—candy, a quarter, another rusty chain.

Lydia had hidden the chain underneath her panties in her top dresser drawer, and one day, as Mattie cleaned the girls' room, she found it. "Where did you get this chain from?" she asked Lydia.

"Darol gave it to me," she said.

"What do you mean Darol gave it to you?"

"He just gave it to me."

"You mean to tell me you've been takin' stuff from that boy?"

Lydia stood silent, not answering her mother.

"I told you you're not allowed to be courtin' no boy."

"But Ox has a boyfriend," Lydia whined.

"Eileen is almost sixteen."

"But why can't I have a boyfriend?"

"Because I said so. And if I catch you round that fast ass boy again, you're gonna wish you'd never seen a boy. You hear me?"

Lydia ran to her room and slammed the door.

Angie sat on the floor, watching television. "What's the matter with you?" she asked.

"Nothing. Mind your own business."

"Don't be getting mad at me cause Ma said you can't see that dirty boy no more."

"Shut up, you Roach."

"I ain't no Roach. And I'm gonna tell Mommy if I see you with him again."

"You're not gonna tell Mommy anything, you ugly Roach."

"You're a Roach, you Duck!" Angie said. Then she ran downstairs to tell her mother about the time she saw them kissing.

24

$\mathcal{M}$attie and the children sat quietly watching the Channel Six news portray the chaos that unfolded when an all-white jury acquitted five white police officers who were charged with the death of Arthur McDuffie, an African-American motorcyclist. It was May 17, 1980, and the Miami Riots were on.

An unsettling feeling rose up inside Mattie—all the same feelings she had the night of Roy's stabbing. She kept them tucked away from her children, for their own good, she reckoned. But now she wasn't so sure, as she observed the looks on her children's faces. She couldn't help but wonder if they understood this was the type of cruelty that was connected to their father's death. She had a mind to turn off the television, but something more powerful gnawed at her.

A phone ringing in the other room roused Mattie's

thoughts. When none of the children made a move to answer it, she went to the telephone herself. It was Eloise calling. "Mama, what's wrong?" Mattie asked, alarmed, as she heard Eloise sobbing on the other end.

Eloise stayed quiet.

"Mama, please tell me what's wrong." Mattie said urgently.

"I . . . I done left Isaac," Eloise finally said in a tiny voice.

"Where are you now?"

"I'm stayin' with Maybelle."

"Do you want me to come and get you?"

Silence.

"Mama, me and John are coming right away," Mattie responded.

Eloise sat on the sofa look-ing out at the trees that circled Maybelle's home. It had been some years since she returned to be with Isaac, the man who had promised he was no longer the same person that left their home like a thief in the night so long ago. In the end, however, the old Isaac showed his face. It had started with the name-calling, and then came the beatings. This time, Eloise didn't wait for a lifetime to pass. She fought

Eloise and Isaac, after Eloise returned to him.

back. When she no longer had the strength to fight, she left with only the clothes on her back and half a will to survive.

Mattie and John arrived at dawn. Eloise had been sitting up all night waiting for them. As soon as Mattie saw Eloise, it pained her heart to see how frail and broken Eloise had become. They embraced without words.

Mattie was the first to speak. "Mama, where's your stuff?" she asked.

"I ain't got no stuff!" Eloise said.

"What about all your clothes, your pictures, all the things you brought with you?"

"I left them."

"Do you want John to go and get them?"

"No. I don't want nothin'. I just want to get as far away from here as I can."

Mattie felt her face go hot. Part of her wanted to go where Isaac was—to tell him all the things that had tortured her mind for the past thirteen hours, and her heart for the past thirty years. But the look in her mother's eyes made her think better of it.

Few words were exchanged on the ride back to Philadelphia. Their silence carried a lifetime of grief, and a future filled with hope.

25

*E*loise was just about to sit down to her dinner when she heard a familiar tap on the door. The savory smells of fried pork chops and collard greens greeted Lydia. Eloise had gotten used to the familiar knocks, usually around dinnertime. She wasted no time fixing her granddaughter a plate.

After Eloise had returned and moved into a two-bedroom rowhouse around the corner from where they lived, the children began asking a lot of questions. Lydia, especially, was curious to know her grandmother's side of the story. She found it hard to believe her grandmother had lived through what Mattie had told them. She plopped down in front of the plate that Eloise had made for her, ready to start prying.

"Mama, it smells so good," Lydia said. "You got any hot sauce?"

"Girl, you don't need no hot sauce on those chops. You

gon' take away all the flavor." Eloise went to the stove. "You want some cornbread?" she asked.

"Yes, ma'am," Lydia answered.

She watched her grandmother slice the cornbread. She could almost taste it before it hit her plate. "Did Mommy tell you about my poems?" she asked with ease.

Eloise replied absently as she cut into her meat, "Yes, that's good baby. You keep it up. I always knew you were a smart one."

"Do you like poetry, Mama?"

"Well, I like some of the words in the music I hear on the radio sometimes and the records I play on my record player." Eloise stopped to think for a moment. "I spose you can call that poetry. I reckon I do like it," she said, smiling.

"What else do you like?" Lydia asked.

A puzzled look came across Eloise's face, like no one had ever asked her what she liked, or really cared for that matter. She paused and closed her eyes, as if she had to go to a far-away place to conjure up things. "Well," she said faintly, her voice even, "I like music. I like to dance. I love my chi'ren and my grandchi'ren. I like to cook, too." After that, Eloise really had to think hard.

"Did you like living down South?" Lydia asked.

Eloise stared at Lydia, and Lydia could sense the sadness welling up inside her grandmother.

"Yeah. I loved livin' down South befo' I met your grandfather."

"Did I ever meet him when I was little?" Lydia asked with curiosity.

"No. He left way befo' you were born."

"Where did he go?"

"He went back down South," Eloise said, without reflection in her voice.

"Mommy said he left when she was just fifteen."

"Yeah, I spose she was 'bout that age."

"Mommy said you lived down South with him before you came to live with us."

Abruptly, Eloise got up from the table and began clearing away their plates. "Why you being so nosy? Ain't you got nothin' betta' to do?" she said, rushing away.

Lydia studied her grandmother's face. She could see that Eloise had the same look in her eyes that her own mother sometimes got. They finished the dishes in silence.

After a short while, Eloise asked, "Why you want to know so much anyway?"

Lydia found herself lost for words. Part of her wanted to know because she wanted to understand her family's past; and part of her wanted to know, just to know. "I don't know," she answered. "I guess I just want to know more about my grandfather."

Eloise stared out the small window that sat above the sink. She could tell that Lydia was itching to know more. "Well, Isaac used to be a good man," she went on. "At least, he was good for a while."

"What do you mean?"

Eloise got quiet, looking into the distance. "Well when we were courtin', Isaac was so charmin'. Always comin' round and sittin' on the porch with me." Her cheeks flushed at the thought of it all.

Lydia listened intently, trying to envision the times that her grandmother spoke of.

"We used to have good times in the beginning, but I guess nothin's meant to last foreva'," Eloise said.

Lydia looked over at her grandmother and saw her face change again. "So what happened? Why did Granddaddy leave?" she asked.

Eloise thought about it. "Baby, I really don't know. All's I know is that he changed. Just woke up one day and he was a changed man. Like somethin' got hol' of him. Wasn't nothin' but the devil."

"You mean he was evil?" Lydia asked incredulously.

Eloise sighed with frustration. "A chile like you shouldn't be concerned with those sorts of things. You need to be outside playin' or somethin'. You too young to be worried about what happened in the past. Let the past rest itself," Eloise said.

Lydia sat quiet for a while. Although much was left unsaid, her grandmother had revealed enough for her to realize that her grandmother and her mother had come through some things that shook them to their core. She wiped down the table and put the last of the dishes away.

"Your mama is still very angry with her daddy," Eloise said out of the blue.

"What for?"

"I spose she never forgave him for all the things he did. But she need to forgive him before he leaves this earth, and for her own peace of mind."

"Did you forgive him?"

Eloise took a seat. "Yeah, I did the first time, when I went back down South to live with him."

"Mama, why'd you go back?" Lydia asked bluntly.

Eloise gave this some thought. "I thought I still loved

him, and in a way, I did. I was hoping he'd changed. Thought maybe there'd be some mo' rocks to turn over between us."

Lydia was fascinated by the way her grandmother crafted her words to make them make sense. "You think my mother will ever forgive Granddaddy?" she asked.

Eloise got sad again. "No, I think she ain't never gon' forgive him. Isaac was a good provider, though. He did the best he could to take care of me and them young'uns."

Lydia pondered how her grandmother could curse Isaac in one breath and praise him in the next.

"I stuck by Isaac because he did the best he could for us. He wasn't always the most lovin' man but love come in strange ways." The faint quiver in Eloise's voice made Lydia tear up. She wished she could wash away all her grandmother's sorrow, take away all her pain.

The sunlight pressed against the window, trying to make its way into the room. Lydia thought it best not to ask any more questions, but her tongue got the best of her. "So do you regret going back to him?" she said, reaching for more.

"No, I don't regret goin' back. I know Mattie and them could never understand why I did it, but I reckon I had to find out for myself."

"Do you think I'll ever get to meet him?"

Eloise smiled. "Girl, why on heaven's earth would you want to do that?"

"I don't know," Lydia said thoughtfully. "I guess I just wanna meet the man everybody seems so afraid of."

26

March 30, 1981. John Hinckley shot President Reagan. Roy Jr. ignited a war with the Youngstons. Eileen got sick. Anthony won a scholastic award. Lydia heard the results of her first poem that had been submitted for publication. And Angie turned eleven, got her period, and started hearing voices.

The smell of bacon lit up the whole house. Mattie awoke the children early so they wouldn't be late for Anthony's award ceremony. He was receiving a scholastic award for achieving the highest grade point average at Vare Junior High School, as well as being recognized as one of the few students selected to attend Southwalk High, a school for scholastically gifted children.

Mattie was nearly bursting with pride as she watched her son adjust his black-rimmed bifocals. He looked so handsome in the navy blue pinstriped suit she had bought for him to wear to the ceremony. No one in the family had ever been so highly honored. Mattie was fixing to have a party to celebrate Anthony's award and Angie's birthday.

Roy Jr. didn't seem enthused about the party or anything else for that matter. He had been acting weird for days. Soon, he was going to have to face Junior Youngston and turn over the money he failed to make on behalf of Junior's cause.

Eileen spent most of the morning sprawled out on the bathroom floor, hovered over the toilet. When not even a whooping would keep her from sneaking calls to Derrick, after her best friend Karen had introduced them, Mattie finally relented and let her have boy company, but only on weekends and only if she followed the rules. "You better not let that boy fool you. You hear me?" Mattie had warned her. And now there Eileen was, sprawled over the toilet—giving it all her body had to give.

Lydia was excited to get to school. Today, she would find out if she'd been selected to participate in the Young Poet's Contest. She had submitted two poems weeks ago, and she couldn't wait to hear the news.

Angie was missing. Mattie went upstairs to check on her and found her sitting on the edge of her bed. Her pajama top was buttoned in all the wrong places, making it look awkward on her. One of her ponytails was facing the ceiling, while the other was matted behind her ear. Her hands were resting together in her lap, and her eyes were fixed on a teddy bear sitting on top of her dresser.

"Girl, what's ailing you?" Mattie asked.

"I'm not feeling good today," Angie whined. "Can I stay home?"

"Stand up," Mattie said.

When Angie stood, Mattie could see that her pajama pants and light blue blanket were covered in blood.

"My Lord. You got your period on your birthday. Come on with me to the bathroom. I hope I got some pads in there."

Mattie banged on the bathroom door. "Eileen, I know you're not still in this bathroom. You've been in there all mornin'. Open up this door."

The loud knock startled Eileen. She quickly lifted herself off of the floor and flushed the toilet. She ran cold water on her face and checked her clothes before opening the door.

"Why are you locked up in this bathroom every mornin'? If you make us late this mornin', I'm gonna knock you into next week."

"I haven't been in here that long," Eileen groused.

Mattie rolled her eyes. "Angie got her period. I want you and Lydia to help her over the next few days. Come on in here, Angie, so I can show you what to do. Eileen, you go on downstairs and make sure that bacon don't burn. Hurry up so we can get on outta here."

Angie followed her mother into the bathroom, and Eileen dragged herself downstairs. The smell of the bacon made her gag. Lydia stared at her sister, wondering why she looked like paste.

Roy Jr. finally made it downstairs.

Anthony refused to eat anything for fear he'd spill grits on his new blue suit.

The ceremony went off without a hitch.

Mattie made it on time and watched proudly as her son accepted six awards. She, Eloise, and the children sat in the front row, grinning from ear to ear.

Mattie had left Angie at home. Something just wasn't right with the way she had acted that morning. She seemed lost, almost like her mind was in another place. When Mattie asked if she was okay, Angie mumbled something that didn't make any sense. Usually, Mattie could sense when one of the children was coming down with something, but this morning, Angie's behavior left her puzzled. She made a mental note to keep an eye on her.

• ◆ •

"You got my money?" Junior asked, the strong pitch of his voice sluggish and his eyes narrowed.

Roy Jr. fidgeted uneasily, too intimidated to hold Junior's stare.

"Well do you?"

"No. I don't have no money," Roy Jr. answered slowly.

"Where's my stuff at then?"

"At home."

"What do you mean at home? I know you don't think you're gonna keep my shit and my money."

"I'm not tryna keep your stuff," Roy Jr. said, his voice shaking. "I'm gonna give it back to you. I just didn't want to bring it to school."

"What do you mean you're gonna give it back to me? You're spose to sell it and bring me the money."

"I'm not doin' it anymore. I just want out," Roy Jr. lamented.

"You don't tell me when you want out! You're gonna do what I tell you to do and when I tell you to do it! You hear?"

Roy Jr. said nothing as he studied Junior, who gave him a hard look.

"You hear what I said, nigga? Now I expect you to bring me my money tonight. Don't let me come lookin' for ya ass."

Roy Jr. felt the blood rise to his forehead. His mouth was dry, and his legs were like putty. He didn't dare make a move for fear that Junior would pummel him.

⁕

Mattie changed out of her dress and put on her cleaning clothes, the ones she always wore when she gave her house the kind of cleaning it deserved. She checked on Angie before she started in on the boys' room, her mind absorbed by the news she'd just heard about President Reagan. Mattie moved around the room swiftly—making the beds, sweeping the floor, and putting away clothes. As she picked up a pair of Roy Jr.'s jeans, something fell from the pocket—a small plastic bag. Mattie opened it and inspected it with her nose. "I know that boy ain't done brought drugs into my house," she said. Then she ran downstairs to tell John.

⁕

By the time the final school bell rang, Eileen wished she could fly home. She had gotten used to the nausea and dizziness, but the cramps and tugs she felt in her stomach for the past few days worried her.

As soon as her foot hit the front door, she ran to her bedroom. She lay curled in bed, her knees pressed against her chest, listening to the rain thrust up against the window. The pain and the sound made the room spin.

•◆•

The news that Lydia received from her English teacher was very discouraging. "Unfortunately, your poem has not been selected, but we can try again next year," Mrs. Lanaham told her. Lydia was certain she'd at least be considered, especially after everyone kept telling her how talented she was. She reached into her book bag and pulled out the letter Mrs. Lanaham had given her and began tearing it into small pieces. "I didn't want to win that stupid contest anyway," she mumbled to herself.

She hurried home, threw her bag into the closet, and rushed to get through her chores. It wasn't until she started to make Eileen's bed that she found her curled up under the covers.

"Are you all right? You really need to tell Mommy," Lydia said, giving her sister a strange eye.

Eileen lay there, holding her stomach. "I'm fine," she moaned, trying to sit up. "Can you do me a favor?"

Lydia's usual contempt melted when she saw how pale her sister looked. "What?" she asked.

"Can you do my chores for me today?"

"Okay," Lydia agreed. She went into the closet to get the vacuum cleaner and began vacuuming the floor, but Eileen motioned for her to stop.

"No, don't vacuum," Eileen said, holding up her hand.

Lydia turned off the vacuum and walked over to the window and pulled down the shades, shielding the room from the faint glare outside. As much as she sometimes despised her sister, it was times like this—when she looked so weak and tiny—she felt sorry for her.

. ◆ .

Mattie's adrenaline was elevated.

It took some willpower to stop her from going up to Roy Jr.'s school. She thought better of it; he'd have enough trouble answering to her.

After he didn't come straight home from school, Mattie fetched her jacket and was just about to get her pocketbook when she heard his voice. She grabbed the bag with the drugs and hurried downstairs. "Boy, where have you been?"

"I was at the playground."

"I suppose you forgot to take this with you." Mattie took the small bag out of the pocket of her housedress and flung it on the table.

Roy Jr. froze.

"Where did you get this? Are you on drugs, boy?"

Roy Jr. was too afraid to look at his mother. "No, I ain't on drugs," he said in a low voice.

"Then why'd you bring this in my house?"

"Junior Youngston gave it to me."

Mattie could sense the panic in his eyes. "You mean Gladys' boy?"

He nodded.

"Why did he give it to you? I told y'all I don't want y'all hangin' around those boys."

"I ain't been hangin' around him. He just gave it to me and told me to get rid of it. He wants me to sell it for him."

"You mean to tell me you've been sellin' drugs outta my house?"

"No. I told him that I didn't want to do it," he said too quickly.

Mattie stood with her hands on her hips, glaring at her son. "Well, I'll tell you what. I'm gonna make sure you don't do it anymore. We're gonna take these drugs back to him and I'm gonna talk to Gladys about it. You come on with me," she said, reaching for her pocketbook.

"Ma, we can't do that," Roy Jr. complained.

"We're gonna see what we can't do all right. Now I ain't gonna tell you but one more time to get your behind out that door."

Roy Jr.'s legs felt like lead as they walked the eight blocks to the Youngstons' house. Along the way, he weighed his options: What his mother would do to him versus what Junior Youngston would do to him. A whooping from his mother seemed like a cakewalk compared to the whooping that Junior could lay on him.

When they arrived at the Youngstons', Mattie knocked on the door with a force that would get a deaf man's attention.

A young boy opened the door.

"Is Gladys home?" Mattie asked.

From the looks of them, the boy could tell this visit wasn't a social one. He left the door open and didn't offer to have them come inside. Mattie didn't budge.

"Well, looka' here," Gladys said, when she came to the door. "How you doin' Mattie? I haven't seen you in a long while."

Gladys was a small, frail-looking woman, not much taller than her youngest boy. She had skin the color of coffee and cream, and her face was so hard and tight you could see the crevices for each of the eleven children she raised. Her salt and pepper hair was pulled back into a ponytail, and she walked like she had purpose—and could set you straight in a minute.

"I'm fine, Gladys. I came to talk to you about somethin'."

"Well, come on in then." Gladys moved to the side, making way for them.

"I'm sure you know my eldest boy here," Mattie said, getting right to it. Roy Jr. stood looking at the floor, like it held more truth than what his mother was about to say.

"Boy, you look a spittin' image to your father," Gladys said, smiling at him as though he were a long lost relative and they were getting reacquainted at a family reunion.

Roy Jr.'s eyes left the floor long enough to acknowledge her.

"I came to talk to you about this." Mattie pulled the small bag from her pocketbook. She handed the bag to Gladys. "I believe my son got it from Junior."

Gladys took the bag and inspected it.

"Now Gladys, you've known my family for a long time. Roy and your husband used to run these streets together, and you know how hard it is to raise children on your own," Mattie said. "I have enough to worry about, and the one thing I don't allow in my house or around my boys is drugs. As a mother, I'm sure you understand where I'm comin' from." Mattie's eyes never left Gladys'.

"You say Junior gave this to you," Gladys said, dangling the bag toward Roy Jr.

Mattie shoved him. "Speak up, boy!"

"Yes, ma'am," he replied.

Gladys walked over to the stairwell and hollered up the steps. "Junior, you come on down here right now!"

Junior plummeted down the steps. He grimaced when he saw Roy Jr. and Mattie standing in their living room.

"I know you know Roy Jr., right?" Gladys said.

"Yeah, I know him," Junior said tightly.

"Now, Mattie tells me that you gave this hea' to Roy Jr. Is that true?" Gladys spread her hand open, revealing the small bag in her palm.

Junior looked down at his mother's hand and then up at Roy Jr.

Roy Jr. felt queasy, refusing to return Junior's gaze.

Gladys raised her voice. "I said is it true?"

"Yeah, I gave it to him," Junior answered, his words dragging.

"Didn't I tell you that I didn't want you messin' round with those drugs no mo'? You gonna end up right back in that place. I thought you done learned your lesson."

Mattie kept watching Roy Jr. She could see that he was intimidated by Junior.

"Do you have any more of this stuff in my house?" Gladys asked Junior.

"No."

"Don't you lie to me, boy!" Gladys said. "Now I'ma ask you one more time, and I expect you to tell me the truth."

Junior considered his mother's words. "I have a few more in my room," he finally admitted.

"You go on upstairs and bring them all to me now!" Gladys said.

When Junior came back down the stairs, this time he moved more like a camel whose hump was displaced. He handed four more of the same bags to his mother.

"I swear you ain't gonna learn yet. I'ma tell you what I'm gonna do with this." Gladys gathered the small bags in her hand. "I'ma flush every bit of it down the toilet. And if I catch any more in my house, I'ma keep on flushing. You hear me?"

"Yeah," Junior said, barely audible.

"And I want you to stay away from Roy Jr., too."

Junior didn't answer his mother.

More concerned about having to face Junior at school the next day, Roy Jr. half listened to the talk that he got from his mother and John.

"You just go the other way when you see that Junior at school," Mattie said, as if sensing his fear. "You don't need to be afraid of him. He's just a punk. I can tell that he barks louder than he bites. You stand up to him if he comes at you."

Roy Jr. nodded slightly. It wasn't only Junior he was concerned about. It was the whole Youngston bunch and all of their gang and drug-toting friends.

"Now you come on downstairs and eat something," Mattie said.

Mattie called the other children down, too, and they all sat around the table for dinner. They could have heard a pin drop it was so quiet.

Without warning, their meal was interrupted by a loud thump and the crash of glass. John and Mattie hurried into the living room. A large bat with dark scribbling on it rested on the floor. It read: *You're dead.*

Mattie's skin crawled. "That little punk," she blurted. "He's got some nerve throwin' a bat through my window."

"Ma, see. I told you we shouldn't have gone around there. Now look what happened," Roy Jr. shuddered, lumbering into the room.

"What do you mean we shouldn't have gone 'round there? What was I supposed to do, let you sell those drugs for him?"

"You should've let me handle it by myself."

"How're you gonna handle it by yourself? You barely looked at the boy when we went around there," Mattie said.

"But going around there only made it worse!"

"Well, I'll tell you what I'm gonna do. I'm gonna call the police and file a report," Mattie said between set teeth.

Two hours later, the police stood in their living room.

"Unless you saw the person that threw the bat through your window, there's really nothing we can do. If they assault you or your home again, you can call us and we'll launch an investigation."

Mattie grimaced. "So what you're tellin' me is that my son's gonna have to get killed before y'all are gonna do something about this. Is that what you're tellin' me, officer?"

"We're sorry, ma'am, but we've got no proof that Junior Youngston was the one that assaulted your home. We can't go around arresting people based on hearsay."

Mattie looked at him sharply. "Fine then. I guess I'm gonna have to take matters into my own hands."

"Ma'am, you don't want to do something that's going to make it worse off for your family. We know Junior Youngston very well. Sooner or later, he's going to end up right back where he belongs. Just keep your family away from him."

"How am I supposed to keep my family away from him when two of my children go to the same school as him? What am I supposed to do, take them out of school?"

"That's not what we're suggesting. Maybe you can go up to the school and inform the principal about what's going on."

Mattie thought about what the officer said. "Well, all right then. Maybe that's all I can do for now." She took the card the officer handed to her.

The next morning, Mattie marched right up to Roy Jr.'s school and told the principal everything.

"We've been trying to get Junior and his gang out of the school," the principal said. "He's already on academic probation, and he's a convicted juvenile, so I can assure you, he isn't going to do anything on school property. He knows we're watching him."

Mattie felt a small surge of relief before she thanked the principal and left. She thought long and hard all day about what needed to be done. By the time she finished cleaning Mrs. Levitsky's home, she had made up her mind. The only thing to put a stop to it was to confront Junior.

This time when Mattie and Roy Jr. went around to the Youngstons' house, Gladys wasn't home. Roy Jr. stood next to his mother, the sweat pouring from his forehead.

"What do you want?" Junior said when he opened the door. Three of his menacing friends stood behind him.

"I want you to leave my family alone!" Mattie said.

"I'll leave your family alone when your son pays me back for the drugs he took from me."

"He didn't take any drugs from you! We gave them back to you and your mother."

"Well, you know what happened to them, don't you? She flushed them down the toilet, and now he owes me for them."

"He doesn't owe you nothin'! We returned the stuff to you, and you need to take it up with your mother."

"My mother didn't know nothin' 'bout no drugs till you came struttin' round here."

"And I'm gonna keep on struttin' round here until you leave my son alone."

Junior gave Mattie a vicious look. "Well, we'll see about that."

"Are you threatenin' me?" Mattie shot back, the adrenaline percolating inside of her like boiled over coffee.

"I ain't threatenin' nobody. I only make promises that I keep." Mattie saw the muscles in Junior's jaw tighten. She tried to match his stance but was distracted by the way he peered at her son.

"All right," Mattie finally conceded. "I'll pay you for your petty drugs, but not because I believe you deserve it. I'm payin' you for the sake of my son. And after today, I want you to stay away from him and my family. We don't want nothin' to do with your kind."

"How you know if I want your money now? Maybe I just want to take it back in my own way." Junior eased a switchblade out of his pocket.

At that moment, Mattie realized what her family was up against. *Don't let them take your strength. Fight back*, the voice inside of her cautioned. She gave Junior an uncompromising look. "I'm gonna offer to pay you one more time. Now do you want the money or not?"

"Give me sixty dolla's," Junior finally said.

"Sixty dollars?" Mattie blurted. "Those drugs ain't worth sixty dollars."

"It's five dolla's for the bag he had, plus five dolla's for the four other bags my mother flushed."

"That's still only twenty five," Mattie said.

"And it's another twenty five plus interest for savin' your son's life."

Mattie could feel a racing in her heartbeat. Her veiled eyes never left Junior's as she pulled her pocketbook from her shoulder and reached inside to take out the sixty dollars that she'd earned that day for cleaning Mrs. Levitsky's home. "Here, take it!" She thrust the money at him. "I don't want to see or hear that you were anywhere near my family. And if you so much as lay one finger on my son, I'm gonna see to it that you spend the rest of your life in hell!"

A few weeks later, the principal called Mattie. "The police picked Junior up this morning for a probation violation. I wanted to thank you for taking the time to come up to the school and inform us about what he'd done to your family. It's parents like you that make it possible for us to get thugs like Junior off the streets."

Mattie smiled when she hung up the phone. Her son was safe, and Junior Youngston was where he belonged.

But nothing could ease the disappointment and anger that Mattie felt a short time later. News that her sixteen-year-old daughter had just had a miscarriage hit her like a ton of bricks.

Mattie and John stood up and watched Eileen walk out into the hospital's waiting area after the doctors had released her. Mattie looked at her daughter with anguish and disappointment all mixed up inside her. She was too weary to be angry, too tired to preach.

It had been one hell of a winter.

27

$\mathcal{M}$attie stood at the sink in her housecoat and slippers, cleaning collard greens. The midmorning sun glared through the kitchen window, lighting up her face like honeydew. The last few years had been heavy on her. After the Youngstons' incident, and Roy Jr. had gotten a taste of earning some fast money, he decided to try and become another Junior. That choice had landed him in jail overnight and later brought him into court. The judge reduced the charges to a misdemeanor after Mattie showed up and pleaded with the judge. Later, Anthony's grades at Southwalk started to slip after he took off his bifocals and discovered girls. Then, Eileen got pregnant again soon after her high school graduation, but fortunately she and Derrick decided to marry and they moved into a small apartment. On top of it all, Mattie had been back and forth at the hospital with Lydia, who had begun having *problems* after she got her period. And then they found out that Lydia wouldn't be able to bear any children at all. And finally, Mattie felt helpless as she watched Angie's behavior turn from odd to very strange. She was deeply concerned. She took Angie everywhere searching for an answer but the things they told her just didn't add up.

Aside from all the family crises, it was mornings like this, with the smells rising from the stove and Shirley Ceasar's sultry voice simmering in the air, that Mattie felt at peace—a kind of peace that helped her put all of her troubles on hold. She thought about John, who had been her rock, the last ounce of strength when she had no strength to give. He'd been with her through it all, oftentimes carrying the weight when she was too overwhelmed, or sad, or just plain tired.

John had gotten into the habit of handing over his paycheck to Mattie and saying: "Get the kids their school clothes," or "Here's a little something to put down on a new living room set," or "Here's this month's rent or money to buy food." His contribution to the family was significant, and Mattie loved him and often wondered what her life would be like without him.

A sudden ringing of the phone interrupted Mattie's thoughts. Eileen was on the other end.

"Ma, guess what?"

"What?" Mattie asked, hoping it wasn't yet another emergency.

"I'm at the hospital. We're about to have the baby."

Mattie darted over to the large calendar that she kept on the refrigerator. She searched for Eileen's due date that she'd circled. "Ain't you about two or three weeks early?" she asked.

"Yes, but my water broke this morning, and I've been in labor for a few hours now."

"All right then," Mattie said, drying her hands. "I'm gonna get John to bring me to the hospital. I should be there soon."

"Okay, Ma."

Mattie quickly turned off the knobs on the stove and rushed upstairs. She couldn't wait to tell John the news.

"Hi, Ma," Eileen said, looking young and frightened.

"How are you feeling?" Mattie asked.

Eileen patted the large mound protruding from her middle. "I'm fine, I guess. It's very painful sometimes."

Mattie smiled. "I know it's painful. But that's what having a baby is all about."

Eileen gave her a weak smile.

Mattie, John, and Derrick stayed in the room with Eileen until it was time to roll her into the delivery room.

"We'll be right out here," Mattie called after her. "Derrick, you let us know as soon as the baby gets here."

Derrick nodded and walked behind Eileen's rolling bed, looking a bit lost in it all.

Less than an hour later, Derrick emerged. "It's a boy!" he said with excitement.

"A boy?" Mattie repeated. "You mean I have a grandson?"

Derrick nodded and smiled.

"How's Eileen?"

Derrick's face lit up. "She's fine. Both of them."

"That's good," Mattie said. "That's really good." The joy that sprang from her face radiated all around them.

28

"Ma, I can't walk," Angie said, limping down the stairs. She looked shrunken inside her pajamas, and her eyes sunk deeply into her ashen face as she looked at her mother, trying to find the right words to describe the voices inside her head.

Mattie examined both of Angie's legs. There was no obvious swelling, no cuts, no bruises. "Let me see you walk over there," she said, pointing toward the living room.

Angie turned around, took three steps, and began hopping. "It hurts really bad," she whined, collapsing on the sofa.

"Where does it hurt?" Mattie asked, pressing down on her thighs and knees.

"All over."

"All over where?"

Angie went silent. Then she muttered something that didn't make any sense.

Mattie rushed upstairs and woke up John. "Something's not right with Angie," she said.

"What's wrong with her?" John said, coming out of sleep.

"I don't know. She's been actin' really strange lately, and now she says she can't walk."

Mattie looked toward the window, trying to make sense out of something that was senseless. "She came downstairs this mornin' limping. She ain't been right for a while now."

John sat up in bed. "What did they say when you took her to the medical center a few weeks ago?"

"Those people 'round there don't know what they're talking about. They just said her behavior is normal for her age, that maybe she's just going through puberty or something."

"That don't make any sense."

"Well, it don't make any sense to me, either. I think we better take her to the hospital so she can see the right kind of doctors."

Mattie and John dressed quickly, and then Mattie helped Angie get dressed. As they drove to Pennsylvania Hospital, Mattie let her mind slip back to when she had first noticed Angie's strange behavior. It had started with her sleeping more than usual. Then the walking around with a glum look on her face, like she was so deep in thought that you needed a fishing rod to yank her back to reality. Then the one-sided conversations, addressing things that she only imagined. Next came the isolation, and then total withdrawal. Finally, limping down the stairs this morning, claiming paralysis.

As soon as they arrived at the emergency room, the attendant took their information and told them to have a seat. "Someone will be with you shortly," she said matter of factly.

Mattie waited patiently with Angie next to her while John stepped out for some air. Two hours later, Mattie heard them call Angie's name. She jumped from her seat so quickly you would have thought her name had just been called for the lottery. "Come on, Angie," she said, as she hoisted her up by the arm. Angie held onto her mother and limped through the white flapping doors.

The nurse pointed to the hospital bed. "Have a seat. So what brings you here today? Did she hurt her leg or foot?"

Mattie looked over at Angie and then back to the nurse. "No, I don't think she hurt it. She says she can't walk any-more, and that she's hearin' voices."

The nurse gave Mattie a concerned look, then turned to Angie. "Why don't you tell me what's wrong with you, honey," she said to Angie as though Mattie was the one who had been hearing voices since Angie's limp had nothing to do with a bizarre state of mind.

"My legs don't work no more," Angie said slowly. "And I keep hearin' things."

The nurse put her hand on Angie's leg. "What do you mean your legs don't work anymore?"

Suddenly, Angie's whole body shook and she started heav-ing and crying, tears flowing down her face like a river.

"See, she's been actin' this way for a while now. I took her to a few doctors, but they all keep saying the same thing," Mattie said.

"What did they say?"

"They just said that her behavior may be normal for her age; she turned thirteen in March."

The nurse removed the stethoscope from around her neck

and listened to Angie's heart, and then she took her blood pressure. "Follow me so I can get your weight, sweetie," she said.

Angie hopped down off the bed. Mattie grabbed her by the arm and helped her to the scale.

The nurse moved the meter back and forth to steady the dial. She pushed the meter further to the right until the dial settled on one hundred sixty-two pounds. She scribbled something in the file. For the first time, Mattie noticed how much weight Angie had gained.

"Have a seat, and the doctor will be in shortly," the nurse told them.

Angie lay down on the hospital bed and shut her eyes. Mattie stared at her, trying to remember exactly when her youngest child had changed—when she had gone from a happy, playful child to the person that lay on the bed across from her. She thought about the day Angie turned eleven, a few years ago.

After a while, the doctor finally showed up. "I'm going to run some tests, draw blood, and have the staff psychiatrist talk to her. We may decide to admit her overnight just to keep an eye on her for a while," he told Mattie.

After a litany of tests and talk, and more tests and more talk, Mattie was asked to sign a consent form giving them permission to admit Angie. The doctor threw words at her that she had never heard of. Then he said, "I've prescribed a mild sedative to stabilize her. We want to monitor her for the next few days and have her see a child psychiatrist. Do you have any questions?"

Mattie cleared her throat. "Well . . ." she began, her voice was low, nearly inaudible. "Is she gonna be okay?"

"It's too early to tell. I want to see how she responds to the medication," the doctor replied, not committing to anything.

Mattie looked square into his eyes, then she looked at John as though he could help explain what was happening to her youngest child. But John seemed as bewildered as Mattie, and he shrugged his shoulders without explanation.

"Okay," Mattie said quietly. She felt profoundly tired all of a sudden, like all the energy had been snuffed from her. She stood up, and her legs felt heavy, like a load of bricks were tied to them, as if she had Angie's legs.

"Why don't you go on home, Mrs. Madison, get some rest, and come back in the morning? We'll make sure that Angie's well cared for. She's going to be all right." Something in his voice sounded superficial to Mattie, like he had said those words too many times before.

It was sometime after midnight when John left the hospital. Mattie stayed with Angie. She stayed by her daughter's side for the next two days as they probed and pried and probed some more. On the fourth day, they released Angie with a prescription and the name of a child psychiatrist they recommended she see immediately.

Sleepless nights overtook Mattie. The thought of whether she'd caused her daughter's condition haunted her. All kinds of horrible thoughts crowded her mind: Was there something she did or didn't do? Did she give her enough attention? Was she too strict? Should she have taken her to the doctor sooner and not allowed those incompetent people to blame puberty?

Mattie kept trudging around, dragging her heart along with her. After several visits to Dr. Phillips, the child psychiatrist, Angie was diagnosed with a manic-depressive and schizophrenia disorder. When Mattie heard this news, it felt like someone had balled up their fist and sucker punched her in the chest. She cried inside, not wanting Angie to see how torn apart she was. How could a vibrant, happy child be playful and joyful one day and schizophrenic the next? She could feel herself falling apart even as Dr. Phillips went on trying to give her hope.

Angie, age 12, before she was diagnosed.

"With medication, proper treatment, and counseling, she may get better over time," Dr. Phillips told her. "She's so young, she's capable of bouncing back."

Mattie could hear him, but the words sounded all bunched up like they had no structure or meaning. She closed her eyes to push back the tears that threatened to stream down her face. She held on tightly to the arms of the chair, squeezing till her fingers hurt. The room closed in on her as she tried to steady herself. Then suddenly she stood up. "My child ain't gonna be all right, is she?" she said to him, more like a statement than a question. She instinctively held out her hand and took the prescription. She turned and grabbed Angie's hand and helped her hobble out the door.

In early November, a few weeks after Dr. Phillips diagnosed her, Angie had her first *episode*. That's what the doctors labeled it, an *episode*, like she was this long lost character inside of a soap opera gone bad. Angie was hospitalized the same night that Wilson Goode won the election and became the first black mayor of Philadelphia.

Mattie sat in the chair across from Angie's hospital bed, watching her chest slowly rise and fall. The medication calmed the voices in Angie's head, making her look at peace as she slept in the large, steel-framed bed that seemed to swallow her.

Mattie listened to the announcement on the television that hung over Angie's hospital bed. Everyone was overcome with joy as Wilson Goode walked up to the podium and thanked his constituents. Mattie couldn't help but feel elated and sad all in the same moment. She was glad that a black man was elected, but sad to see her baby laying there zoned out on Lithium.

She couldn't believe that in a few short months so much had changed. Wilson Goode was elected the first black mayor of Philadelphia, Vanessa Williams was selected as the first black woman to become Miss America, and Ronald Reagan signed a bill designating January 15 a national holiday for Martin Luther King Jr.'s birthday. But from where she sat on the fourth floor in the Psychiatric Ward at Pennsylvania Hospital with her thirteen-year-old daughter, the world looked bleak.

The television appeared to get smaller and smaller as the tears fell down Mattie's cheeks, flooding her vision. She grabbed her daughter's hand, holding on to it, a quiet prayer parting her lips.

29

For two days now, Lydia had been preparing for the New Year's Eve party that Lloyd was taking her to. She and Lloyd had met the summer before her sixteenth birthday, and though she wasn't allowed to have boy phone calls, they talked and saw each other secretly until she became of age.

Lloyd was one of the cutest boys Lydia had ever met. All the girls on 25th Street had a crush on him, but it was Lydia that he pursued. At first, Lydia was reluctant, because she had heard he was trouble. In fact, he'd been in and out of detention centers ever since he was eleven years old, for almost every type of crime—stealing cars, selling drugs, possessing a weapon. You name it, he'd apparently done it. But everything that Lydia had heard about him just didn't fit the boy that showed up on her porch that summer.

It was the previous summer that Lloyd's family had moved in with his grandmother, who lived only a few doors away from Lydia's family. When they first met, Lloyd's magnetic smile beamed at her. He was so pleasant and charming. And when she asked him about his past, he told her he was no longer that person. He wanted things out of life—wanted to finish high school, wanted to go to college. He had goals and dreams and desires. "That's why my family moved out of Passyunk Projects and bought a house in the suburbs—to get us away from all the trouble," he had told her.

Lloyd was good to Lydia. He took her to the movies, out to dinner, to the park to listen to her recite her poems. He loved her poetry and encouraged her to write more. "You are so creative," he told her one day when she read one of the poems that she had written for him.

He had even come up to the hospital to see her when she was hospitalized and later learned that she couldn't have any children. "You're gonna be all right," he had told her. "Maybe someday we can adopt." Lydia clung to the *we* word. Already, he was planning a future with her.

They had been together for a year, and now Lydia was preparing for the holiday party. She rushed to put on the new outfit she had bought just that day: a red top, black slacks, and black patent leather shoes.

Lydia could sense Angie's eyes on her. "Where you going?" she asked from her bed.

"To a New Year's Eve party with Lloyd," Lydia answered, not turning from the mirror.

"I went to a New Year's Eve party today," Angie said unexpectedly.

Lydia turned and smiled at her sister. She finished dressing and admired herself in the mirror. She looked very pretty. Even Angie told her so.

Lydia couldn't help but feel sorry for her sister. She watched her mother take Angie to every specialist known in the area, trying to find a cause or cure. But they all seemed to tell her the same thing and did nothing more than prescribe more drugs. Angie's sickness was like a double-edged sword—without the drugs, she would hear and see things, have *episodes*; with the drugs, she was lifeless, floating around on air with only enough energy to sleep.

As soon as Lydia heard her mother calling her, she grabbed her stuff and ran downstairs. The sight of Angie made her sad, and she didn't want to be sad on New Year's Eve.

"Hi," Lydia greeted Lloyd.

"Hi. You ready?" he asked. He seemed nervous, as he twirled the keys to his father's car in his hands.

"Yes, I'm ready." Lydia turned to get her jacket. "Mom, we're leaving now."

Mattie came out from the kitchen. "Y'all have a good time," she said.

Lloyd held the car door open as he helped Lydia get into the old Buick. As he started the engine, he told her that he needed to make a stop.

"Okay," Lydia said, not really caring they would be late for the party.

Lydia was surprised when she noticed they were heading in the direction of Passyunk Projects, the place where Lloyd had moved away from. When he stopped the car, she was about to get out and follow him, but he told her to wait. "I won't be long," he said.

Lydia sat in the car, staring out the window, with the doors locked. Half an hour later when Lloyd finally came out, she was relieved.

He barely looked at her when he got into the car and started the ignition.

"Are you okay?" Lydia asked.

"I'm fine," he said quickly, trying hard not to look flustered.

Lydia stayed by Lloyd's side the whole night. He wasn't himself. He seemed on edge, she thought. Just as they were ready to leave, she spotted one of her classmates. "I'll be right back," she told him.

Lloyd grabbed her by the arm so tightly she could feel his nails digging into her flesh. "We're leaving!" he said, pulling her out the door.

"Ouch! You're hurting me," Lydia winced.

"I'm gonna hurt somethin' else if you don't get your ass in the car."

"Excuse me. What's wrong with you?"

"I said shut the hell up and get in the car."

"I'm not getting in that car with you. Something must be wrong with you if you think you can talk to me like that." Lydia pulled away from him and marched down the street.

Lloyd caught up to her, and with a single gesture, he swung his fist—hitting her precisely on her bottom lip. Lydia was stunned for just an instant, before she fell to the ground. She lay on the cold cement, her breath uneven, her body heaving. She could hear him coming closer to her, and she stayed still. She didn't move. She didn't say another word.

"See, look what you made me do," Lloyd crooned, his voice hinting at disbelief. "I told you to get in the car and not to say anything."

Lydia stiffened as he approached her. "Get away from me!" She sat up and looked around for her jacket and purse, the purse she had borrowed from her mother.

"Lydia, I'm so sorry. I didn't mean to do it. I just lost my head for a minute."

"Stay away from me. I hate you!" Lydia struggled to sit up.

"You don't mean that. You know how much I love you. I just lost it for a minute. Please don't treat me like this."

Lydia wiped the stickiness from her face and tried to balance her thoughts. Her voice came from deep within her, toneless and coarse. "Don't treat *you* like this? What do you mean don't treat *you* like this? You hit me, and I'm the one that's treating you like something?" She crawled over to the car and started putting her stuff back in the purse—coins, the eye shadow case, lipstick, the New Year's Eve card that she had made especially for him with one of her poems inserted in it. She shoved the card into the purse and tried to lift herself off the ground. Lloyd reached his hand out to help her.

"Leave me alone!" she said, knocking away his hand. She stood and limped over to her jacket.

"Come on now. You know I didn't mean it. I'm trying really hard to do the right thing," Lloyd said, following her.

Lydia looked at him, her anger melting slightly. "If you're trying to do the right thing, then why do you keep going back to Passyunk? Why did you go inside that house for half an hour? You think I don't know what you've been doing?"

Her questions surprised him.

"Yeah, I know what's been going on," Lydia said. "You've been taking drugs. You think I can't tell when you show up at my house with your glassy eyes and slow talking. I've known for a while now."

Lloyd moved closer to her. "Lydia, I'm so sorry. I promise, I'll never put my hands on you again."

Lydia's shoulders relaxed. She wiped the tears away from her cheeks and looked off into the distance.

Lloyd reached for her. "I love you. I promise I'm gonna get myself together, leave the drugs alone."

Strangely calm and forgiving, Lydia fell into him and put her head against his shoulder. Minutes passed before they released their embrace.

They drove home in silence.

With her bottom lip raw and swollen, camouflaged by pink lipstick, Lydia avoided her mother like the plague. She had forgiven Lloyd, so there was no need to worry her mother. After all, Lloyd wasn't himself; the drugs had made him do it, she told herself. And when she saw him the next weekend, he looked like his old self again, charming and loving.

Lydia and Lloyd went on seeing each other every weekend and during the week whenever they found the time. He seemed to go out of his way to make her feel comfortable. He bought her candy and poetry books, whatever he thought would win her heart again. In time, he did manage to do just that, making her feel like she had once felt. He even found a job and stayed away from Passyunk. Or so she thought, until one weekend when she went to visit him.

Lydia found Lloyd in his bedroom. He was in a strange

mood. His eyes were glassy, and as soon as she settled in, he started accusing and cursing her for being unfaithful, a lie that one of his friends had told him.

"Whoever told you they saw me with another boy is lying. I don't want to be with anybody but you," she told him.

But Lloyd kept on about it, telling her there must be some truth to it, especially since she rarely made time for him anymore.

"I work now. You know that I don't get off until six o'clock, and by the time I get home and do my homework and chores, my mother ain't gonna let me come back out to see you. I'm not supposed to see you during the week anyway," she said.

He hovered over her, looking down at her with a smirk on his face. There was something else bothering him. Something he wasn't saying. "You act like you're better than me since you've been workin' at that place," he finally said.

Lloyd's words surprised Lydia. She took in her breath and stared at him. "What!" she said. "That is the most ridiculous thing I have ever heard."

Lloyd's body stiffened, his eyes narrowed, and the bones in his jaws tightened. "I know you ain't talkin' down to me again," he said tightly.

A tremor of fear swept over Lydia. She had seen this side of him before, had felt the love turn to hate, seen him transform. She softened her voice. "What do you mean I'm talking down to you?" she stammered. "How am I talking down to you? I'm just surprised you would say something like that."

Lloyd gawked at her. "I don't know why you brought your ass over here today anyway. You should just go and be with your high and mighty friends at that job."

Lydia picked up her purse and looked for her jacket. "You know what . . . I don't have to listen to this. I'm leaving."

"You ain't going nowhere till I take you home." Lloyd stood in front of the door.

"I don't need you to take me home. I'm gonna take the bus." She put on her jacket and walked toward the door.

"I said you ain't going nowhere without me." Lloyd grabbed her arm and shoved her to the bed.

"Don't you put your hands on me, boy," Lydia said. "Don't you ever put your hands on me again!"

"I told you, you ain't gonna talk to me like no punk. All you bitches are the same."

"I know you didn't just call me a bitch. Move outta my way. I'm leaving." Lydia stood up and tried to push past him. As soon as she reached for the doorknob, Lloyd struck her. She lost her balance and fell back, her head hitting the dresser. This time, he didn't stop at one punch. He stood over her and pounded her for what seemed like an eternity. She kicked and screamed and fought back, but it wasn't until Lloyd heard a knock at the door that he stopped beating her.

"Lloyd?" his mother called out. "Is everything okay in there?"

Lydia wanted to cry out, flee him, but he grabbed her mouth and held her down.

"Yeah, everything's fine. We're just having a little disagreement."

"Well, it's getting pretty late. Maybe you should take Lydia home soon."

"I will."

Hearing his mother leave from the door, Lloyd finally let

Lydia go. She lay there a while before she tried to push herself up off the floor. Finally, she stood and looked Lloyd squarely in the eyes. "I'm gonna leave this time, and if you try to stop me, I'm gonna call the police when I get home. Just move outta my way so I can leave!"

Seeing the look on Lydia's face, Lloyd stepped out of her way. As soon as Lydia reached the hallway, she could hear the television downstairs, could hear his mother moving around in the kitchen. She waited to collect herself.

"Lydia, are you leaving?" Lloyd's mother called out from the kitchen.

Lydia became still. "Yes," she said quietly.

His mother came out of the kitchen. "Well, you have a safe trip home, and maybe I'll see you next week."

"Okay," Lydia said quietly, her eyes fixed on the floor.

"Are you all right? And where is Lloyd? Ain't he gonna take you home?"

"No, I told him that he didn't need to take me home. My brother's coming to get me," Lydia said, standing in the dark foyer.

"Well, all right then. You sure you're okay?"

Lydia nodded and then turned and left. She walked slowly to the bus stop. Her face stung and her body reeked pain. She could feel the swelling rising.

An hour later, she boarded the bus, paid her fare, and walked to the back. She looked out the window and cried silently. She was ashamed that she had allowed herself to be in this situation. She had known for a while about Lloyd's behavior. New Year's Eve was the first time he had struck her, but it wasn't the first sign. Before that night, there were other signs—a shove here, a push there, the periodic name-calling. But she always forgave him, allowed him to blame this or that, never holding him accountable.

Lydia never told her mother any of it and had only confided in her best friend, Dana. "You need to leave him alone," Dana had told her more than once. But Lydia wouldn't listen, and tonight she thought about what Dana had said to her. She wished that she'd taken her advice, but it was too late to think about that now. Tonight, she was alone with a bruised face, an aching body, and a broken heart, and she told herself that she never wanted to see Lloyd again, never wanted anything more to do with him.

"Lydia, is that you?"

Lydia froze and quickly straightened up, as she heard her mother's footsteps coming down the stairs.

"I thought that was you. I didn't expect you for another two hours."

Lydia forced a smile and turned her sad face away from her mother.

"What's ailing you girl? Why are you actin' so strange?"

Lydia stood still, keeping her eyes focused on the large picture of Jesus that hung above the sofa in the dark living room. "Nothing's wrong with me. I'm just tired, that's all."

Mattie gave her an inquisitive look. Lydia shifted her stance, kept her eyes on Jesus.

"You come on in the kitchen with me so I can see what's ailing you."

"Ma, ain't nothing wrong with me. I'm just tired. I just want to go to bed."

"You just want to go to bed?" Mattie said in a raised

voice. "You just want to go to bed? Well you can go to bed after I see what's ailing you. Now I said get on in that kitchen."

Lydia hesitated, and then dragged herself into the kitchen.

As soon as Mattie turned and looked at her daughter, she saw it all. "What done happened to you? Why are you cryin' and why is your face red?"

Lydia took a deep breath. "Nothing happened to me. I was just crying because Lloyd and I broke up."

Mattie studied her daughter's face. "Somethin' more happened than just you and Lloyd broke up. That boy ain't done put his hands on you, did he?"

Lydia felt the tears stinging her eyes. She raised her gaze to the ceiling to keep the tears from falling. "No boy put his hands on me. I told you, Ma. We just broke up, that's all," she said, then she turned and rushed up the stairs.

Lydia stayed in her room until she heard her mother finally shut her bedroom door. She quietly made her way to the kitchen and wrapped some ice in a paper towel, to keep the swelling down.

During the next few days, Lydia managed to stay out of her mother's sight. Lloyd called nonstop, but she refused to take his calls.

A week later, she went to see the school nurse, complaining of severe cramps.

"Are you on your period?" the nurse asked.

"Yes, I have really bad cramps, too."

After the nurse examined her, she wrote a pass for Lydia to be released early from school. By the time her mother got home from work, Lydia could barely stand up.

"I'm gonna have to take you to the hospital. You hurry up and get dressed," Mattie said.

The attending physician examined Lydia and ordered all kinds of tests.

Mattie and Lydia sat in silence for a long time, a silence broken only by the rushing noises outside their door. Mattie knew that Lydia had been in a lot of pain lately—in more ways than one. A feeling was in Mattie's stomach, the kind that made her hope something serious wasn't wrong with her daughter. She thought about the night that Lydia had come home in tears and then the days that followed when she stayed in her room, avoiding everyone. Mattie wondered if there was something more that Lydia wasn't telling. Her thoughts were suddenly interrupted by the doctor entering their room. Lydia sat up as the doctor stepped in closer to her bed. Mattie came closer, too.

"Unfortunately, a tumor has grown, and we are going to have to perform a hysterectomy to stop the swelling and bleeding," the doctor said. Because Lydia was not of age, the doctor went on, he needed Mattie's permission to perform the hysterectomy. "I have ordered more blood work and a sonogram. Once I get the results, we'll schedule the surgery for tomorrow morning."

Mattie nodded blankly.

After the doctor left, the nurse came in and drew blood from Lydia and arranged to take her for the sonogram. Several hours later, the doctor returned to her room. "Mrs. Madison, we have some unexpected news," he said.

Mattie felt the weight of his words closing in on her. She held her breath.

"It appears that your daughter is pregnant. The blood test and the sonogram results have confirmed our findings."

His news cut through Mattie like a sharp knife. Lydia lay motionless.

"*Pregnant?* She can't be pregnant. We were told she couldn't have any chi'ren," Mattie stammered.

"Who told you that?" the doctor asked, baffled.

"Dr. Kapow did. The gynecologist she's been seeing all this time."

"Well, I don't understand why she would have told you that. The results clearly suggest otherwise."

A small amount of time had lapsed when Mattie realized the magnitude of what the doctor had just said. Her surprise turned to sheer anger. "I'm gonna kill you, girl," she said to Lydia. "I can't believe you've been lettin' that boy fool you."

"Mrs. Madison, can I speak to you outside please?" the doctor asked, embarrassed to see that Mattie had to find out about her daughter's condition this way.

"Whatever you gotta say you can say in front of her, because I want her to know what I'm gonna do to her when she get home!"

The doctor nodded his head in understanding. He gave Lydia a sympathetic look and turned back to Mattie. "Ma'am, please join me in the hallway."

Mattie gave Lydia a warning look and reluctantly followed him out of the room.

"Mrs. Madison, I know how upset you are, but maybe you should think about this," he said delicately. "Now, before your daughter ended up here today, you and your family were told she couldn't bear any children; maybe her doctor told you that at the time because of her condition. However, you might want to examine this from another angle. If she wasn't pregnant and we had performed the hysterectomy, it would have been a one hundred percent certainty that she would never be able to have children. Please, Mrs. Madison, perhaps you should take some time to think about it."

A rush of emotions flooded through Mattie. "Maybe you're right," she finally said. "Maybe I need to take some time to think about it."

"Now, we have some other decisions to make," the doctor continued. "Obviously, the pregnancy precludes us from performing the hysterectomy. There's one other thing that I didn't want to tell you in front of your daughter."

Mattie felt faint.

"It appears the pregnancy is lodged in her tubes. We were able to confirm this from the test results, as well."

"So what are you saying?" Mattie asked, puzzled.

"I'd like to see if the fetus will find its way to the uterus. If so, then perhaps the pregnancy could be salvaged. I would also suggest that you and your daughter take some time to discuss whether or not she would like to keep the baby. You may want to give it some serious thought, especially since she will be unable to have any children if we abort this pregnancy and proceed with the surgery."

Mattie's mind was numb. "How long will it take before we know anything?" she asked.

"I want to give it at least four weeks."

"All right then," Mattie said quietly.

"I would like to release her tomorrow morning and prescribe medication for the tumor and to relieve the bleeding and pain. In the meantime, I want her to stay off her feet for four weeks and reduce any stress or physical activities until she returns to see me. Do you have any questions?"

Mattie shook her head from side to side.

"Very well. I'd like to discuss this with your daughter if that's okay with you."

Mattie gave a faint nod.

That evening after Mattie and the doctors left her alone, Lydia rested her hand on her abdomen, wanting to feel the life that was spawning inside of her. She instinctively picked up the phone and dialed it.

"Hello."

Lydia held her breath.

"Hello, who is this?" Lloyd said again. Then he heard a dial tone.

Two weeks later, Anthony called Lydia downstairs. As soon as she saw Lloyd standing there, she could see from the look on his face that he knew.

"Can I talk to you?" he asked tentatively.

Lydia nodded and went over to the sofa. Lloyd followed her.

"I know that I've hurt you really bad," Lloyd said, taking his time. "I told myself over and over again that I don't deserve you. That's why I stopped calling. But when I saw your brother in town and he told me about what happened to you . . . I want to be by your side through this. It's as much my responsibility as it is yours."

Lydia felt like leaving the room, but she couldn't bring herself to walk away.

"I want to do the right thing. I want to be a good father if you decide to keep the baby. And I think things turned out this way for a reason. I think this could be a sign that we're supposed to be together. I'm not asking you to take me back right now, but just think about it. Okay?"

During the last few weeks, as much as Lydia had felt alone and wanted to call him, her pride wouldn't let her. And now she couldn't bring herself to forgive him, to let him back in. Not just yet.

Lydia awoke bright and early the morning of her appointment. A fierce nausea tugged at her. She had watched Eileen go through terrible morning sickness, and now she took back every bad thought she'd ever had about her sister during that time. She got up and went to the bathroom, relented her morning sickness to the toilet, splashed cold water on her face, and brushed her teeth.

"Here," Mattie said, shoving a plate in front of Lydia when Lydia joined her for breakfast. "You need to try to force something on your stomach. Try to eat these grits." Lydia and her mother barely spoke anymore.

Lydia picked up the spoon and took small bites. After she was done, she got her jacket and waited for her mother in the living room.

They arrived at the doctor's office at exactly ten thirty.

Lydia and Mattie sat in the waiting room, glued to the black-and-white clock, watching the big hand move slowly around with the little hand ticking closely behind. The wait was unbearable. Mattie had prayed over the past few weeks that her daughter would be okay—if it was God's will for Lydia to have this child, she would love her and the baby all the same. Lydia's heart ticked like the clock as she prayed she would come to have this baby, love it, and raise it like her mother had raised her.

Interrupting their thoughts, the nurse arrived to tell them the doctor would now see them.

"I have good news," he said, as soon as they took a seat in his office. His voice sounded distant, and the room got still and small and moved slowly around Lydia. She imagined seeing the words slowly roll from his lips, like a ventriloquist.

"The fetus has found its way to the uterus, and the pregnancy appears to be stable. Although the tumor is still there, there is no indication the pregnancy has made it any worse. In fact, she has responded very well to the medication."

Mattie looked at the doctor, and then at Lydia, a mixture of emotions enveloping her.

"Do you have any questions?" the doctor asked.

They both shook their heads no.

"Very well." The doctor jotted something in his file. "So have you made a decision about the pregnancy?" he said, looking up at them again.

Mattie didn't know how to speak the words she'd been intending to say for weeks now. "Well," she said softly. "I decided to let Lydia make the decision. I'll support whatever she decides." She turned and looked at her daughter.

The doctor turned to Lydia. "Well Lydia, have you made a decision?"

Lydia's heart pounded so fast she could feel it beat against her throat. "Ummm, yes. I . . . I think I've made a decision," she said cautiously. She looked timidly at her mother. "I, um . . . I think I would like to keep the baby, if it's all right with my mother."

Mattie's heart felt like it was about to rip in two hearing the pity in her daughter's voice. "It's all right with me," she whispered.

The room got quiet.

"All right then," the doctor said at last. "I'm going to put you in touch with a very good obstetrician, and I would also like to continue to see you, as well." He reached into his top drawer and pulled out a book that held the names of his most esteemed colleagues. He jotted down a name onto a card and handed it to Lydia. "I think you are making a very brave decision, young lady. I hope someday you will make your mother proud." He stood and reached out his hand.

Lydia took it with a blank face. She thought it odd the way he was talking to her, like she had just won the Pulitzer Prize or something—as though she were not a scared seventeen-year-old who was about to become a mother, a woman. But when she looked at him and saw his smile, she realized he was only trying to prepare her for the next phase of her life, prepare her for what lay ahead.

30

The day that Deller called to give Mattie some news, the April skies opened up and poured rain so hard the streets flooded all over Philadelphia. The rain, Deller's news, and Mattie's somber mood carried on for days.

"Daddy's sick," Deller had said, as soon as she heard Mattie's voice on the other end of the line.

Mattie went numb. The last time she and Deller had seen their father was more than twenty-five years ago; and the only other time they'd been in touch with him was when their mother had gone back to Kingstree to live with him. But the brief phone calls were barely memorable now.

"He's in a nursing home," Deller continued. "They say he's been in there for a while now. He had a stroke after Mama left him."

Mattie stayed quiet; she was detached and silenced by the thought of her father.

"The only thing he remembered was that he had a daughter who moved to New York to get married. He couldn't remember my last name. The nurses felt so bad for him they spent the last few months trying to track me down. Can you believe they were able to find me?"

Mattie didn't move, didn't say anything.

"I can't believe Daddy remembered all this time that I was the one who married and moved to New York. They say it's a miracle he even remembered that much because the stroke has left him pretty bad off." Deller waited for some kind of response from Mattie. Anything.

"Anyhow, they contacted me because he's got no family down there. I think we need to go see him, Mattie. Maybe bring him up north."

They were over two hundred miles apart, but the tension in the air was so thick it crossed state lines. A full minute passed before Mattie replied. "You know, I'm sorry he's sick and all, but I'm really not interested in seein' him, nor do I care to have him around my family."

"Mattie, I know he ain't been the best person, but he's still our father. We can't just act like we don't know him. He's sick. He needs us." Deller moved her ear closer to the phone, hoping that she had gotten through to her sister. "Mattie please don't make me do this on my own. You know that you and I are the only two that can do something. I don't think we have a choice," Deller said dismally.

Mattie wiped away the one tear that managed to push its way down her left cheek. The fact that he was an old sick man didn't make it any more desirable for her to suddenly want to rescue him. It puzzled her, however, that Deller was ready to forgive him for all he'd done. To be sure, she had suffered her share of torment from him. And now here she was on the other end of the line asking Mattie to put her life on hold for him. Well, that wasn't going to happen. Not now. Not ever. If Deller wanted to let him back in, then that was her business. "Well, I hope you have a safe trip," Mattie said curtly and hung up the phone.

Within days, Deller made arrangements to go to Kingstree. She would travel by train. The drive would be too much for her, since she was going alone. She packed lightly, taking only the necessary things. She'd plan to stay with Aunt Maybelle while she finalized the plans for their return trip. She took a late train out of New York City's Grand Central Station. The trip would be sixteen hours.

When Deller arrived in Kingstree, Aunt Maybelle picked her up at the train station and drove her to her home. Deller rested for only a few hours before Aunt Maybelle drove her to the nursing home.

"I'm here to see my father, Isaac Bingham," Deller announced, as soon as they arrived. She was so nervous she could hear her own teeth clatter together as the words fumbled out of her mouth.

"Sign here," the desk attendant said. He looked up her father's information and scribbled the room number on two yellow passes. "Isaac Bingham is in room 315. Take the elevator to the third floor, then turn right. His room is on the left."

Deller nodded, and Aunt Maybelle followed.

As the elevator accelerated to the third floor, Deller could feel her stomach drop to her knees. Suddenly, she was sixteen again, not forty-two. Today would be the first time she had seen her father since the day he threw her and Ben and their newborn baby out of the house. That day was as vivid in her mind as the bright light that lit up the numbers above the elevator door.

Isaac sat in a wooden chair, the television glowing in front of him. He wore blue khaki pants and a gray cotton sweater that seemed to swallow him. His skin was chalky, his hair gray. His hazel eyes had specks of yellow with a tinge of gray tint, and they were sunk deep in their sockets. He was frail and gaunt, no longer the giant that ruled the kingdom on Boston Street.

At first he didn't recognize Deller. She favored somebody he once knew, perhaps his own mother. He knew that she had to be one of the eldest girls. The nurse had told him the one from New York City was coming. Deller. His Deller.

Deller grabbed his thin, bony hand. "Hi, Daddy. It's me, Deller. You remember me, don't you Daddy?" she coaxed.

Isaac had to strain to look up at her. "Del-la. Del-la. Is that who you say you are?" he said, struggling to pronounce her name in his aged voice.

Deller smiled at him as her heart swelled and her eyes moistened. "Yes, Daddy. It's me. It's Deller."

Isaac gaped at her, then his expression changed. "Yeah, I memba' you, gal. I memba' Del-la," he said.

Deller squeezed his hand, rubbed his arm. "Daddy, I came to take you back home with me. The nurses told you already, didn't they? I want to take you back to New York City with me," she said, nearly shouting.

He smiled a weak smile and squeezed her hand lightly.

"Is that okay with you, Daddy? Would you like to go to New York City with me?"

Isaac nodded his head; his left leg jumped uncontrollably. "Yeah, that's all right with me. I like New York City," he slurred.

The fear that was stuck in the pit of Deller's stomach suddenly melted. No longer was she afraid of him. No longer was he a giant. Isaac sat in his chair, speaking almost too loudly, trying to control his jumping left leg. He was worn over, and time had gotten the best of him. He needed Deller, and he needed forgiveness.

"I have a few things to take care of so I can take you back with me. I'll be back tomorrow to get you," Deller said. She released his hand, giving him another long hug.

The next day, Isaac was sitting in the same chair, wearing the same clothes. His gaunt eyes lit up when Deller came through the door. His things were already packed.

"Okay, Daddy. I took care of everything. We can go now. Do you want to say goodbye to anyone before we leave?"

Isaac shook his head and tried to stand on his own.

"All right then. Let me help you," Deller said. She helped him up, grabbed his one bag, and walked behind him as he took slow baby steps toward the door.

Over the next week, Deller took time off from her job to stay with her father. She arranged for a nurse's aid to come sit with him three days a week, dispense his medication, and check his health.

In time, Isaac grew comfortable with Deller. He began to gain some of his weight back, and the chalky look of his skin softened. He talked more, and bits and pieces of his memory came back. He liked being in a place that seemed familiar. It wasn't Deller's home that was familiar but her presence. Deller had told him about his children, his grandchildren, and his great-grandchildren. She told him about each one of them: who they belonged to and where they lived. She reminded him of the good times on Boston Street, leaving out the bad stuff. In time, spurts of Isaac's life came back to him—the time he spent in Baltimore, then later in Philadelphia. He barely remembered his wife, Eloise.

"She was very pretty," he told Deller one day.

"Yes, Mama is a beautiful woman, Daddy."

Isaac smiled.

Deller thought it was peculiar how God seemed to have a sense of humor and a big heart. The way He had erased the turbulence from Isaac's mind, the evil from his heart. And Deller thought that if God was big enough to forgive him, then who was she to hold him in contempt?

Every day, Deller spent time with her father, helping him to get stronger, as strong as anyone could expect. Then the letter came, the one that told her she and Isaac had broken the law. It was a letter from the state of South Carolina's Parole Office. *Isaac Bingham is in violation of his parole for leaving the state of South Carolina without written permission from his parole officer*, the letter read.

Deller panicked. She called his parole officer and explained she wasn't aware of the parole violation. She explained her father had had a stroke, the nursing home had contacted her because his health was declining, and that she had decided to move him back to New York with her since he was given a short time to live. At no time was she or her father trying to break the law, she told him. In fact, the stroke had damaged her father's memory. He barely remembered most of his life, and she was certain he had lost all knowledge of his parole.

After a few calls and a full investigation to verify Deller's story, the state agreed to allow Isaac to stay in New York with her. Given the seriousness of his health and his age, they saw no reason to press any charges. However, Deller had to complete a parole form every month, verifying his address. If the form was not returned on time each month, Isaac would be in violation of his parole, and they would extradite him back to South Carolina.

Deller agreed and explained everything to her father. He just nodded, not really understanding what she was talking about. He had no memory of his crime, no knowledge of the grief that he had caused his family. Yet something in the back of his mind caused him great distress. He sensed an unsettling feeling about one of his other daughters, the one that Deller had told him about. He wondered what it was, where *she* was.

Where was Mattie?

31

Lydia let her fingers slide across the page of her notebook. She tried not to smudge the ink with the tears that had just fallen.

My mind is lost
my body's growin'
things done happened
that I ain't been knowin'
I'm shifting

I got secrets in my head
hurt in my heart
a baby on the way
and my heart's been torn apart
I'm shifting

I had dreams for my future
wanted to go to college
didn't choose this path
didn't ask for all this mileage
I'm shifting

I feel so alone
holdin' it on my own
done let my Mama down
went from child, to grown

I'm shifting

  I'm shifting

    I'm shifting

She sat on the edge of her bed in her white panties and bra and her protruding belly. Over the past few months, she had become more aware of her changing body—the emergence of her belly, the fullness of her breasts, the roundness of her hips, and the way the child inside her had shifted her from a child to a woman, making her look and feel almost out of place.

She inserted the poem into her composition book and shoved it back under her mattress. She stood up clumsily and walked over to the closet to grab the gold cap and gown. Today was her high school graduation, and she would be walking down the aisle five months pregnant.

Her mother, grandmother, John, Anthony, Lloyd, and even Angie were all planning to attend. Since Lloyd had shown up at her doorstep after hearing about the baby, Lydia had dug deep and mustered up a sprout of forgiveness. She knew he didn't deserve her, but the baby didn't deserve to be fatherless, either. As far as she could tell, Lloyd was off the drugs and working, and he'd been there seeing her through her pregnancy so far. But no matter how hard she tried, she couldn't forget about the times he had beaten her.

Lydia blinked hard to suppress the tears brimming at her eyelids. Today was supposed to be a happy day. She was graduating with honors. She had no reason to feel so wretched, except that she would be one of several girls sashaying down the aisle in her gold cap and gown, the white dress underneath covering her bulging belly.

"Are you ready?" Mattie asked, when Lydia finally made her way downstairs.

"Yes, I'm ready," Lydia answered with a sigh.

"Well you need to put something on your stomach for that baby before we leave here."

"I will."

"I made some grits. Go on and fix yourself a plate, and be sure to take your vitamins when you finish eatin'."

Eloise stood in the kitchen dressed in a peach and white satin dress with white patent leather shoes. A string of large white pearls adorned her neck, and a matching wide brim hat with small white roses and a sheer veil that covered one side of her face was cocked on her head. She even wore white gloves and carried a matching white patent leather purse. "How you feelin' this mornin', baby?" she asked Lydia.

"I'm feeling fine, Mama. I'm just a little nervous about the graduation."

"Well ain't no need to be. You gon' do jus' fine."

"Thanks, Mama," Lydia said.

"I can't believe how fast you chi'ren done grown up. Seem like only yesterday y'all were runnin' round in your diapers. Now looka' you. Done finished high school and got a chile' on the way ya'self." Eloise walked over to Lydia and rubbed her stomach. "You carryin' that baby high. Looks like a girl to me."

"You want some of these grits?" Lydia asked her grandmother.

"No, chile. I already done ate. Had my grits and coffee real early this mornin'. You gon' and worry bout feedin' that young'un of yours. I'ma take me a seat before these here shoes I got on give me an arched foot."

As soon as Eloise took her seat, Angie came downstairs. Her eyes were lost inside of her bloated face. Her tan pants were pulled high up over her belly. One side of her blouse was tucked in, the other side hanging down.

"Hi, Mama," Angie said, her voice flat.

"How you, Angie? You look pretty today," Eloise said to her.

A bleak smile came across Angie's face.

"You want something to eat?" Lydia asked.

Angie didn't answer. Lydia fixed her a plate anyway.

Mattie returned, dressed in a lavender dress, black shoes, and a matching black purse. "We better be on our way before we're late. Y'all go on outside. I'm gonna grab my camera."

Lydia felt nauseous. The baby was doing somersaults inside of her. Her mood had changed since earlier that morn-

ing, when she awoke in a fog, absorbed by sadness. Now she
felt the magnitude of her accomplishments, the significance
of the day. She knew that her future held promise, as she
looked over the many faces in the crowded auditorium. She
could see her family from where she stood. It wasn't hard to
spot them, since Eloise's hat stood out amongst the crowd.
She smiled as she watched them looking around, waiting
patiently for the ceremony to start.

"Line up, seniors. We will be starting the march in about
five minutes," Principal Bell called out.

•◆•

The summer heat exhausted Lydia. The weight of the
baby made her tired all the time, and when September rolled
around, she was counting the days to her delivery.

She had kept her job as a clerk typist and had been saving
to get her own place and go to college. She wanted what was
best for her and the baby, and she'd come to realize it wasn't
Lloyd.

Although he hadn't beaten her like he had done before,
occasionally he still called her names and shoved her around.
One time, he slapped her so hard one side of her face was red
for days. He claimed it was an accident, and she accepted his
apology and buried the truth. But it was obvious that real
change was difficult for him. As the baby grew inside of her,
so did her plans for the future. She didn't want to end up like
most of the other girls who walked around Wilson Park with
poked bellies and damaged prides, harboring dark secrets.
The baby was due in less than six weeks, and she wanted a
clean break. She'd already put down a small deposit on an

apartment that would become available in January. Tonight, she planned to tell Lloyd.

"Lydia, are you all right in there?" Mattie called out to her in the bathroom.

"I'm fine. I'm just washing up."

"Well, Lloyd is downstairs."

"Ok. I'm coming."

Lydia had already planned on how she would tell Lloyd her news. Not in the house. She would tell him on the porch, so if things got out of hand, she was close enough to home to escape him.

"Hi. How you feeling?" Lloyd asked her when she finally came downstairs.

"I'm fine. I had a really long day at work," Lydia said, her heart beating fast already.

"I told you before how I feel about you working at that job so close to the baby coming. You should quit. I'm making enough right now to buy the baby the rest of the stuff it's going to need."

An interminable minute passed before Lydia spoke again. "Can we go outside on the porch? I have something I want to talk to you about."

Lloyd gave her a puzzled look. He had noticed lately that she was becoming more distant, that they were spending less and less time together. It seemed to him that ever since she learned about the pregnancy, she treated him differently. But he just shoved it off. "Don't read too much into her behavior," his mother had advised him. "She's probably just getting nervous about the baby and all." Now there she was asking him if they could go outside for a minute to *talk*. Suddenly, whatever she had to tell him required privacy, like she didn't even want him in her house.

Lloyd followed Lydia out onto the porch. She pulled the door shut behind her, left it unlocked.

"Well," she said quietly, "I don't quite know how to say this so I'm just gonna say it."

Lloyd stared at her, the same perplexed look on his face.

"I think it's probably best that we just be a mother and a father to this baby and not try to be boyfriend and girlfriend anymore."

Lloyd's eyes locked on hers. She turned away from him.

"What I'm trying to say is that I don't think we make a good couple anymore. I got things I wanna do and now that the baby's on the way, I realize I need to be more serious about my future, our future. I mean me and the baby's future."

Her words stung Lloyd, hitting him in the chest like a fierce bullet. "So you think you're too good for me now?" he said, his words clipped.

Lydia was slow to respond. "I think it's best if we just be friends and try to do right by this baby."

Anger collected in Lloyd's eyes. "You fuckin' bitch. I know you don't think I'm gonna let you just walk away and keep my baby from me."

"I ain't trying to keep this baby from you," Lydia said. "I told you that I want us both to be part of the baby's life."

"You think I'm gonna take care of some fuckin' baby while you go be with some other nigga'. You must be crazy, bitch."

"What are you talking about? I ain't been with anybody else."

"Oh, you think I don't know what this is all about? You think you gonna just dis me, talkin' about we can do right by this baby. Fuck you, you bitch!"

"Fine then." Lydia said. "You can think whatever you wanna think. I already said what I had to say."

As she turned, Lloyd lifted his foot, arched it, and plunged it into her stomach so hard Lydia felt the baby ball up inside of her. She twisted her body as she fell to protect the baby. As she lay crumbled and terrified, he hurled off and spit on her before he walked away.

Lydia could hear the cars passing by, a dog barking in the distance, her heart thumping. She waited before she slowly lifted herself up part way. Minutes passed before she was able to stand and walk inside. She could hear her mother running her bath water in the tub, the television playing in the background. She tiptoed past the bathroom and went to her room.

She went to her bed and lay down. She lay there in the stillness and quiet, listening to Angie's snores. After an hour, with the pains still coming, she finally got up the nerve to call her best friend. "Dana, can you meet me at Smith Playground?" she said, sobbing into the phone.

"Okay, I'm on my way right now," Dana said.

When Lydia heard her mother return to her bedroom, she snuck past her mother's partially cracked door and into the bathroom. She could feel the moisture in the crotch of her pants, and when she removed her pants and sat on the toilet, she saw the blood. She quickly cleaned herself up and changed into a fresh pair of underwear and clothes. Then she snuck downstairs and left, slowly walking the six blocks to Smith Playground.

"What's wrong? What happened to you?" Dana said, a frightened look on her face.

Lydia cried so hard, her whole body shook. When it felt like all the tears had poured out of her, she told Dana what Lloyd had done.

"Oh my God," Dana cried. "We gotta do something. We gotta tell somebody. We gotta tell your mother."

"No. I don't want to tell my mother. She's gonna be really mad at me if she knew what's been going on," Lydia said, trying to compose herself.

"But what if something happened to the baby?"

"Let's just walk for a while. Maybe the pain will stop if we just walk for a while," Lydia said out of desperation.

Dana gave her a strange look. She was caught between doing what she felt was right and doing what Lydia wanted. She didn't want to betray her friend, so they walked.

After walking and stroking her belly for more than two hours, the pain in Lydia's abdomen began to subside, and she could feel the baby's movements again.

"So what should we do now?" Dana asked her.

"I think I should go back home and lay down for a while. I think the baby's gonna be okay. I don't feel the pains anymore."

The concern on Dana's face deepened. "I still say you need to tell your mother. I just don't feel right about this."

"I know, Dana. But right now I've got no other choice. I don't want to disappoint my mother any more than I have already."

They walked back to Lydia's house in silence.

Dana hugged Lydia and told her to call if she needed her. When Lydia shut the door, Dana broke down in tears.

— ◆ —

Lydia moved around the kitchen slowly, putting dishes away. Her belly poked out in front of her like a ripe melon waiting to be cracked open. Cramps had been tugging at her all morning. When she was done with the kitchen, she went into the living room and dusted the furniture. Anything was better than just sitting around, anticipating the pain. But another fierce cramp struck her so hard she had to grab hold of her stomach and grip the vacuum cleaner she was pushing.

The baby was due any day now. Lloyd had called many times, begging for her forgiveness. But she wanted no part of his sorry excuses. She knew more than ever what she wanted and what she didn't want. She didn't want Lloyd. That was settled.

The key turning in the front door prompted Lydia to push herself up from the sofa and meet her mother at the door. "Ma, I think the baby's about to come. I've been feeling pains in my belly and back all day. I think it's time," she said.

"You need to get off your feet then, if the baby's on its way. Go on and lay down on the sofa. I'm gonna make you some tea," Mattie said.

Lydia watched her mother move around the kitchen.

"Well, you're gonna have to wait till the contractions get five minutes apart before we go to the hospital. How often do you feel the real sharp pains?" Mattie asked.

"I don't know. They've been coming and going all day. I haven't been keeping track of them."

"Well, you let me know when the next one hits you. I'm gonna start timin' them now."

Lydia lay down on the sofa. The contractions came hard and in spurts with no regard for her body or time. Sleep was difficult; the pain kept her from it. Her mother sat with her while her screams pierced the night. By the time the sun shined its orange-yellow rays over Wilson Park, it was time for them to go to the hospital.

At 2:44 p.m. on Sunday afternoon, October 21, a baby girl came tumbling into the world, screaming at the top of her pear-sized lungs with flailing little arms and legs, pink-tinted skin, a corn shaped head, and her father's eyes.

They weighed her and then wrapped her in the hospital blanket, handing her to Lydia. Tears of joy filled Lydia as she buried her nostrils into the smells of the newborn. Then the nurses took the baby and handed her to Lloyd, who had come to the hospital as soon as Lydia's mother called him. He smiled and held on tightly to his daughter, forgetting that less than six weeks ago, he had nearly snuffed away her little life. Walking over to her with the baby tightly in his arms, he reached for Lydia. She snatched her hand away and motioned for him to hand the baby to her.

She held the baby close and kissed her. Then she thought about the name she had chosen for her—Treasure. She was indeed a small little treasure that had come to her under less than the best circumstances. And Treasure was her strength, her reason for wanting a better life, her gift from God.

Lydia handed Treasure to the nurse. Then she turned her back to Lloyd and closed her eyes, wanting to shut him out and rest before her new life began.

32

Three months later, Lydia, Dana, and Treasure moved to a one-bedroom apartment clear across town. It was all they could afford, and it was as far away from Lloyd and Wilson Park as Lydia's money could buy.

Lydia sat stiffly on the thrift-store-bought green velvet sofa, holding Treasure, who lay sleeping in her arms. She watched the television with disbelief, as the flames engulfed everything on Osage Avenue. "Sixty-one homes have been destroyed, and two hundred and fifty are left homeless," the Channel Six news reported. By the time it was all over, an entire community was devastated and the city of Philadelphia was brought to its knees.

"It's believed that eleven members of the Move group may have perished in the fire," the reporter went on, "some of which are believed to be children." When Mayor Goode appeared and talked about how they had done all they could to contain the situation, Lydia covered her ears. She couldn't bring herself to hear the first black mayor of Philadelphia try to rationalize how a bomb could be dropped on a black middle-class community. She was so overcome with disgust, she got up and turned off the television.

She carried Treasure into the bedroom and put her down in the crib. Then she returned to the living room and tried to force herself to study, but her good mind was gone. The only thing she could think about was all the chaos, the flames, and the black faces.

She was too tired to think after the long day at work and then her class, which she was taking three nights a week since moving into the apartment. There were nights when she would stay up studying until two a.m., and then she would have to get up at six to take Treasure to daycare, report to work, and then drag her tired mind and body to class. Whenever she felt overwhelmed, she reminded herself of the stories that her grandmother and mother had shared with her. She would immediately be inspired, telling herself that if they had survived their circumstances, who was she to complain.

The news about the bombing of Osage Avenue carried on for weeks, a terrible start for the summer of 1985. As though nothing worse could happen, Lydia got a call one sweltering evening in July that changed her family's life.

"We're at the hospital," Mattie said. "Angie tried to kill herself."

"Is she all right?" Lydia asked. She shut her eyes, expecting the worst.

"Yeah. She's gonna be fine, but they're keeping her here for a few days."

"What happened?"

"She took a bottle of pills," Mattie said, the pain and sadness audible in her voice.

"Do you want me to come to the hospital? I can get Dana to watch Treasure."

"No, you stay home with that baby. I just wanted to let you know what happened."

Lydia wanted to go to her mother, hold her in her arms, and let her cry on her shoulder. "It's going to be all right," she wanted to say to her mother. But suddenly, those words seemed too trivial, inappropriate. How do you tell a mother whose fifteen-year-old daughter has just tried to take her own life that *it's going to be all right*?

"Mama's here with me," Mattie said, reading Lydia's mind.

"Well, I'll come to the hospital tomorrow then," Lydia said. Silence trailed the line.

"Well, I better get back in there," Mattie said softly.

"Ok, Ma. "I'll see you tomorrow, all right?"

After Lydia hung up the phone, she picked up Treasure and held her tightly in her arms. She couldn't imagine what it would be like to almost lose her child. It had to be worse than any pain a mother could ever know. She closed her eyes and said a silent prayer for her mother and sister.

The next day, Lydia skipped her classes and took the bus to Pennsylvania Hospital. As soon as she walked through the automatic glass doors, the stale air hit her and made her gag. She hated the sterile smell and the way it exuded sickness. Although she had been in the hospital many times, she could never bring herself to get use to its stench. The only time she ever recalled feeling remotely happy in a hospital was the day her daughter was born.

She took the elevator up to the fourth floor and was met by John pacing in the hallway.

"Hi," Lydia said. "Where's Mommy?"

"She's in the room with Angie."

"How is Angie?" Lydia asked.

"As good as you can expect," John murmured.

Mattie sat in a chair next to Angie, who lay in the bed, her head propped up on two pillows. Lydia looked at her sister, and her heart sunk.

"Hi," Lydia said to Angie. But Angie just stared at her, too overcome by the drugs to respond.

"How long has she been like this?" Lydia asked Mattie.

"Ever since she woke up, after I found her. They say it's normal for her to be this way after an episode. She did say a little somethin' earlier today."

"You found her?" Lydia asked, alarmed.

Tears surfaced in Mattie, and when she blinked, they came rolling down her cheeks. "Yes. I found her upstairs in her bed with the bottle on the floor. I may have found her just in time." Overcome with emotion, Mattie broke down with a choked cry.

Lydia moved closer to her mother, intending to take her in her arms and hold her. But she stopped. A part of her wanted to, but she couldn't bring herself to do it. It was something she had never done before, something they had never shared.

The hospital released Angie a week later and sent her home with more drugs. Lydia called her mother daily to check on her. She knew that Angie's sickness was too much for her mother to handle, and she thought if her mother had to deal with one more thing, she would break. So when Lloyd showed up at her door one evening, it was just one more secret she chose to keep from her mother.

She had just put Treasure down to sleep and was in her bedroom studying when Dana knocked on the door.

"Lloyd is out here," Dana yelled through the closed door.

Lydia's nerves suddenly felt like they were jumping over boulders. The last time she had spoken to Lloyd was when he called and said he wanted to work things out. She told him the only thing they could work out was anything having to do with their daughter. He had yelled at her, called her names, and then hung up on her. He even showed up at her job one day, but her supervisor told him that Lydia hadn't come to work that day. After he left, Lydia's supervisor talked to her. "You may be fooling everyone else," she said, "but I know what's been going on. I've been where you are."

Lydia looked at her supervisor, surprised by her comment.

"If you ever need to talk, I'm here for you," she told Lydia. But she was too ashamed to tell her.

Lydia took a deep breath, pulled herself together, and walked out into the living room. Lloyd was standing at the door.

"I just wanted to talk to you," he said, sounding sincere. "Can we please talk?"

Although something in Lydia's gut told her to ask him to leave, she invited him into her bedroom anyway.

Lloyd followed her and shut the door behind them. Lydia stood next to the closet as Lloyd went over to Treasure. He picked up the sleeping Treasure as she tussled and stretched

her arms. She opened her eyes and smiled. He sat down on
the bed and held her tightly, looking like he belonged there.

"Look, I know that I haven't done my part and that I've
treated you wrong in the past, but I really have changed," he
finally said to Lydia. "I'm gettin' myself together. I don't mess
with drugs anymore, and I been workin' steady. I know it's
going to take some time for you to forgive everything that
I've done to you, but I was hopin' that we could be together,
be a family."

Lydia didn't say anything, just listened to her heart that
was ticking like a time bomb inside of her.

"Look. You don't have to give me an answer right now. I
just want you to think about it, okay?"

The air grew tight around Lydia, and something that felt
like bravery pushed up inside of her. "No. No, it's not okay,"
she managed to say, looking squarely at Lloyd, her voice
cracking.

Lloyd got quiet, and his face flushed. He stood and put
Treasure down on the bed. "Why can't you at least think
about it?" he asked, his voice edgy.

Lydia stepped back and knocked against the closet.

"Why are you actin' like you're so scared of me? I ain't
gonna do nothin' to you."

Lydia felt her body tensing, could feel the fear kick-start
inside of her. "I already gave it some thought, and I told you
how I feel. We just need to be friends and take care of
Treasure," she answered in a small voice.

Lloyd lurched forward, inches from her face. "Be friends?
Be friends? What the hell you mean be friends? How we
gonna be friends when I'm the baby's father? Can't nobody be

just friends when they got a baby together. It's all or nothin'."

"Well, I guess it's gonna be nothing then," Lydia said, her voice trembling.

"Oh, so it's like that, huh? Just cause you're a college girl now you think you can just toss me away? Well, I'm gonna show you who's tossin' who." Lloyd reached under his shirt and pulled out a small black pistol. He wrapped his finger around the trigger and pointed it to Lydia's head. "So, Miss High and Mighty, tell me who's gonna be callin' all the shots now?" he said in a raw voice. "I bet you ain't got nothin' to say now, do you?"

Lydia felt her muscles tense up. She closed her eyes, severing the tears that were flooding her face. Her life flashed before her as she slid to the floor, raising her arms over her head.

"You ain't got nothin' to say now, do you bitch?" Lloyd said, still pointing the gun to her head.

Lydia said nothing and did the only thing she knew how to do, the same thing her grandmother and mother had done: she prayed. She asked God to save her baby, to have mercy on Treasure. And when she thought she heard Lloyd pull the trigger, she screamed. But it wasn't the trigger that she heard or the gun's explosion—it was his fist hitting her. She huddled on the floor, covering her face with her hands. Then she became aware of Treasure crying, and she let out a wail that shook the room and brought Dana knocking on the door.

"Lydia, are you okay?" Dana yelled. But Lydia was too overtaken by Lloyd's blows to call for help.

When Dana got no answer, she swung open the door. Lloyd was on top of Lydia, pummeling her. Dana jumped on his back. "Leave her alone!" she screamed. "You leave her alone!"

Realizing that Dana had come to her rescue, Lydia fought back. They both charged at him like two preyed-upon wild animals.

Lloyd was no match for them. "Y'all bitches are lucky I ain't got no bullets, cause if I had some, you both would be dead bitches," he said. Then he went over to Treasure, picked her up with one hand, and kissed her, as though that was the sanest thing to do. He put her back down and looked at Lydia. "I ain't done with you yet," he said and left.

Hearing the front door slam, Lydia rushed over to the bed to hold her frightened daughter. Dana joined her, and together they cried.

"Lydia, you gotta do something about this," Dana sobbed. "You can't keep living like this. You gotta tell somebody."

Lydia listened, but the truth was too heavy for her. The secrets, and the possibility of what Lloyd might do to her and Treasure, consumed her. She'd thought if she could just make peace with him, perhaps he'd come to his senses and they could raise the baby together. But after tonight, she realized that was out of the question. Lloyd had no interest in *doing what was right for Treasure.* "It's all or nothin'," he had told her. And for the first time, she believed him.

"I will," Lydia finally said, looking up at Dana. "I'm gonna do something."

"Lydia, I'm not trying to tell you what to do," Dana said sympathetically, "but you've got to do something. Maybe you can take a protection order out against him. What if he did have bullets in that gun? What then? We might not be

around to talk about this. Promise me you'll think about getting a restraining order."

Lydia's head was full of confusion. She wanted to do what
was right, what was best for Treasure. But she was afraid that
getting a restraining order might ignite more trouble from
Lloyd. And Lloyd was Treasure's father, the only father
Treasure would ever have. She didn't want to have her daughter grow up like so many other children born out of
wedlock—babies without their fathers, and fathers without
their babies. Treasure deserved more than that.

"Dana, I just don't know what to do anymore," Lydia
said, drawing her breath. "I feel like if I get the authorities
involved, then that's going to create all kinds of problems
for Lloyd, and then he'll never be a father to Treasure. I
just don't know what to do. I wish I could talk to my
mother about it, but she's got so many other things going
on right now with my sister. Things I haven't even told
you about."

Dana didn't say anything at first, just looked at Lydia
with concern on her face. "But what if something more serious were to happen like tonight," she said after a while.
"What if he would have hurt you and Treasure? Do you think
your mother wouldn't want to know what's been going on all
this time? What if you were to go to the police? You wouldn't
be doing anything but protecting yourself and your child. In
fact, you may be doing Treasure a favor. He doesn't deserve to
be in her life. Don't be so hung up on trying to save a relationship that ain't there to save."

That night, Lydia lay restless. Dana's words had been
emphatic, and she had paid attention. She was going to do

what was best for her and her daughter. She planned to tell her mother, to finally be rid of Lloyd.

All in due time.

. ◆ .

Lloyd made no attempt to contact Lydia after that fateful night. He was already on parole, and he didn't need any more trouble. He had decided to try a different tactic. Lydia figured this out when she got a phone call from his mother.

"You know Lloyd really cares about you and Treasure," his mother said. "He don't mean to do the things that he's done to you. He just don't know how to express himself sometimes. Maybe you should think about letting him spend some time with ya'll. I'm sure you'll see that he's really trying to change."

Lydia forced herself to stay calm before she gave his mother a piece of her mind. "Did Lloyd tell you that he pulled a gun on me?" she said abruptly, bringing a halt to any more of her words.

"Well, he told me that you and him had a disagreement. You know he wouldn't do nothing to hurt you or that baby."

"Well, I have spoken to someone about it, and they told me that if he ever tries to do something like that again that I should press charges against him."

Lloyd's mother was surprised by Lydia's response. This wasn't the same young girl she knew. "Lydia, Lloyd is really sorry for what he did. He ain't gonna cause you no more problems," she said. "I think he's learned his lesson this time."

"Well, like I said, I'm going to press charges against him if he ever threatens or touches me again," Lydia said pointedly before she hung up the phone.

The next day, Lydia went to her supervisor and confided in her about everything. After their heartfelt talk, Lydia felt relieved.

"I have a close friend who works for a women's group. I think you should call and talk to her," the supervisor advised.

It took Lydia two whole days to summon up enough nerve to dial the number. The counselor was so understanding and easy to talk to that before long, Lydia told her everything. When she was done pouring it all out like a river that had run its course, she felt embarrassed.

"Don't be afraid to reach out to us," the counselor said. "That's what we're here for. We're here to help battered women like yourself."

Lydia thought it strange that the counselor referred to her as *battered*. Even the word sounded too harsh, unfamiliar. Besides, Lloyd had never really *battered* her, she thought. He had only beaten her a few times, called her bad names. *Battered women* were women who were married to or lived with their abuser. And since she was neither, she thought she shouldn't be put in the same category. Lydia twisted her lips to make the word roll off of her tongue. *B-a-t-t-e-r-e-d*, she kept repeating to herself. I am *b-a-t-t-e-r-e-d*. I am what my grandmother was, who my mother was.

I am that.

My mother, my child
in both I see
a vivid concoction, of what's in me
so strong, yet weak
she holds her throne

so timid, meek—she does no wrong
once the captain, the leader of her scout
yet when from sea, the rabbity peeks out
her coyness, the authenticity
of who she is, what she be
no impostor can clone her style
she is unique, she is frail
her flaws are her woes, her courage her strengths
she need no perfection
no excellence
she is a mother, proud she be
she is a child, with such purity
within these reflections, I clearly see
a genuine concoction of what's in me
My mother, My child

*L*ydia pulled herself from her bed and rubbed at her puffy eyes. She'd had a fitful sleep the night before, dreading what lay ahead. She was scheduled to appear in court for the protection order she had filed against Lloyd. And she had been feeling sick ever since she filed the complaint.

Since Lloyd had threatened her with his gun the previous summer, he had managed to stay away for a while. But then out of the blue he turned up at her job, and when she refused to talk to him, he attacked her. Noticing that Lydia's right eye was puffed and partially shut, her supervisor encouraged her to contact the counselor. "You need to file a protection order against him," the counselor told her as soon as Lydia explained what happened.

"Is there any other way?" Lydia asked in a subdued voice.

"Unfortunately, there is no other way. For your sake and

the sake of your daughter, you have to do this Lydia."

Lydia moved around the kitchen slowly. As soon as she put on the grits and scrambled the eggs, she heard Treasure moving around in her crib. She went into the bedroom and changed Treasure's diaper. Treasure was walking now and was more than curious about everything in her sight. She trundled along behind her mother into the kitchen and raised her arms to be lifted into her high chair.

After she had fed Treasure, Lydia poked the fork around on her own plate; her food was cold and her appetite lost. She quickly cleaned the dishes and bathed and dressed Treasure, then she went into the living room and turned on the television. She was jittery and needed something to take her mind off the things that were pulling at her. She flipped through the channels until she came upon a news reporter announcing, "It's a chilly morning here at the Kennedy Space Center in Cape Canaveral, Florida. But it's no less an exciting time as we await the liftoff of the Space Shuttle Challenger."

Lydia thought about what it would be like to just leave and go to a place where there was no confusion, no fear. She envied the seven astronauts.

The countdown started and Lydia counted with it, Treasure mimicking her. "Ten—nine—eight—seven—six—five—four—three—two—one." Orange-yellow flames flushed out its bottom as the Challenger slowly accelerated toward the sky.

"There it goes, folks. The Space Shuttle Challenger has just lifted off," the reporter announced excitedly.

Lydia watched as the rocket glided into the clouds. "Look, Treasure," she said, as fired up as the Challenger.

"Look baby, can you see the rocket?"

An excitement came over Treasure's small face as she pointed and flailed her little arms toward the television. Lydia grabbed Treasure's hands and started clapping them together. But just as the shuttle's liftoff had lifted their spirits, their joy suddenly came to an abrupt halt. The television's audio went silent as a puff of smoke and a big ball of fire engulfed the television screen. Something terrible had happened!

Lydia held Treasure close against her heart.

The Space Shuttle Challenger had exploded in mid-air, just seventy-three seconds after it lifted off from the Kennedy Space Center. By the time Dana came home, Lydia was so grief stricken she told Dana she didn't think she'd be able to make the three o'clock courthouse appointment.

"You have to pull yourself together and go," Dana told her.

Two hours later, Lydia stood in front of the judge, answering his questions. In less than ten minutes, the whole ordeal was over. The judge granted her petition. But the two-page document he signed and gave to her made her feel no more safe. She felt just as vulnerable as the Space Shuttle Challenger.

By the time the frigid air moved on and the trees began to take shape, Lydia thought maybe she was finally free of Lloyd and that he'd taken the protection order seriously—until his mother called one warm evening in April. "Lydia, Lloyd was arrested last night," she said.

"What did he do?" Lydia asked in a cold, clear voice.

"Armed robbery. They say he robbed a Seven-Eleven."

As soon as Lydia hung up the phone, she cried, mostly out

of relief. She was relieved because she knew the gun he had used at the Seven-Eleven was probably meant for her. But what made her sad—overwhelmingly sad—was the anger she felt. She was angry because Lloyd had just destroyed any possibility of being a father to Treasure. It was as if he had purposely decided that if she was going to shut him out, then he was going to shut out Treasure. She was more enraged about that than his wanting to harm her. She was strong enough to withstand whatever he did to her. But Treasure, Treasure was an innocent victim, and Lloyd's actions had just guaranteed her a spot in the Hall of Fatherless Fame. All the pain that Lydia had endured and the peace that she'd prayed for had just been tossed away.

The night Lloyd took that gun and walked into the Seven-Eleven, he had committed two crimes; he had not only robbed the store, he had also robbed Treasure. Now, Treasure had only one hope, one last option for unconditional love: her mother—the young woman who finally had the courage to protect herself, the one who would do whatever it took to protect her Treasure.

34

As soon as Lydia walked through Mattie's front door, the savory aroma hit her nostrils so hard she almost dropped the bag and Treasure. She always enjoyed coming to her mother's house for a good home-cooked meal. She thought that there was something special in her mother's touch to be able to season the food and cook it up just right.

"Hey, Ma," Lydia said, as she put Treasure and the bag down.

Mattie sat in the living room, staring out the window, a copy of *True Story* magazine clutched in her hand.

"Are you all right?" Lydia asked.

Treasure bounced over to Mattie and tried to find a comfortable seat in her grandmother's lap.

"Yeah, I'm fine," Mattie said in a thin voice.

"Well, you don't look fine. Did something happen? Is Angie okay?"

Mattie looked away from Lydia. "I just got a call from Deller. She says Isaac is really sick, and she wants us to come and see him."

"Are you going to go?" Lydia asked slowly.

"I don't know. I just don't know."

"Well, maybe you should go," Lydia said, coaxing her mother. "Maybe if you don't go now, you may never get a chance to see your father again." Lydia moved closer to Mattie, choosing her words carefully. "Ma, you gotta let the past go. Sometimes it just ain't worth the pain."

An expression of defiance clouded Mattie's face. "What do you know about pain? Y'all don't know the kind of pain I've been through," she said, her voice hovering between grief and pride.

Lydia took a seat next to her mother, trying to hold her gaze. "You're right, Ma. I may not know the kind of pain you've been through, but I do know pain."

The room got quiet. Mattie embraced Treasure tightly, making her squirm. "I know you've been through somethin', too. I've been waitin' for you to come to me about it."

A look of surprise crossed Lydia's face. "You already knew?" she said, her voice tempered.

Mattie looked at her again. "Yeah, I always suspected that somethin' wasn't right between you and that boy, even when I asked and you wouldn't tell me the truth. I figured you'd come to me in your own time."

Lydia sat quiet for a moment. She looked down at the shiny, waxed tile floors, too embarrassed to look at her mother. Tears fell from her cheeks and through the cracks of her hands that were resting in her lap. "The worst part of all," she said, still afraid to look at her mother. "The worst part was that I wanted so badly for Lloyd to be a father to Treasure, for Treasure never to know the kind of pain that you've been through with your father."

Mattie's heart swelled, hearing Lydia open up to her in this way.

"That's why I think you gotta go, Ma. It just ain't worth all the pain."

Mattie suddenly stood and handed Treasure to Lydia. "I think my food's burnin'," she said and rushed into the kitchen.

Lydia stayed in the living room, burying her tears in Treasure's hair. Mattie moved quietly around the kitchen and silently wiped away her tears.

That night, after eating their dinner in complete silence, Lydia and Treasure joined Angie in her room. Mattie got out her telephone book, looked up Deller's number, and dialed it. When she answered, only three words came from Mattie's mouth: "We're gonna come." Then she quickly hung up the phone.

• ◆ •

The morning of their trip, Mattie got up early to bake pies for the cookout Deller had planned. It was Memorial Day weekend, and the weather reports called for temperatures in the mid-eighties.

After the pies were done, Mattie went upstairs to wake Angie, along with Lydia and Treasure, who had stayed the night. After breakfast, they all piled into John's car, picked up Eloise, and headed toward the Walt Whitman Bridge.

Eileen, Roy Jr., and Anthony would be there with their families, too.

As soon as they crossed the Goethals Bridge into Staten Island, the palms of Mattie's hands started pouring sweat. They were less than fifteen minutes away. She had told herself she wasn't going to clam up, wasn't going to let her nerves get the best of her. She thought it was silly that she was feeling so nervous, so fourteen again. But she wasn't fourteen, she reminded herself. She was more than grown, had raised five children of her own, and even had grandbabies. But no matter how much she tried to rationalize her thoughts, still she wasn't ready to see her father again.

When the car pulled into the driveway, Deller came rushing out the front door, waving. "I can't believe y'all made it," she said. "I wasn't expectin' you for at least another hour." She went over to Eloise and helped her out of the car, giving her a big hug and a kiss.

"Yeah, we got an early start," Eloise said, stretching her legs. "You know how John like to beat the traffic."

"Hi, Mattie. How you doing?" Deller asked.

"I'm fine," Mattie said. They hugged awkwardly.

Lydia grabbed Treasure's hand and motioned for Angie to come along, as they walked toward the house. She was filled with anticipation, wondering what it would be like to finally meet Isaac, the patriarch behind all the stories. She tried to imagine what he would be like. Would he be tall or short? Handsome or ugly? Nice or evil looking? She had made up so many images in her mind about him.

"Has anyone else arrived yet?" Eloise asked.

"Not yet. But I'm sure they'll all be here soon. Daddy's in the backyard," Deller said.

Isaac sat in the yard in his iron chair, the one he sat in every day. The seat was slightly damp from the morning dew. He looked out at the bed of roses Deller had planted for him. He hadn't been feeling well lately, and Deller was thinking he might take a turn for the worse. But when she told him all of his family was planning to come and see him, his spirits were lifted. He wondered what it would be like to finally meet the family Deller had been telling him about. It was nearly impossible for Isaac to grasp that he had eight children, eighteen grandchildren, and six great-grandchildren. Whenever Deller showed him pictures of everyone, he barely recognized anyone at all.

Mattie took a deep breath as they turned the corner to the backyard. From a distance, Isaac didn't look at all like the same man who had walked out on them so long ago. But as she got closer, all the emotion she had carried for so many years struck her like lightning.

Deller took Mattie by the hand and pulled her toward him. "Daddy, this here is Mattie. Remember, I told you about Mattie, the one you say you remember as a little girl. She's the daughter that lived down South with us before you brought us up here," Deller said, nearly shouting.

Isaac's eyes met Mattie's as she stood there looking down at him, an awkward smile on her face. She could see the deep lines in his face, each telling a story of struggle.

"Yeah, I memba' her." Isaac perked up. "Wha' you say her name was?"

"It's Mattie, Daddy," Deller said, still holding onto Mattie's hand.

Isaac stretched his neck toward her and squinted his eyes. A shallow smile came across his face. "Yeah, I memba' Mat-tee. Mat-tee was the other chile right?"

"That's right, Daddy. She was the second child."

Mattie suddenly felt silly standing there with Deller speaking for her. She reached her hand out toward him. "Hi, Daddy," she said stiffly. "How you been feelin'?" A handshake was all she could muster.

Isaac shifted in his seat and reached out his fragile hand. "I been feelin' fine lately. Been a whole lot betta' since I been here with Della," he said, slurring his words through droopy lips.

Eloise was standing behind Mattie when Deller reached for her and moved her closer to Isaac. "And Daddy, you remember Mama, don't you? Y'all were together for a long time, remember?"

Isaac turned his head slowly and looked toward Eloise. She stood there like a wax figure, watching him, wondering if he could remember her, remember any of the pain he had caused her. But when he looked at her, it was like he was looking at her for the first time. "Who you say she was?" he said, peering at Eloise with a strange eye.

Eloise shifted her weight, feeling something twitch inside of her heart as she watched the man that had caused her so much pain struggle to recognize her.

"It's Mama. Your wife, Eloise. Remember, I showed you her pictures?"

Isaac strained his eyes, twisted his drooped lip, and leaned in a bit closer. "Oh yeah," he said excitedly. "I memba' now. You say her name is Elo-eez?" He released Mattie's hand and offered it limply to Eloise, inviting her to take it.

Eloise took his hand and was taken aback by how cold it felt in her own.

"How you?" Isaac asked.

"I'm fine, Isaac. How you?" Eloise replied.

He nodded his head. "I'm doin' okay," he stammered. "I been feelin' much betta' lately since y'all got here."

"That's good," Eloise managed to say.

Then Deller introduced him to Lydia, who'd been waiting patiently in the background. When Lydia reached out to take his hand, she held onto it a little longer, just long enough to see if she could feel her way to the memories. It seemed strange to finally see her grandfather in the flesh, to hear his voice. And there he was, looking at her with inviting eyes and a face that reminded her of her own brothers.

"The others should be along soon, Daddy," Deller said. "Mama, why don't you and Mattie grab a chair and sit with Daddy while I finish getting the food ready."

"Deller, let me help you," Mattie said. "Mama, you go on and have a seat. I'll be back after while," Mattie took off quickly behind Deller.

Eloise took a seat across from Isaac. It was difficult to believe she had shared almost a lifetime with this man, and time now stood still between them. Seeing Isaac in his condition, she couldn't help but feel sorry for him. All the harsh feelings she had carried for so long suddenly left her, and the only thing she felt for him now was empathy.

"Are you okay?" Deller asked Mattie when she joined her in the kitchen.

Mattie moved the window curtain back and looked out

at her father. "Yes, I'm okay. I just didn't expect for him not to know us," she said.

"Yeah. It's sad, ain't it? All that's happened over the years, and he doesn't remember any of it." Deller joined Mattie at the window. "You know, when I first went down there to get him, I think he recognized me for a brief moment. He remembered bits and pieces. Like he remembered I was the one who moved to New York. For some reason, that stayed with him."

Mattie shook her head; a mischievous look came across her face. "Well you know, he was angry somethin' awful at you for leavin' and marryin' that boy."

Deller smiled.

"It really is a shame," Mattie said quietly. "It's a shame that he was spared all the memories, and we gotta live with them for the rest of our lives. It just ain't right."

Deller glanced at Mattie and nodded her head slightly. "Well, maybe it ain't meant for him to remember. Maybe God spared him for a reason," she said softly.

As soon as their car pulled up, you could feel trouble. Lionel, Walton, and Rollie emerged. They had come alone. No families. Just the three of them bonded together, just like they were as little boys.

For years, they had lived separate and quiet lives, but two things remained in common: their memories and a nasty habit that helped them to forget. By the time they reached Deller's house and got out of the car, they had had plenty of what made them forget.

During the two-hour drive, they boasted about what

piece of their mind they were going to give to Isaac if he even looked at them the wrong way. But as soon as the car turned into the driveway, the fear they felt many years ago surrounded them. And though none of them would own up to it, they were as petrified as they had been as little boys.

They got out of the car and stumbled toward the back of Deller's house. She came rushing toward them. "Thank God, y'all finally made it," she said, as she held her arms out toward Lionel.

Lionel hugged her and then moved out of the way so that she could hug the other two. Then she grabbed Lionel by the hand and brought him over to Isaac. "Daddy, do you remember who this is?" Deller shouted in the same way she had introduced Mattie. "Remember I told you about the oldest boy?"

Isaac tried to stand up. Lionel reached out his hand to help him. Isaac grabbed onto Lionel's left arm as he gripped the cane with his other hand to balance himself. "Lio—no," he slurred.

Deller's eyes lit up. "Yes, Daddy. It's Lionel."

"I memba' Lio-no," Isaac said.

Lionel hugged his father and all the anger, disappointment, and hatred suddenly melted. He felt like he had betrayed the feelings he'd harbored for so long. Now he felt sorry for the old man—the same man who had beaten him to a near pulp in a dark basement so long ago.

Walton held on tightly like it was the first time he'd ever hugged his father, when Deller introduced him. But when it came time for Rollie to greet Isaac, he looked at his father with pure disgust. Maybe it was because of all the vodka he'd drunk, or maybe he could still remember the rat his father made him eat when he was only three, and he still hated him for it. Now a foot away from Isaac, he couldn't bring himself to let go of that memory. When Deller reached for him, he pushed her hand away. "I ain't got nothin' I need to say to him," he announced and stalked away.

"What's wrong, Rollie? Why you actin' like this?" Deller asked, annoyed that he might ruin the whole day.

Rollie turned and looked at her. "Why am I actin' like this? Why am I actin' like this? I'll tell you why I'm actin' like this. Fuck him," he slurred. "Fuck you and him!"

Deller squirmed. "Now Rollie, you don't mean that. Come on. Don't spoil it for the rest of us," she said, rushing after him.

Rollie turned and gave her a hard look. "Don't spoil it for the rest of y'all. What do you mean don't spoil it for the rest of y'all?! How am I supposed to spoil somethin' that's already been spoiled? You think cause he's sick we're supposed to forget everything he did to us? He was evil, Deller. You know it. Mama knows it. All y'all know it. Now y'all actin' like he's some damn king. Like he didn't just walk out and leave us. He walked out on Mama, remember? And he didn't even leave us one red cent!"

Mattie came out of the house and stood on the porch, listening. In a way, she understood how Rollie felt, had even wanted to say the things that he was saying. But she kept silent.

"We all know what he did to us. But sometimes you've got to learn to forgive. People make mistakes. He made mistakes, Rollie. Ain't no need to punish him for it now. He's living in his last days. Why not try to make the time he has left worth something?"

Rollie cut right through Deller's words. "I ain't got nothin' to say to that man. Now, if y'all wanna act like he's deservin' of all this, then go right ahead. I'm gonna sit here in this car till it's time to go."

Rollie opened the car door and slumped down in the passenger seat. He reached under the seat, pulled out the vodka, and took a long swig.

Deller raised her hands in disgust and flagged them at him, before walking back into the house.

• ◆ •

Six weeks after the cookout, Isaac's body gave way to his illnesses. He died in his sleep, in the nursing home that Deller put him in when his health became too much for her to handle.

When Mattie got the call in July, she didn't shed one tear. She figured she'd already shed a lifetime of tears for her father. That morning, she did one thing, the only thing that carried her for so long. She prayed and thanked God for giving her the strength to finally forgive her father. And she asked Him to have mercy on her father and to allow his soul to rest in peace.

Lydia was another story: she cried. She cried for the loss of three generations of fathers—fathers who had been lost to death or self-destruction. And when she had no more tears to give, she did the only thing she could do, the one thing that came naturally to her. She pulled out her black composition book and stuffed her sorrow onto a page.

*Young Isaac, just before
he met Eloise.*

*HE, who was in and out of my life
Leaving things undone, sacrificed
A father's figure, is what I dreamed to have
Instead, I'm left groping, needy, sad
I longed for his love, protection, to feel safe
But I'm lost . . . feeling so, displaced
Often I wonder . . . how could it be
That he's gone—to hell, perhaps heaven, a penitentiary
They were our fathers, just as they came
Making their marks, history unclaimed
And so a loss is grieved, three generations fold
A story undone, a story told*

Our fathers

35

The ringing phone startled Lydia, who had been at her books studying for two hours. She jumped up from the sofa, dropping the papers strewn across her lap.

"Hello?"

"Hello, ma'am. Are you Treasure's mother?" The woman's voice on the other end was so commanding that Lydia snapped to attention.

"Yes, I'm Treasure's mother," she replied.

"Ma'am, I'm calling from the Philadelphia Police Department. We received a call from Treasure a few minutes ago."

Lydia nearly dropped the phone.

"Ma'am, are you there?"

"Yes, I'm here."

"Ma'am, Treasure called claiming that you beat her. Is that true?"

"No. I mean yes. I mean . . . No! No, it's not true. Are you sure it was Treasure who called you?"

"Ma'am, I need to know that no harm has been brought to Treasure. Can you please tell me what happened?"

A surge of panic came over Lydia. "Where did you say you were calling from?" she asked.

"The Philadelphia Police Department."

"There must be a mistake. My daughter has never been abused. I did spank her earlier and put her to bed for the night."

"Then how would she know to call us?" the woman asked sternly.

"Well, I'm not sure, but now that she's four and she and I live alone, I've been teaching her how to call 911 for emergencies."

"Ma'am, I have already dispatched an officer to your home. He should arrive any minute. It would be helpful if you would allow him to talk to your daughter to be sure that everything's okay."

"Okay," Lydia said.

"Why don't we stay on the line until he arrives."

A few minutes later, Lydia said, "Someone's knocking at the door now. It must be the officer."

"Yes, it is the officers. You can go ahead and open the door. I'm going to disconnect the call now."

Two uniformed police officers stood at Lydia's door.

"Hello, ma'am. I'm Officer Godfrey, and this is Officer McDonald. We understand that you've been talking to one of our dispatchers about an abuse call."

"Yes," Lydia said, now getting a little flustered.

"Well, we need to ensure that everything's okay with Treasure. May we come in?"

"Sure. Sure, come on in." Lydia moved to one side to allow the officers to enter.

"Ma'am is your daughter around?" the officer asked, carefully looking around the apartment.

"Yes, she's in the bedroom."

"Can you go and get her. We just need to make sure she's okay."

Lydia didn't hesitate, didn't even flinch. She gave the officer a nod. "Treasure, I want you to come out here right now," she called to her.

Treasure hid under her blankets when she heard the strange voices in the living room and her mother's stern voice.

"N-o-w, Treasure!" Lydia said, as she opened Treasure's bedroom door.

Treasure peeked out from under her blankets. Her quarter-sized almond eyes got wide when she saw the look on her mother's face. She slowly kicked the blankets back and jumped down off her bed, dragging the plastic slippers that were attached to her pajamas.

"Here she is," Lydia said squarely, nodding toward the innocent-looking Treasure.

Officer Godfrey knelt down until he was at eye level with her. "Hi, sweetheart. How are you?" he said.

Treasure rocked from side to side, clutching her teddy bear.

"Treasure, answer the officer," Lydia said tightly.

"Fiinne," Treasure said.

"Well, do you know why we are here, honey?"

"Yeesss," Treasure said quietly.

"Are you okay?"

"Yeesss."

"Do you remember why you called us?"

Treasure glanced at her mother. "Nooo," she answered.

"It's okay, sweetheart. You can talk to me. We won't let anything happen to you."

Treasure twirled her pajama pants with her free hand. "Yeesss, I re-mem-ber."

"Do you want to tell me what happened?"

Treasure gave her mother a look that begged for clemency. "My mommy spanked me," she finally said in a pure voice.

"Has anyone hurt you honey?"

"Nooo," she said, moving her head from side to side.

"Are you sure, sweetheart?"

"Yeesss."

"Okay then, sweetheart. You were very brave to tell me the truth." Officer Godfrey stood and gave Lydia an apologetic smile. "I'm sorry, ma'am. But it's always best to check these things out."

"I understand," Lydia said.

"Well, I think it's very smart of you to teach your child at such a young age what to do in the event of an emergency. So often, parents take it for granted. It's good to see that you've taken the proper steps to ensure her safety."

"Thank you, officer."

After Lydia escorted the police officers out, she turned to Treasure, but Treasure was already out of sight, out of her reach. Lydia walked into her room and found her hiding under the blanket.

"Sit up. I want to talk to you."

Treasure sat up Indian style. She held her head down, looking at the teddy bear in her lap.

"Now, when I taught you how to use the phone to call 911, I didn't mean for you to call them on me."

Treasure kept her eyes down, but Lydia could see the tears beading up.

"Now, why do you think it was all right for you to call the police on me?"

"I don't knooow."

"Do you understand the difference between a spanking and abuse?"

"Yeesss."

"Then why don't you tell me the difference."

Treasure hesitated for a few seconds before she spoke up. "I think a spankin' is when I'm bad an a'bruise is when somebody hurt you real hard."

"Yes, that's right," Lydia said. "Now you're supposed to call 911 when somebody is hurting you or mommy really badly, or when something happens to mommy and she can't make the call herself. Remember how I taught you?"

"Yeesss."

"Then I want you to remember it just like that. Okay? Cause you can't go around calling the police on mommy when she spanks you, because if they think something is wrong, they can take you from mommy. Okay?"

"Okaaay."

"Now, is there anything else you want to talk about?"

Treasure shook her head slowly.

"No one else has hurt you, have they?"

"Nooo."

"All right then. Now I want you to get back to sleep so mommy can finish studying. We have a long day tomorrow."

Lydia picked up Dozzie, the teddy bear, and snuggled it under Treasure's small arm. "Okay, goodnight," she said, kissing Treasure on her forehead.

"Goodnight, mommy."

"And Treasure,"

"Yeesss?"

"Mommy loves you."

"I love you, toooo."

· ◆ ·

Lydia sat on one of the large boxes as she packed the last of Treasure's toys. She and Treasure were moving into a three-bedroom rowhouse in Mount Airy, a middle-class section of the city. It wasn't much, but it was time to get out of the crime infested South Philadelphia neighborhood where they had lived for over a year. Since Dana had moved out of their first apartment to get married, Lydia had moved to a small one-bedroom apartment in South Philadelphia to be closer to her parents so she could finish school. She had graduated from Pierce Junior College and was planning to attend a four-year university. Her life was improving just the way she'd planned.

She loaded the final boxes into the truck that John had rented for her. Then she gathered the last of the odds and ends before gathering up Treasure and heading to their new home.

· ◆ ·

It was late, as late as night became, and the quiet engulfed

Lydia. She had been awake for hours, unable to force her mind to release all the anxiety from her studies. Now she just lay there in the darkness, listening to the sounds of the house until the phone rang.

"Angie's back in the hospital," Mattie said, as soon as she heard Lydia's voice.

"Oh, Ma, not again. Is she okay?"

"She tried to kill herself, and this time, they took her to a maximum-security psychiatric hospital. They say she's gonna have to stay there for a few weeks because she could have hurt other people."

"Why? What happened?" Lydia asked, sensing the worst.

"She went down into the subway and laid across the tracks." Mattie began sobbing. "They say they stopped the train just in time."

"Oh, Ma. I'm so sorry."

"They say they want me to think about putting her in some kind of psychiatric care facility."

"Maybe that'd be the best thing for her, Ma," Lydia said cautiously. "At least she'll get the care she needs."

Mattie had already thought long and hard about what to do. Since Angie took sick, she promised herself, promised God, that she would never abandon her daughter. Even though the doctors and the social workers all seemed to have given up on her, Mattie couldn't bring herself to do it. Angie was her youngest, her baby. How could she just quit on her?

"Ma, maybe you should at least think about it," Lydia said after a moment. "Angie is really sick and this place they told you about may be what she needs. I'll go with you to check it out if you want."

Mattie kept quiet, feeling her heart cave in on her.

.•.

Stonewall Residential Rehabilitation Center located in West Philadelphia was an oversized, redbrick one-story building that sat on the corner of a quiet residential neighborhood. From the outside, it looked out of place, like someone had absently deposited it there. Stonewall took in what the psychiatric world referred to as its borderline cases: those who were still capable of semi-independent living but were two missed pills away from a maximum-security institute. Angie was considered closer to crossing the line over to maximum security but was given one last straw for sanctuary.

It was an odd-looking building with its rectangular shaped windows covered with wooden Venetian blinds. There were four picnic tables and three benches on the side of the building. The yard was dressed in azalea bushes and green shrubs. Yellow roses stood abruptly on each side of the entryway. The door was mainly glass, with the words Stonewall Residential Rehabilitation Center slapped across it in large black lettering. Two days before, Angie had been released from the hospital and was now scheduled to check into Stonewall.

"Come on, Angie," Mattie said, as she opened the glass door.

Angie pulled her obese body through the entranceway. With all the medication she had been taking, it looked as if she were in a deep trance, and the only thing keeping her coherent was the air she breathed.

"I'm here to check my daughter, Angelica, in," Mattie said to the woman behind the desk who was watching a small black-and-white television underneath the counter.

"Oh, yes," the woman said, then she reached over to turn down the volume. "We've been expecting you. You must be the Madison family."

Mattie reached out to shake the woman's hand and looked at her closely. She didn't look like the kind of people Mattie had encountered in the hospitals or at the treatment center. She was a short, big boned woman, with caramel-colored skin and cornrows that were braided down her back. She wore a friendly smile, the kind that was soft and inviting. She had a round, friendly face with mild lines that compromised her age and eyes that told a story. She looked like she was good for Stonewall.

"Yes, that's right," Mattie replied.

"My name is Bonita Jones. I'm one of the group home attendants here at Stonewall. I'll be checking your daughter in today and helping her to get acquainted. Which one of y'all is Angelica?" she asked, looking over at Lydia and Angie.

Mattie pointed toward Angie, who had already found a seat on one of the plaid sofas in the room adjacent to the check-in desk.

"Oh, I see you've already gotten acquainted with the residential hall," Ms. Jones said, giving Angie a warm smile.

Angie sat stiff as a board, unaware she was being spoken to. The walls of the residential hall were bare except for a few sheets of white bond paper with large black lettering that described Stonewall rules. _No Smoking in Your Room_, one sign read. _Don't forget to Take Your Meds,_ another said. _Day Program Starts at 9:00 a.m.,_ a third one read. Two wooden-style plaid sofas sat opposite each other. A matching wooden coffee table that bore only silver tin ashtrays overflowing with cigarette

butts sat in its middle. A nineteen-
inch color television sat clumsily
on top of a dark brown stand with
wheels at its feet. The room had a
feeling of indifference.

*Angie, just before she
checked into Stonewall.*

"Well, let me get all the paperwork, and when you're done filling
it out, I'll go over all the rules. Then
I'll show y'all around," Ms. Jones said. She went behind the
counter, grabbed a pile of papers, and attached them to a
brown clipboard.

"Why don't you have a seat over there." She handed the
clipboard to Mattie and pointed to four white plastic tables
surrounded by gray iron chairs.

Mattie took the forms and walked over to the tables.
Lydia followed her. John went and sat down with Angie.

Lydia watched her mother meticulously answer every
question. It hurt to see the pained expression on her mother's
face, like someone had put a wrench in her heart and kept
turning and turning until all the joy was squeezed out of her.
Even though Mattie had agreed to admit Angie to Stonewall,
something still nagged at her. She wondered if she was making the right decision. It took Mattie nearly an hour to
complete the forms. When she was done, she gathered up all
the papers, putting them back in the order that Ms. Jones
had given them to her.

"All righty. Let me check all the information and make
sure we got everything we need, and we'll be on our way,"
Ms. Jones said, as though they were about to venture into an
amusement park.

Mattie and Lydia watched her as she slowly reviewed all the documents, being careful not to overlook anything. "Okay. It looks like everything is here. Now the only thing I need are her meds. Do you have them? The doctor should have also given you a prescription for her."

Mattie removed the oversized pocketbook from her shoulder and reached inside to pull out a Ziploc bag full of the little brown bottles with white caps and bright orange labels.

"Great! Let me put this away and I'll be right back." Ms. Jones went behind the counter and pulled out a set of keys and a large black marker. They watched as she wrote Angie's full name in big dark letters on the Ziploc bag, walked over to a metal safe the same height as Treasure, and inserted a key into it. The safe made a crackling sound as she opened it and revealed mounds of medication in white containers, Ziploc bags, and brown manila folders. She threw Angie's bag inside the safe and was careful to lock it before she walked back to her desk and put the set of keys back in its place.

"Okay. So why don't we first start with the tour?" she said, motioning them to follow her.

"There are four women and three men here right now, including Angelica," she said, as she opened the door to one resident's bedroom. "The women and men are kept apart, of course. The women's rooms are on this side of the building. We call this the north side. And the men are on the south side. We don't allow fraternizing between them. They all get chores and are responsible for keeping their rooms clean. Every resident must attend a day program, where they get daily counseling and treatment. They are expected to meet with the psychiatrist twice a week. There are no drugs or alcohol allowed on the premises, and an attendant is always here 24/7." Ms. Jones' spiel and the entire tour took ten minutes. "Y'all got any questions?" she asked, nearly out of breath.

Mattie spoke up. "Well, I . . . I just want to make sure my Angie's gonna be okay." The sadness in her voice was palpable.

Ms. Jones gave Mattie a smile and nodded. "Yes, ma'am. She's going to be just fine," she said empathetically. "We take great care of our residents."

"All right then," Mattie said quietly. She turned and looked toward Angie. "You call me if you need anything, you hear?"

Angie looked at her blankly and lowered her head.

"Well, I guess we should go now," Mattie said.

"Okay. Now if you have any questions, feel free to call us." Ms. Jones handed Mattie a small white card with the center's information printed on it.

"Oh, I did have one question," Lydia said. "Where are all the other residents?"

Ms. Jones smiled and then chuckled. "Well, we ain't hiding them sweetie. They're all at the day program. They should be returning home soon, around three. I'll make sure Angie meets them all."

36

*I*t's not that she was looking for a man, but when Donald caught up to Lydia in September, she didn't turn him away. Since the time with Lloyd, she had written off boys—well, men now. She had the habit of sizing up every man that approached her. She dated occasionally, but her job, her studies, and Treasure kept what little time she had occupied. Besides, relationships weren't all that Dana and her other friends had chalked them up to be. At least, they didn't see relationships from her perspective. When you're eighteen and have a gun pointed to your head, you tend to see things a little bit differently, she had told them. But when Donald appeared with teeth the color of white sheets, milky brown skin, and dimples on both sides of his cheeks, Lydia forgot her golden rule and all her defenses came down.

"I see you pass by here every morning," Donald said.

"Where are you going? To work?"

Lydia turned and gave him a sharp look. She was in no mood for small talk. "Yes, I'm on my way to work."

"Well, I just wanted to say that I see you every morning and you make my day." Donald flashed his winning smile at her.

Lydia slowed her pace and smiled. "Well, thank you. That's nice of you to say."

Donald kept up with her pace. "I see you with a little girl sometimes, too. Is that your daughter?"

At first, Lydia wondered how he knew about Treasure. Then she remembered that she had to pass by his building when taking Treasure to daycare. "Yes, that's my little girl," she answered.

"Well, she's just as beautiful as her mother."

Lydia blushed.

"I know this is a bit forward, but do you mind if I take your number? Maybe I can take you and your little girl out for ice cream one day."

Lydia gave him a look that showed her mistrust. It wasn't about him. It was just that she didn't trust many people when it came to Treasure. But there was something different about Donald, something caring, something that felt safe. "Why don't you let me have your number and I'll think about it," she told him.

He kept smiling as he pulled a small piece of paper from his black khaki slacks and then patted his white shirt pocket, looking for a pen. "Do you happen to have a pen?" he asked her.

Lydia reached into her purse to fish out a pen. She made sure she got a closer look at him while he was writing his name and number on the paper. He was handsome, really handsome, she thought; and he looked older than she was. The men she'd been meeting lately didn't approach her in the way he had. They were rude, mostly. But Donald had class. She could tell from the moment he spoke to her.

Lydia waited a week before she called Donald. He answered the phone like he had been waiting for her call since the moment they had met. They talked for three hours straight. And by the time she hung up, she knew she really liked him. He invited her out for dinner the following Saturday, and she agreed.

On their first date, Donald showed up at her house in a brand new tan Ford Escort. He carried a dozen pink roses for her and a small white flower for Treasure. She invited him in and put the roses in a tall glass with water. She didn't own a vase. Never had a need for one.

"I'm sure Treasure's going to like the flower," she told him. "I'll make sure she gets it. She's at my mom's today."

Lydia looked so put together. Donald would never have guessed she spent the entire afternoon thinking about what to wear. After hours of stressing over it, she finally settled on a light blue cotton dress, the one with the scooped neckline, and a pair of black sandals. She had purchased the dress the week before when she was window-shopping on her lunch break. She had walked in and out of the store three times before she finally made up her mind to spring for the eighteen bucks.

Donald took Lydia to the Chart House on the waterfront in Penns Landing. She had never been to Penns Landing, let alone the Chart House. She soaked in the attention he gave her. From where she came, the closest she'd ever gotten to receiving that type of treatment was a weeded flower picked out of some old lady's yard in Wilson Park and a trip to the Market Street movie theatre. If she were really lucky, she and Lloyd would end up at Gino's for a Philly cheese steak and a cherry water ice.

Lydia felt out of place at the Chart House, with all its fancy dinnerware and people. She was so nervous that when the waiter brought out their salads, she waited to see which fork Donald was going to pick up. With two sets of silverware on both sides of the plate, she was confused. The smaller fork seemed like the obvious choice, but she didn't want to embarrass herself.

"Do you come here a lot?" Lydia asked, not wanting to seem like a fish out of water.

Donald smiled sheepishly. "No. This is my first time. I wanted to wait until I found someone special to bring here."

Lydia felt a warmness cover her whole insides.

By the time the waiter brought out the triple German chocolate cake that Donald had ordered for her, Lydia felt so comfortable talking to him that it was like she'd known him for years. They talked about everything: her family, the life she had with Lloyd, and her desire to continue school and make a good life for Treasure and herself. He told her about his work and family. Both of his parents were deceased, and he was divorced, with two little girls himself. He lived alone in an apartment in Germantown, and he was ten years older than Lydia.

By Thanksgiving, Donald and his two daughters were like permanent fixtures in Lydia and Treasure's lives. Treasure had latched onto them immediately. The girls all got along well, like they'd known each other for a long time. Blair, the youngest, was the same age as Treasure, and Victoria took on the role as big sister.

When Donald cut the turkey, for the first time in a long time, Lydia looked happy—happier than she ever remembered being. She sat at the other end of the table, and her face blossomed as she looked around and took in all the festivities. She felt blessed. She had much to look forward to—her independence, her education, her Treasure, and now a life with Donald, Blair, and Victoria.

Her life had never been so sweet.

· ◆ ·

When Valentine's Day arrived, the first that Lydia and Donald would be spending together, the ground shimmered from the light dusting of snow that had been coming down since the afternoon. Lydia was glad to be leaving her last class of the day. She tried not to think about the social science paper that was due the following day. A special evening with Donald—at least what was left of it—was all she was contemplating. She pulled her keys from her book bag and bundled her coat around her as she walked quickly toward her car, a '79 Chevette that she'd purchased for seven hundred dollars at a car auction.

When she reached the car, Donald was waiting there for her, holding an armful of long-stemmed red roses. He had a way of always making her feel special, more special than she'd ever felt. But tonight, he was about to do something that Lydia had only read about in Harlequin romance novels. He walked up to her and lowered his left knee to the cold, snow-covered asphalt. He pulled a small white box from his brown corduroy jacket, holding it out to Lydia. "Will you marry me?" he asked, right on cue.

Lydia's heart thumped wildly. "Yes!" she heard herself say. "Yes, Donald, I'll marry you." Tears rushed down her cold cheeks.

Donald stood and grabbed her and held her tightly in his arms. She held onto him as she felt the snow hit her face and melt with her tears.

• ◆ •

March arrived with the promise for an early spring.

One early afternoon, Lydia received a call from Stonewall. "I have been trying to reach your mother all day," Ms. Jones said. "Do you know how I might be able to contact her?"

"Yes. But I don't have the number here with me."

"I really need to talk to your mother."

Lydia sensed the urgency in Ms. Jones' voice. "If it's an emergency, then I would need to go to her house and get the number out of her telephone book," she said.

"Well, is there any way you can get in touch with her and have her give me a call immediately?" Ms. Jones asked.

"Yes. But can you tell me what's going on? Is something wrong with my sister?"

Ms. Jones hesitated. "I'm not sure. She's been missing since yesterday, and I was hoping your mother would know her whereabouts."

"I don't think my mother has seen Angie since the weekend, but I'll try to reach her and have her give you a call."

"Have her call us immediately. If I'm not here, she can speak with the attendant on duty."

"Okay," Lydia said.

•◆•

Mattie bent forward, pushing the large yellow sponge across the floor. The kitchen was always the last room she tackled before a day's end. She moved the sponge gracefully, as she hummed the words to a song that had shadowed her mind all day.

> *Gonna be a long night*
> *It's gonna be all right*
> *On the nightshift*
> *Oh, you found another home*
> *I know you're not alone*
> *On the nightshift*

She had just heard it on the radio that very morning, the *Nightshift* song the Commodores had recorded as a tribute to Marvin Gaye and Jackie Wilson.

The song played over and over in Mattie's head, and by the time she took off her apron and gathered her things, she had made up her mind: she was going to J.B. Records to buy that song. She needed it. She just had to have it.

•◆•

Lydia drove a little too fast down Broad Street and turned onto Mifflin, taking shortcuts to her parents' house. As soon as she arrived, she parked the car and dashed out, almost forgetting her purse.

"John, we gotta get in touch with Mommy. Angie's counselor called me and said Angie's missing," she said, as soon as John opened the door.

John watched her lips move, but the words floated right past him. He looked like he was about to cry, standing there holding a small white business card. "I found this in the door when I got home." He handed the card to Lydia.

It was a notice from the Philadelphia Medical Examiner's Office advising them to contact their office immediately.

"No, there must be a mistake. I'm going to call them," Lydia said, pushing past John to grab the phone.

The sterile voice on the other end sounded distant, unattached. "Do you know an Angelica Madison?" he said.

"Yes, she's my sister," Lydia answered quickly.

"Can you describe her?"

Fearing the worst, Lydia gave him a brief description of Angie.

"Miss, I'm sorry to inform you that an eighteen- or nineteen-year-old black female fitting that description jumped in front of a train yesterday."

Lydia felt her heart drop.

"Miss, are you still there?"

"Yes," Lydia said softly.

"Is it possible for me to come by and have you view a picture of the young woman? We need to obtain confirmation of identity."

"Yes," Lydia barely heard herself say.

When she hung up the phone, John told her he had already contacted Eileen, Anthony, Roy Jr., and even Eloise, and they were all on their way. By the time the medical examiner came, they had all arrived.

He was a white, heavyset, short man with wire-rimmed glasses that sat awkwardly on his face. He wore tan pants, a white shirt, and a black trench coat. A manila file folder rested tentatively under his left arm.

John asked him to come inside. The man seemed surprised by all the faces staring at him. They prayed he had the wrong family.

He cleared his throat nervously and looked around the room. "Who's the person that I spoke to on the phone?" he asked.

John pointed to Lydia.

"You are the sister, correct?"

"Yes," Lydia said in a whisper.

He gave her a sad look. "I'm going to show you a picture, and I need for you to confirm whether the deceased is your sister."

Lydia nodded slowly.

"Are you ready?"

"Yes," Lydia said, bracing herself.

He pulled a black-and-white picture from the manila folder. Lydia waited, then looked intently at the picture. When she saw Angie lying there on a cold steel table, she let out a wretched cry, and her body slid to the floor. They all knew it was Angie.

"I'm so sorry," the man said, his voice filled with empathy. "This type of news is never easy to deliver." He put his hand on Lydia's shoulder, as she lay there curled up in her pain, listening to the cries of her family.

John collected himself and helped lift her off the floor.

"Come on, Lydia," he said. "Come on now. It's going to be all right."

•—•—•

Mattie walked down Oregon Avenue and cut over to 29th Street, the song still playing in her mind. As soon as she entered the record store, she went straight up to the register. "I want to buy that song the Commodores are singin'," she said excitedly. "I'm not sure what it's called but it goes somethin' like this." She hummed the tune and then sang the words to the chorus.

"Oh, yes," the man said. "You're talking about the song called *Nightshift.*"

"Yeah, that's it. That's the one."

"We just got some more in. They're right over there," he said, pointing to the back wall.

Mattie followed him to the back of the store.

"Would you like the album or the forty-five?"

"I'll take the forty-five," Mattie said.

"Very well."

Mattie smiled as she handed him a five-dollar bill and watched as he slipped the vinyl record into a small brown bag.

"I like that song, too," he said. "It's kinda sad, being that they are singing about those two dead Motown singers. I believe it's about Marvin Gaye, and I can't think of the other singer."

"Jackie Wilson," Mattie said. "My mother used to love to listen to him."

"Yeah, that's right. Marvin Gaye and Jackie Wilson." He handed Mattie her change and then folded the top part of the bag over, creasing it. "Well, enjoy your record."

"I will," Mattie said, smiling to herself.

Mattie fumbled at the door, trying to locate her keys in her purse. Suddenly, the door swung open and Roy Jr. stood there looking straight at her.

"Well, what a nice surprise. What are you doin' here? It must be your birthday or somethin'," she said, smiling.

When Roy Jr. moved aside and Mattie saw all of her family sitting in her living room, she was amused. "Well, did I miss somebody's birthday or somethin'? I know it ain't mine. So what's the occasion?" she said, a smile spread wide across her face.

No one moved; no one spoke up. It was Roy Jr. who finally broke the silence. "Ma," he said in a choking voice. "It's Angie . . ."

Mattie looked at him. The room got still, quiet, as they watched her smile slowly fade.

"Ma . . . Angie's gone. Angie's gone, Ma."

Mattie's heart stopped. The stillness was shattered by her anguished shriek, a sound capable of moving the earth. She fell limply into her eldest son's arms. The brown bag that carried the *Nightshift* went crashing to the floor.

• ◆ •

It was a cool, drizzly morning the day of Angie's funeral.

The choir's voices drifted high across the cathedral ceiling—*Amazing Grace,* they sang, as Mattie, John, Roy Jr., Eileen, Anthony, Lydia, Eloise, Miss Esther, and Mr. Marshall all sat in the front pew, swollen with grief.

The pastor prayed over Angie's closed casket. When he asked the family to come say their final goodbyes, they couldn't move.

Lydia was the first to walk up to the white and pink casket. She wrapped her arms around it and wept, heaving sobs that made her whole body convulse.

She cried for having not spent enough time with her sister, for never telling her that she loved her. She cried for the times that she remembered them playing together—jumping rope, playing hopscotch, watching cartoons. She cried for all the memories past and the memories that would be no more. But she cried most of all for the times she was mean to her— the times she had called her a roach. And when she felt completely drained, Roy Jr. came to her and put his arms around his sister, carrying her back to her seat.

That night, Lydia slept in Treasure's room and held her all night. By the time the sun rose up over the city the next morning, she finally closed her eyes and fashioned a silent prayer. She asked God to take away her mother's pain and give her peace. She asked Him to bless her sister and keep her in the Heavens.

And as her final plea, she asked Him—begged Him—to protect her child, her daughter, her Treasure.

eyes full of pain
heart feels heartless
thoughts confused
voices in her head
gotta' stop the voices
gotta' make choices

Choices that ended it all . . .

years came and rapidly went by
years full of happiness and cries
can't take away the pain because
can't ask for no more than what was
she's happy now, happier than before

but Mama, she ain't commin' home no more

time has lapsed, passed us by
the memories in our hearts will never die
peace and love is now in her heart
can't forget the important parts
of her life, the times she laughed, smiled, and cried
happiness she finally found and much more

but Mama, she ain't commin' home no more

she's in a place, higher than the sky
no longer need to question why
why did she choose to leave
maybe she just wanted peace, love, serenity

eyes look painless
heart is heartful
thoughts unconfused
no more voices in her head
no more choices to be made

she's no longer feeling sad for sure

 Maybe it's better Mama,

   that she ain't

     commin' home no more

PART THREE

Treasure

37

Treasure stuffed her nightgown, a change of clothes, and anything else she could remember into her Little Mermaid backpack. If it had fit, she would have squeezed Dozzie the Bear into it, too.

"You almost ready?" Lydia hollered up the stairs, glancing at her watch and counting the hours she'd have left in the day after dropping Treasure off at Lloyd's folks' house.

Treasure scanned the room one last time before feeling satisfied that she had everything she needed. At nine years old, she was a definite cross between her mother and father, with skin the color of butterscotch and long, dark, coarse hair her mother often pressed for easy combing. Her quarter-sized, almond-shaped eyes were set in a round face that was eager to please, and she had a smile that could light up a maze of underground caverns. She was still too young to understand the essence of her beauty, a beauty complemented by intelligence that her mother had nurtured from the moment she was born.

Treasure's heart thudded wildly with anticipation at the thought of the circus her grandparents were planning to take her to. She'd never been to a circus before, and her breathing felt so heavy with excitement, she thought it would burst open her chest.

Lydia was convinced she'd made the right choice in allowing Treasure to spend time with Lloyd's parents. After Lloyd was convicted, she wanted to erase them from her daughter's life, fearing that they, too, would disappoint Treasure. But there was no sense in keeping her from them, she reasoned. After all, there wasn't much to be gained by it, and she might even feel sorry someday if she had no answers for Treasure's questions, which were bound to come.

Since Treasure had started spending time with her grandparents every other weekend, Donald arranged for his daughters, Victoria and Blair, to visit their mother on the same weekends, giving him and Lydia some time for themselves. She and Donald had been married for a few years now, and they'd long since settled into the life of a blended family. Lydia was proud of the family they'd become, although she sometimes worried about the subtle changes Donald had begun to make, like spending less and less time with Treasure or sometimes showing no interest in her at all. It seemed as soon as the nuptials were sealed between them, Donald had put a stake in the ground between her, Treasure, and his girls. Lately, he'd made it more obvious that he favored Victoria and Blair over Treasure. She especially remembered the day

Donald had gone out and shopped for the girls' school clothes. When he returned, the girls impatiently grabbed at the bags, curious to see what their father had brought back for them. He opened up the packages and handed small denim skirts and blouses to Blair and Victoria, but he'd gotten nothing for Treasure. "Why didn't you bring something back for Treasure?" Lydia wanted to know. The only response she got was, "I thought you were going to go school shopping for her." During times like that, Lydia was doubly thankful she'd made the choice to let Treasure spend time with her grandparents, so she would feel as special as other little girls.

The weekend had passed quickly, and before long, Lydia heard the knock she always listened for when it was time for Treasure's grandparents to bring her home.

"Welcome home, sweetie," Lydia said, as soon as she opened the door. Treasure squeezed from between her grandparents and quickly rushed past her mother and up the stairs.

"I guess she's just tired," Treasure's grandmother said. "We had a very long day."

Lydia smiled warmly at them. "Y'all wanna come in for a minute and thaw out?"

"No, we better be on our way. We got a long day tomorrow."

Lydia nodded and let her invitation fall on deaf ears, as it had done every time she asked them to come inside. She didn't think much of it, no more than what she'd always thought: although they were spending time with Treasure, deep down, there still seemed to be shreds of embarrassment about their son. They never looked Lydia in the eyes without their own being covered with shame.

Lydia was puzzled by Treasure's behavior and decided to check in on her. "Hey sweetie, how was your weekend?" she asked.

Treasure lay in bed with Dozzie tucked under her arm, her back to her mother.

"Are you okay, sweetie?"

Treasure kept her eyes to the wall. "Uh-huh," she finally answered, sounding glum.

"All right then. I'll come and get you when it's time for your bath."

After Lydia shut the door to her room, Treasure wrapped Dozzie tightly under her arms, squeezed her eyes shut, buried her thoughts deep into her pillow, and tried to force sleep to come.

38

*T*reasure sat with her back and shoulders slumped and her eyes stuck on her mother. As Lydia turned on the small television that sat atop the kitchen counter, she reached inside the freezer and grabbed the meat for thawing. Treasure had plunked her small body down at the kitchen table, placed her head into the cradle of her arms, and became lost in her thoughts. Her heart throbbed wildly as she tried to push the fear up from out of her and curl her small lips to form the words that had been stirring inside of her for more than two weeks now. But the words always got caught in the same place, no matter how hard she tried.

Treasure's secret was as frozen inside of her as the meat that needed thawing, and her thoughts made her head feel woozy and her heart fill with guilt and shame. Her eyes left her mother long enough to catch a glimpse of the snow cascading against the kitchen window. It reminded her of how she'd been feeling lately—cold, damp, and hollow—a feeling that seemed to follow her around like a magnet.

Lydia hurried around the kitchen, trying to get dinner started while following the news about a car bomb that was planted in New York City's World Trade Center. The news slowed down her pace, as she took notice of the faces covered in soot splashed across the small television screen. She was so immersed in the news, she wasn't aware of how closely her daughter watched her every move, trying to find the courage to tell her mother what had been eating away at her.

"At least six people are believed to have died and hundreds more injured," the CNN anchor announced. "Let's go back to the scene, where one of our correspondents is standing by."

A familiar mood passed over Lydia while sadness spread out around her as she watched the devastation unfold. She could only imagine how the families were feeling, waiting to see if their loved ones were trapped inside the building. She imagined that they must be having the same feelings her family had only a few short years ago. She never believed that time would heal her family, especially her mother. But it did. And she was glad when the burden had been lifted, because it was difficult for her to watch how her mother had closed in on herself and deteriorated until she had nothing more to hold onto but her grief. Lydia prayed every day—twice a day, in fact—that her mother would someday find peace. But how could her mother ever find peace when she'd lost a child?

More than a year after she and Donald married, when she had gone to visit with her mother, Lydia noticed something different about Mattie. When she asked her mother what had changed, her mother told her Angie had come to her in a dream. "She looked really happy," she told her, with eyes that seemed clearer, brighter. "One night, she just came to me and rang the doorbell. When I answered it, she was surrounded by a bunch of young people, and she was smiling. She told me that I could let her go now, that she was all right."

Lydia could tell immediately that her mother, too, was going to be all right. After that day, the dark veil that had covered Mattie for so long had been lifted. She had let go of the grief, let go of Angie. Now, Lydia stood in front of the television hoping those who had just lost loved ones would receive the same blessing as her mother.

Treasure let out a huge sigh. She wished her mother would pay some attention to her. Since that awful thing had happened to her, she was no longer the same happy and trusting child. Instead, she was sad and guarded, and she wanted the secret that was lodged deep in her heart to go away. It was a secret that was like tempered glass waiting to burst.

It tortured Treasure to keep this secret. She had never before kept anything from her mother. She'd always told her mother everything, no matter what. But this wasn't something she could tell just anybody, especially her mother. If she told, she would be putting her and her mother in danger. But her mind and heart were just too fragile to carry such a big secret.

She knew something just wasn't right about the way he had touched her and the things he'd said to her. "You betta' not tell no body, or I'ma hurt you and your mother real bad," he'd said. And she believed him, too, knew in her heart that he'd meant those words. She knew her mother would be very angry about what had happened to her, and she would take whatever measures necessary to ensure it would never happen again.

One day, Treasure thought about calling 911 like her mother had taught her so long ago, but she didn't want to get anybody in trouble. She just wanted it all to go away, just wanted to feel like the little girl she was before all this happened—before he snatched away her innocence, making her cave in on herself like a butterfly encased inside its wings.

Finally, when she thought the secret was going to burst inside of her, Treasure confided in one other person, but she made her cross her heart and hope to die and stick a needle in her eye if she were to ever break her promise not to tell. And when her best friend, Stephanie, took her small finger and made an "x" across the center of her small chest, Treasure blurted it out. At first, she was surprised by Stephanie's response. When she told her, Stephanie's eyes lit up, as if they had a common secret. And they did. Stephanie told her the same thing had happened to her and that she had never told anyone. "Just keep it to yourself, Treasure," Stephanie had told her. "If you keep it to yourself, then one day you're gonna stop thinking about it, and it'll just go away like mine did."

Treasure tried that, tried forcing it to a tiny place in the back of her mind. But every day when she awoke, and her bed was wet and her stomach felt queasy, she knew it wasn't going to go away. It would never just go away unless somebody made it go away.

The time was coming when she'd have to be alone with

him again, and she didn't want to have to go through the same thing. She needed to tell somebody. She needed for it to go away.

. ◆ .

On the morning she was to go to her grandparents' house, Treasure was fidgety, counting down the minutes until it was time for her mother to take her there.

"Treasure, you got all your stuff packed that you're taking?" Lydia asked. "Hurry up. We gotta be going soon."

Treasure's face had become solemn, stony. She shook her head no.

"What do you mean no?" Lydia rushed over to Treasure's closet to find the small backpack. "Why are you not packed?" she said, turning the empty Little Mermaid bag upside down.

Treasure turned away from her mother.

"Answer me, Treasure!"

Treasure's eyes were fixed on the floor as she felt the words filling up inside of her. Her eyes were brimming with tears, and she slowly raised them to meet her mother's. The room became motionless, and time seemed to have slowed itself. In a small, subdued voice she said, "Mommy, he hurt me. Granddaddy hurt me, mommy."

Treasure's words fell hard on Lydia's ears. And when Treasure moved her eyes from her mother's and stared blankly into space, Lydia knew. She felt the room spinning around her and her heart spinning with it. She reached for something to steady herself, as she felt Treasure's eyes watching her, waiting for her to crumble.

The chalky sound of the chair scraping against the wood

floor, the chair that Lydia was squeezing tightly, was the sound that broke the silence. Her heart was beating so fast she could feel it thumping like a hammer in her chest. She wanted the word *hurt* to have another meaning, any meaning but the one her good mind was telling her.

"What? What did you say, baby? What do you mean he *hurt* you?" Lydia heard herself ask, barely a whisper.

Treasure sat there for a minute, letting the courage once again build up inside. Her big brown eyes looked sullen, lost. Tears flowed slowly down her butterscotch cheeks, and her voice sounded so tiny. "I'm . . . I'm sorry, mommy. He made me do it," she said, her eyes pleading with her mother's.

"Oooh, baby," was all that came from Lydia. She opened her arms and went to her daughter. Treasure leaned into her, feeling her mother's arms embrace her so tightly the only sound between them was their sobs and their hearts beating in unison.

After Lydia explained everything her confused, broken Treasure needed to hear, she went straight to the phone. She didn't mince words or listen to excuses. She got straight to the point and told Ralph Sr. that she planned to see to it that he would never hurt another little girl the way he had hurt her baby. When he tried to escape the truth, she hung up the phone in his ear and called the police.

Following months of police, lawyers, courts, and counseling, Lydia waited impatiently at the Philadelphia Child Protection Agency. Treasure sat close to her mother. There wasn't an inch of room between them. She still had trouble concentrating, even on the things she used to like to think about. She was tired of all the questions and the sympathetic faces that everybody gave her. She liked Mrs. Juniper, though, the counselor who had started coming to her house twice a week since the day she told her mother what granddaddy had done to her. At first, Treasure was afraid to talk to anyone other than her mother and her Nana about it. But Mrs. Juniper had a way of making her feel like she understood, like she knew how lost and ashamed she felt inside. She didn't want to answer any more questions, but Mrs. Juniper told her that today would be the last time she'd have to talk about it, unless she wanted to. "Besides," Mrs. Juniper said, "your mother and I are both gonna be right by your side. You don't have anything to worry about." Treasure nodded and leaned in closer to her mother, as she bravely sat waiting to be called into the office of the court-appointed psychologist.

After Treasure told the psychologist what her grandfather had done to her, it was more than the judge needed to hear. Ralph Sr. was given a sentence of seven to ten years in the state penitentiary.

Lydia continued to ensure that Treasure got all the support she needed, hoping that her daughter's wings would someday unfold and she'd be as free and unabashed as she was before her life was turned upside down. In time, Lydia noticed bits and pieces of her Treasure's vibrancy returning. There were other times when Lydia could still see the hurt and shame in her daughter's eyes; those were the times that Lydia's heart would split open, and she'd cry herself to sleep. It was her mother who had told her time and again she needed to be strong. "The Lord will take care of him," Mattie told her one day when Lydia broke down crying on the phone. "You need to be there for your daughter. You must be strong for her. Treasure's young enough that she'll be able to put this all behind her. But you're gonna have to keep it together until she does."

Lydia listened to her mother, took in her words, and used them to mend the broken places of her heart. And in time, each day got a little bit easier, each hour brought hope, and every minute brought Treasure back to her youth.

39

*T*reasure gazed at the letter she held loosely in her fingertips. She squinted as the noonday sun crept its way through her window blinds, softening the hard edges of her sullen face. The letter had arrived early one Saturday morning, and she had forced herself to ignore it ever since her mother handed it to her. There were many thoughts running through her mind all at once, as though the world had suddenly unloaded a wave of emotions on her. She had always wondered what it would be like to talk to him, to hear his voice, to see his face. But somehow in the midst of her turning nine, then ten, and later eleven, the years had managed to push her curiosity into the abyss. Now that she was twelve, she no longer had the desire, nor the longing, to know him.

She remembered how she sometimes felt jealous about the closeness that Victoria and Blair had with her stepfather,

Donald. And though Donald was mostly nice to her, she could tell there was a difference in the way he treated them. She would have given anything, even her left arm, to have her father be a part of her life in the way she saw other little girls with their daddies. But she had come to accept that her father was never going to be in her life the way she had often dreamt about.

She felt her heart warm as she peered down at the letter, thinking about how this was the first time she had ever heard from him. The only things she knew about her father were what her mother had told her. She often tried to stretch her mind, hoping to remember the last time he held her when she was only two. But she was too young to hold onto such a memory. The only memories she had were the ones she gathered from her mother.

The moment Treasure was old enough to know the truth, Lydia told her everything, being careful not to sugarcoat or make up stories. Treasure could remember the words her mother used, the tone of her voice, and the way she had told Treasure she never wanted her to feel that it was something she had done to make her father not have a relationship with her. "The choices he makes are his choices, and he must own up to them. It has nothing to do with you, so I don't ever want you to feel like it's your fault," Lydia told her. But as much as she tried to make Treasure understand it was not her fault, still Treasure wondered if she was the reason her daddy had made the choices that he did.

Treasure moved her fingers slowly across the envelope, wanting to feel her way to the words inside. Part of her wanted to rip the letter to pieces and dispose of it the way he had disposed of her. Another part of her wanted to reveal his words, words she'd dreamt about since she was a small child. It was that part of her that made her feel like she hated her father for leaving her—and hated her mother for doing whatever *she'd* done to push him away. There were times when she wanted her mother to tell her anything other than what she'd told her. She couldn't fathom that it was just so plain and simple, that Lloyd had just gone out one day and did what he had done without ever thinking of her.

She sat quietly, feeling the stillness of her room. The air felt thick, hot, as it beamed across her face. The air, the envelope, and the tightness around her heart overwhelmed her, making her feel like a tiny gnat just waiting to be crushed. She had waited all twelve years of her life to finally meet the man she'd dreamt about for so long. And now there he was: all wrapped up in a stupid white envelope with a serial number next to his name, her name and address printed neatly across its center.

Treasure hesitated as she opened the dresser drawer and put the unread letter inside. Reluctantly, she shut the drawer, returned to her bed, plopped down, and buried her face into her pillow. She lay there for hours, as she watched the noonday sun go gray. Sleep tugged at her. As her eyelids grew heavy, she stared at an imaginary spot on the ceiling until her body and mind gave in and she was swept away into her sweet dreams.

A sudden knock on her bedroom door stirred her. "Treasure?" she heard her mother's voice drifting nearby. She felt stuck between her dream and her awareness. It was the same dream she'd always had: she was sitting in a park next to her father, and he was telling her how much he loved her and missed her, and he promised he'd never leave her again. She wanted so much to stay in the dream, in the park, to be with her father. But she could feel her fused eyelids opening. And she could see her father melting away as her mind slowly came back to her. "Yes," she mumbled.

Lydia stood on the other side of the door with her hand on the doorknob, considering whether to go inside. She knew how confusing a time it was for her daughter, but she didn't want to pry. "You've been in there for a long time. You sure you okay?"

"Yes, I'm fine."

"All right then," Lydia said, her hand falling from the doorknob. "Well, dinner's almost ready, so you come on downstairs soon. Okay?"

"Okay," Treasure said.

Hearing her mother's footsteps descend the stairs, Treasure got up and walked over to the dresser. She took the envelope out of the drawer. Her heart thudded so hard she could feel it rising inside of her chest. The envelope felt strange, so official, so detached.

With the letter in hand, she pushed herself back until she rested comfortably against the headboard. She turned the envelope over and used her thumb and forefinger to peel back the flap. Once open, she pulled out the ruled, white, neatly folded paper. Tears stung her eyes as she took a deep breath and began reading the words.

Dear Treasure,

How are you? I know how difficult it is for you to even open this letter. By now, you're probably wondering why I have chosen to write after all this time. Baby girl, I don't blame you one bit if you choose not to read this letter and don't want to hear from me ever again.

I've been meaning to write to you for so long, but I just needed time to get myself together. Being in prison gave me a lot of time to think and to learn how to become a man.

When you were born, I truly loved you, and believe it or not, I have never stopped loving you. I'm sorry that I have not been around. I know now that I've done wrong and would give anything right now to change the past. But that's something I can't do, and the only thing I can do is to try to make it up to you. I realize that you probably hate me, and I don't blame you for that. If I were in your shoes, I would hate me, too.

I've been blessed to find Allah, and He has changed my life. I'm a different person now, and I hope that someday you will find it in your heart to forgive me. I'm doing so many positive things now. I got a job and I'm even taking classes in here.

With Allah's blessings, I am up for parole, and hopefully I'll be leaving this place by the end of the year. I can't wait to see you, baby girl.

Well, I don't want to put too much on you in this first letter. I promise to write again soon, and I hope you will find it in your heart to drop me a line sometime. I'm also enclosing a picture. I wanted to send you a picture so that you can at least see who I am.

Be safe and walk with Allah.

Peace,
Your father
Rasheek

P.S. I forgot to mention my brothers have given me a new name.

Treasure felt mute, deflated. All that she could feel were the words from her father's letter drumming in her head. She now knew that no matter how much she wanted to hate her father, no matter all the bad things she had wished upon him, no matter how long she had forced herself not to think about him, there he was—finally revealed, his words forcing themselves upon the most tender places of her heart.

She picked up the small picture that had fallen into her lap. Lloyd stood next to a block concrete wall with a face that reminded her of her own. His skin was the color of her skin, his eyes the shape of her eyes. He looked to be not much taller than Lydia, and his body seemed to bring form to the orange-tangerine jumpsuit that he wore. He was, in no uncertain terms, her father.

She ran her fingers across the picture, wanting to touch him. At that moment, she couldn't think about anything except for the way his eyes seemed to look back at her and speak to her with the words she had wanted to hear all of her young life: *I love you Treasure. I miss you*, she heard a strange voice saying inside her head.

"Treasure, it's time to eat. Hurry up and wash your face and hands, and come on down here for dinner," her mother's voice interrupted.

Treasure folded the letter at its creases and stuffed it back into the envelope. She tucked it inside the top drawer, where she kept her diary and other things she wanted to keep from her mother. Just as she was about to close the dresser drawer, she glanced down at the letter once more and touched it.

• ◆ •

It was a long-awaited day for Lydia. She looked frantically around the room, searching for the black shoes she planned to wear to her graduation. It had taken more than ten years for her to earn this bachelor's degree, and now she had almost overslept. She was going to kick herself if she missed being handed that diploma.

As soon as Lydia pulled the graduation gown over her tan dress, she rushed down the hall to hasten Treasure, who seemed to be spending an inordinate amount of time in her room lately.

As soon as Treasure heard her mother, she jumped from her bed and quickly hid the letter in the drawer. For months now, she had been reading and rereading the same letter, and every day she checked the mail to see if he'd sent another. But none had come. She had written countless letters to him, but she couldn't bring herself to mail them.

She sealed each letter she wrote in an envelope and stuck it in a shoebox underneath her bed. Every now and then, she'd pull his letter out and read it, looking for words that she thought she'd imagined. *Didn't he promise to write again? Was he expecting me to write him back before he sent another letter? Maybe I should have mailed the letters I wrote. Maybe I never should have read that stupid letter.* Treasure tortured herself with questions that had no answers, and answers to superficial questions. When no more letters came, she was crushed. She hated herself for feeling this way, for just wanting more of him.

Treasure thrust the drawer closed and quickly put on her shoes. She ran out of her room and collided with her mother.

"How do I look?" Lydia said, twirling around in the cap and gown.

"Okay, I guess," Treasure said in a flat voice.

"That's all you can think to say?"

Treasure rolled her eyes and sighed.

"Never mind. You'd think you'd be a little more happy for your mother."

"Whatever," Treasure mumbled.

Lydia grabbed her purse and keys. "Let's get out of here before we're late," she said to Donald.

Treasure followed them, trudging slowly behind.

40

By the time her thirteenth birthday rolled around, bringing her period along with it, Treasure's body had moved beyond puberty, finally catching up to the mind that had long since ripened.

She excelled in school and in everything she put her mind to. Lydia didn't cut corners with Treasure, always reminding her daughter that no goal was too high for her to reach. But the more Lydia insisted on Treasure's development, the more Treasure seemed to retreat and turn loose a rebellion that sometimes made Lydia think twice before letting Treasure's tongue get the best of her.

Lydia had no way of knowing that Treasure had been on Lloyd's mind every day for the past ten years. Lloyd had been angry with himself for a long time, especially after he'd been sent to prison. The first few years were hard. Life on the inside was no joke. Although he'd spent time in a juvenile facility, prison was tenfold harder. Finally, he met Brother Ahmad Mohammed, who taught him how to see things in a different light. "This cage is meant to bury you, man. But you are a better man than this cage. You can't let it take away your strength. Now, are you going to let these walls take it from you? Or are you gonna be the man you're supposed to be?" Brother Mohammed chided Lloyd after he was released from solitary confinement for fighting another inmate. It took Lloyd three years to fend off the violence and a lot of time spent in solitary confinement before he turned his life over to Allah.

It had taken long days and nights for him to muster up the courage to write to Treasure. And when he did find the guts to mail that one and only letter, and Treasure never wrote him back, he thought maybe it was just not the right time. He'd talked to Brother Mohammed about it, even prayed with him about it. After some intense prayerful meditation, he realized he needed to get out of there to really make a difference in her life. "It's impossible to father her when you're surrounded by bars," Brother Mohammed had told him. So Lloyd made up his mind right then and there that he would not send another letter, would not make another attempt to contact her, until he was a free man. It was only a few short months away.

· ◆ ·

December arrived with old man winter clinging at its heels, showering Philadelphia with so much snow the city looked almost magical.

As much as Treasure tried to force her father from her mind, the longing for him had become even more powerful. A cloud followed her everywhere, and the only outlet she had was her diary—the place where she dumped all of her strange and unexpected feelings and locked them away with a small metallic key, securing her most private thoughts.

Two disturbing calls came one Sunday morning. The first came from Mattie.

"Ma, is everything all right?" Lydia asked, as soon as she heard Mattie's voice.

"Mama's sick," Mattie answered. Her voice was strained, like those two words pained her.

"What's wrong with her?" Lydia asked, as the grits made gurgling sounds, popping bubbles on the stove nearby.

"They say it's serious. They say it's cancer."

"CANcer?" Lydia flung the word out like a bad taste in her mouth. She hissed at the hot grits that had popped on her arm and the word that stung her ear. "How could she have cancer? She's never been sick before."

"We've been at the hospital with her all night," Mattie continued. "She's been goin' to the doctor for a while now. They had told her she was sick, but she never told us. Then yesterday she called sayin' that she wasn't feelin' good."

Lydia moved away from the stove and walked toward the window, looking out at the snow that had picked up. It was coming down in flakes the size of nickels. "You mean she already knew she had cancer, and she never told you?" she asked, her voice cracking.

"Well, she says she been feelin' fine, and she didn't believe those doctors knew what they were talkin' about."

"Are they gonna be able to help her?"

"They say that she's gonna need treatment. I have to take her to a specialist on Tuesday."

"Oh, Ma. I'm so sorry. How's Mama feeling today?"

"She's feelin' better. They're gonna keep her for a few more days."

"I'm gonna come by tomorrow to see her as soon as I get off work," Lydia said. "But I want to call her right now. Do you have the number to her room?"

As soon as Mattie gave Lydia the number, she hung up and called the hospital.

Eloise, just before she became sick.

Eloise's voice sounded as strong and healthy as it had every other time Lydia had spoken to her. There was no evidence of sickness, no evidence of cancer.

"Hi, baby," Eloise said, as soon as she heard Lydia's voice.

"Hi, Mama. Mommy told me you haven't been feeling too well lately."

"I'se feel jus' fine. These doctors don't know what ail' me. I feel as good as I been feelin' any other mornin'."

Lydia chuckled. "But Mama, you're gonna have to listen to the doctors. They probably are right, even though you've been feeling okay."

Lydia heard her grandmother suck the air between her teeth.

"Shoot, I ain't been dependin' on no doctors befo'. Prayer is what done kept me."

"I know, Mama. But you've got to listen to the doctors. I'm sure they don't tell you something for no reason."

Eloise sighed and went quiet.

"Mama, are you still there?"

"Yeah, I'm still here. And I'm gon' continue to be here long as I put my trust in the Lord."

Lydia smiled. "I know, Mama. But you gotta listen to the doctors. Okay?"

Eloise didn't answer.

"Okay, Mama?"

"All right," Eloise was slow to say. "I reckon you right. But I still think I was doin' a whole lot betta befo' those doctors got hol' of me."

"Now Mama, stop that. You said you're gonna listen to the doctors. Right?"

"I know what I said, girl. I ain't done lose my mind, too."

Lydia let out a small chuckle. "Well you be good in there. Okay? I'll come and see you tomorrow as soon as I get off work."

"All right, baby. I will. And how's my great-grandbaby doin'?"

Lydia hesitated. She didn't want to tell her grandmother how she sometimes wanted to just ring Treasure's neck. "She's fine. She's doing well in school. Getting more grown every day, though."

"Well, I spose she is. She done turned into a teenager. Ain't much you can do bout' that. Just be patient with her."

Lydia smiled into the phone. "Well, you get back to your rest. I'll see you tomorrow."

As soon as Lydia heard the dial tone, she said a silent prayer for her grandmother.

"I'll get it," Treasure shouted. The second disquieting phone call of the morning was about to come.

"Hello," she answered in a half-cheered voice.

"May I speak to Treasure?" a deep and unfamiliar voice responded.

"This is Treasure."

"Hi, Treasure. This is Lloyd. Your father."

Treasure's heart stopped as the phone fell from her ear and thudded to the floor.

"Girl, why'd you drop that phone like that?" Lydia snapped.

Treasure stood with her hand covering her mouth, a stunned look on her face.

"What's wrong with you? Who's on the phone?"

Treasure's almond eyes bore into her mother's.

"I said who's on the phone?"

Treasure picked up the receiver and handed it to her mother.

"Hello," Lydia shouted into the phone. "Who is this?"

The caller hesitated. "This is Lloyd," he finally said.

The kitchen grew quiet, except for the sound of water splashing down into the sink, hitting the soaking dishes.

"Hi, Lloyd," Lydia said, staring at the wall in front of her. She was trying to decide whether to hang up or hold on.

"I was hoping to talk to Treasure," Lloyd said.

Lydia twisted her lips in an effort to hold back her tongue.

"I've been home since Thursday, and I wanted to see her," Lloyd said gravely.

Lydia was slow to put the phone down and turn to where Treasure had been standing, but she had already disappeared.

Lydia went to find her. "Treasure, can I come in?" she asked, leaning into Treasure's bedroom door.

She opened up to let her mother in.

"Why did you leave? Didn't you know it was your father on the phone?"

Treasure stared out the window. "Yes, I knew it was him. But I don't want to talk to him."

"Don't you think you should at least tell him why you don't want to talk to him? I think you're old enough to tell him how you feel."

"Why can't you tell him? You're the one that had a baby with him!" Treasure's voice was on the verge of cracking.

"Don't you speak to me like that. You aren't that grown yet that you can talk to me like that!"

Treasure sucked in her breath and folded her arms.

"Now you go on down there, pick up that phone, and tell your father how you feel."

Treasure's memories of the letter began to stir. She stomped past her mother and trotted down the stairs.

⋆ ◆ ⋆

Lloyd's hands were folded on top of the red-and-white-checkered tablecloth, rubbing together, a bad habit he'd picked up in solitary confinement. A habit he often wished would go away because it showcased his weakness.

More than a month had passed since he'd made that first call to Treasure, and it had taken several more calls to convince her and Lydia to agree to a meeting.

As soon as Lloyd saw a young girl emerge from the passenger side of a dark blue sedan, he knew immediately it was Treasure. He needn't be close up to tell that she was a part of him.

Lydia got out of the driver's seat and looked toward the pizza shop. Lloyd got up from his seat and walked to the door. He was no longer the young juvenile punk that Lydia remembered; instead, he looked older, wiser than his twenty-eight years.

For a short while, not one of them moved or said anything.

Treasure figured she was much too wise to fall for the things she'd fallen for when she was younger. Even though she had finally agreed to meet Lloyd, she didn't intend to forgive him. It was going to take a whole lot more than a slice of pizza and a Coke to win her over.

"Hello, Lloyd," Lydia said, as she held out her hand.

Lloyd wiped his sweaty hand on his jeans and reached out, taking hold of hers. "Hi, Lydia. How you been doin'?" he stammered.

Treasure was too afraid to look at him, too afraid those feelings she managed to bury would come tapping at her again.

"Hello, Treasure," Lloyd said in as tender a voice as he could muster. He reached out to touch her shoulder, but Treasure flinched. She took her time before she looked at him. A quick *hi* was all she managed.

Lloyd suddenly felt silly for being there, trying to worm his way back into her life. He felt himself fighting an urge to walk away. It was Lydia's soft voice that halted him.

"Y'all wanna have a seat? Maybe we can order some pizza or something," Lydia said.

They took a seat at the table where Lloyd had been sitting.

"So how have you been doing?" Lydia asked Lloyd, breaking the ice.

"Fine. I've been staying with my mother until I get myself settled. You know, find a job, get my own place. Everything seems so different now. I'm not sure where to start."

Lydia nodded and looked past Lloyd. It felt strange to be sitting across from him and not have the same feelings: feelings of fear and inferiority. In a way, as odd as it was, she had Lloyd to thank. She wondered what her life would be like if she had never met him, if he had never made her want so much to not be like her own mother and grandmother. Instead of sitting across from him, loathing him, she sat in that seat and secretly wanted to thank him for strengthening her and for giving her Treasure.

Treasure was stubbornly silent as she watched her father struggle to earn a sliver of respect from her and her mother. She had wanted to ask him why he'd done the things he'd done, why he had never been the type of father she so often dreamt about. But after the first hour had passed and she heard the contrition in his voice and the way he seemed to want so much to be a part of her, she felt her heart betraying her. Lloyd told them about all of the things he'd accomplished in prison, the way it had changed his life. And by the time Lydia said it was getting late and that she and Treasure needed to be getting home, Lloyd was eager to make plans to see his daughter again.

"Why don't you and Treasure spend some time getting to

know each other over the phone first," Lydia told him.

"All right. I understand. I'm in no rush," Lloyd replied. He moved slowly toward Treasure and held her for what seemed like a lifetime before releasing her. Treasure took a step back, trying to compose herself and take control of her heart, which tethered between forgiveness and disdain.

"Well, y'all get home safely," Lloyd said.

Treasure smiled awkwardly at her father and then raised her hand, waving it slightly to say goodbye.

Lydia and Treasure

"Bye, Treasure. I hope to see you soon."

"Me, too," Treasure said in a gentle voice.

Over the next few weeks, Lydia could see immediately how different her daughter seemed since she'd been talking to her father on the phone.

"He's really nice, Mom," Treasure announced as they stood shoulder to shoulder, washing and drying dishes.

Lydia kept her focus on the dishes.

"Did you know he got an associate's degree while he was in prison? I think that's so cool."

Lydia was happy to see the light shine in her daughter's eyes again. As much as she didn't want to admit it, she was grateful to have Lloyd back in Treasure's life—especially since Donald seemed to be taking less and less interest in Treasure.

Lydia had talked to Donald about his indifference toward Treasure, and she was taken aback when he retorted, "She's your daughter, not mine." From that day forward, Lydia had decided they were no longer a family; she and Donald were married, but Treasure was her responsibility, and she didn't expect him to be a part of her life anymore.

"His girlfriend is really nice," Treasure went on, bringing Lydia's attention back.

"Is she?" Lydia said absently.

"I think she really likes you, Mom. She said she has never met anyone who is as nice as you are."

"Well I think she's nice, too."

"And guess what, Mom? She said she got me a gift and she's going to give it to me when I visit them."

Lydia looked intently into her daughter's glowing face and held her smile for a moment. "That was very nice of her," she said at last.

"Yeah, I know. I really like her, Mom."

Lydia turned to put away the last of the dishes. "How did your dad and Cheryl meet? Did he tell you?"

"Yes. They met while he was still in prison. She had gone to the prison with one of her girlfriends who was visiting her husband, and he introduced them."

"Oh, that's nice," Lydia said thoughtfully.

The smile on Treasure's face lit up. "I can't believe she waited three years for him to get out of prison."

Lydia dried her hands. "Well, I hope he realizes he has someone special," she said.

Treasure soon forgot about the lost years between her and

Lloyd. It didn't escape Lydia that Lloyd was buying lost time by taking Treasure to malls and showering her with gifts. And one weekend when Lydia told Treasure she'd rather she stay home, Treasure called her father and told him her mother wouldn't let her visit. Lloyd immediately called Lydia.

"Why can't she come this weekend?" he demanded to know.

"Because she can't. She has things to do at home this weekend."

"Why do I feel like you're callin' all the shots? She's my daughter, too. I have every right to see her."

Lydia thought carefully about her next words. "You know, I welcomed you back into her life with open arms. Even though you've not been there to help raise her all these years, I tried to be fair and ignore the past. How dare you tell me what *rights* you have! And if you start allowing her to manipulate both of us, it's only going to bring trouble."

Lloyd ignored Lydia and tried to force *his rights,* as Lydia watched her daughter change from a quiet, respectful child into a manipulative adolescent that knew how to play one rooster against the other.

It wasn't long before Lydia saw the contrite man who showed up at the pizza shop disappear and glimpses of the old Lloyd return. This time, it wasn't a matter of abusing her or taking away her self-esteem. It was something far more damaging. Lloyd was imposing a fate on something more precious to her—her Treasure, the daughter she'd loved and nurtured the past thirteen years.

41

Treasure listened to the train whistle in the distance. She stretched her long limbs forward, scrubbing the bathroom floor, careful to wash behind the toilet where she was sure her mother would check. She wrung the rag a final time before giving the floor an extra swift wipe. She had been cleaning all morning, making sure each room was spotless, the way her mother liked it. Saturday was housecleaning day, and Treasure was expected to have all of her chores done by the time Lydia returned home from her early morning class and errands. After Treasure finished with the bathroom, she quickly made her way to the kitchen. She was hopeful that the care she took with her chores would soften her mother's mood.

Treasure liked spending time with her father and his girl-friend, Cheryl, because they gave her the freedoms her mother would never allow. Like staying up half the night watching television and sleeping until noon the next day. Lately, Treasure was feeling a strong urge to ask her mother if she could live with them. She desperately wanted to get out from under her mother's wing and away from all the structure and rules. One night when Lydia refused to let Treasure stay out past her curfew, Treasure screamed that she'd much rather live with her father. Her words stung. "You know what?" Lydia slung back, "That's exactly where you're going to end up, with your father. I won't have you living in my house disrespecting me." Lydia knew her words came only out of anger. She'd never allow Treasure to live with Lloyd. And it wasn't just Treasure she was concerned about. When she first met Cheryl, she noticed how her eyes carried the same emptiness that her own eyes had once carried. Cheryl seemed to shy away with an all too familiar stigma.

There was something going on with Lloyd, and even Treasure could sense it. She could tell when his dark side was about to emerge, and he'd take all his frustrations out on the world, including Cheryl. She remembered the time he struck Cheryl across the face with a closed fist. The blow stunned Treasure. "Dad, please don't ever hit her like that again," she pleaded.

Lloyd gave her a callous look. "You don't know nothin', so keep out of it." After Lloyd left, Treasure went to Cheryl and held her. She felt odd, being so young and comforting a woman who was supposed to be stronger than her.

Once Treasure returned home, she was shaken but decided against telling her mother about the incident for fear that she'd never see her father again.

As soon as the professor announced that class was adjourned, Lydia headed straight to the Radio Shack to pick up the small Apple computer she'd put on layaway months before. Although it was a very expensive gift, she had decided to get it for Treasure's birthday, even if it meant sacrificing a few things.

She stopped at the movie theatre to pick up two tickets for a matinee. It had been a long time since she and Treasure had shared some quality time, and she was looking forward to celebrating Treasure's fourteenth birthday together.

She'd been thinking hard about her daughter and trying to find ways to resolve their differences. She had shared her frustrations with her mother, who suggested she was maybe being too overprotective of Treasure. "If you don't try to work it out with her, you'll lose her. I know you love her and want the best for her, but she's a teenager now and you gotta give her some space. Sometimes you gotta let a butterfly go in order for it to learn to fly," Mattie had told her. Lydia knew her mother's words came from a deep place that still lurked in her heart, a place Lydia never wanted to know.

The moment her foot crossed the front door, Lydia was welcomed by the scent of lemon Pine Sol. She fumbled with the groceries, trying to pull the key out of the keyhole while using her right foot to push the door far enough open, allowing her to enter. She could tell that Treasure had had a busy morning.

"Hi, Mom. Where you been? I thought you would have been home earlier," Treasure said.

Lydia noticed the softness in Treasure's voice. "I know, but I had a few errands to run."

Treasure helped Lydia put away the groceries. She stole small glances at her mother, waiting for the right time to ask her permission to spend the weekend with her father. She glanced at the clock. It was nearing the time she was supposed to meet Lloyd at the train station.

"You did a great job with the house today," Lydia said.

"I cleaned your room, too," Treasure said, smiling.

"You did? Well, thank you. I really appreciate it."

Lydia looked at Treasure, thinking about how much more mature her daughter already seemed. Thirteen had been a strange age, a struggle for them both, with Treasure's moodiness yanking them around.

"What other plans do you have today?" Treasure asked cautiously.

A proud look came across Lydia's face. "Well, I thought you and I could spend the weekend together and celebrate your birthday. I have already taken care of everything. All you have to do is get dressed, and we'll be on our way."

"What? My birthday isn't until Monday," Treasure said, her face turning red.

"I know, but I wanted to celebrate it this weekend since Monday is a school night and we won't have enough time to do all the things I planned."

Treasure felt her good mood easing away. "But I already have plans," she whined.

"What do you mean you already have plans? What plans do you have?" As soon as the words came from Lydia, Treasure knew she needn't tell her what her plans were. She already knew.

Treasure's lips pressed together in a grimace. "I was waiting all day for you to come home so that I could tell you," she said, her voice unsteady.

"How come you're making plans without even talking to me first?"

They both stood there, waiting for the other to relent.

"Well, I'll tell you what," Lydia finally said. "You need to

go and change those plans because I ain't breaking mine."
The words snapped off her tongue like crisp twigs.

Treasure stood with her arms wrapped tightly at her chest.
"So are you telling me that I can't go and spend the weekend
with my father?" she asked, about to break into tears.

"That's right. We're gonna do what I have spent the last few
weeks planning. So you might as well go upstairs and get ready."

Treasure's stare penetrated her mother. Before she could
catch hold of her tongue, the words had already left her. "You
Dumb Bitch. I Hate You. I Wish You Would Die!"

Lydia's open palm was already in the air and across
Treasure's face before she had time to think. The blow was so
fierce it sent Treasure hurling to the floor.

Treasure jumped up and lunged at her mother.

No matter how much Lydia tried to fend off her daughter, her strength was no match for all the anger and
resentment Treasure harbored. It seemed that the earth had
stopped moving, and Lydia's world was pulled out from
beneath her before Donald rushed through the door and
pulled Treasure off of her.

"What's going on here?" Donald demanded to know.

Lydia wiped away the blood that trickled from her nose.
She felt her heart throbbing, ready to erupt.

It was Treasure who broke the silence with words that cut
through her mother.

"I hate that bitch. I hate her. I wish she were dead!" As
though she hadn't already broken her mother's heart enough,
Treasure leaned in close to Lydia and spit in her face. "I want
to leave this stupid house and go live with my father," she
announced coldly.

Lydia's chest was rising as quickly as her breath heaved. She did not try to match words with her daughter, nor hatred. She spoke only briefly: "Take her to her father," she told Donald, in a voice that scratched her throat. Then she turned and walked away.

Treasure left with nothing but the clothes on her back.

When Lydia heard the front door close, she felt her heart close with it. She knew without a doubt how much disdain her daughter had for her. She had felt it in her blows, saw it in her eyes. And when Lydia's heart had no more to give, she went to her room and pulled out the black-and-white composition book she kept tucked under her mattress. She took hold of the pen and scrawled the words that had been stirring in her for a long time.

Birthed, nothin' shone that would appear
a child so lost, soul so bare

A stake was woven through my heart
the day my child's eyes lost its spark

A shallow glance, here—sometimes there
solitude, those eyes of hers appeared not to fear

How could this be, often I'd swear
my child could possess a soul so rare

A woman-child, torn—must she feel
life's long journey has no real appeal

A distant father perhaps stole her pride
left her heart empty, stripped the glint from her eyes

A lost stare her beautiful eyes portrayed
searching for love that went astray

How could this be, often I'd swear
my child could possess a loveless tear

Detest, now and again, bore her stare
antipathy—lay lost with no care

A fruitless heart, squashed with no love
for a mother, self, or the good Lord above

I beg of you, Almighty Thee
to reinstate her eyes with that purity

Humbly, I'm at the altar, my precious God
begging for the sparkle—to be put back
in my child's eyes

42

The first night Treasure spent with her dad and Cheryl in their cramped one-bedroom apartment was awkward for all of them.

The apartment was already too small, and even though they'd managed to make it work when Treasure had come to visit, the thought of her staying longer than a weekend seemed burdensome. It had taken Treasure two whole days before she'd conjured up enough nerve to tell her father she wanted to live with him. His only response was a nod and an uncomfortable, patronizing smile. It made Lloyd flinch to see how much his daughter reminded him of himself, the way she seemed to harbor a stubbornness that hardened her in ways that were unnatural for a girl.

After Lydia made no attempt to contact them, Lloyd and Cheryl realized they'd have to support Treasure themselves. It was an unexpected expense their small budget could not handle, since Cheryl was the only one working—a sacrifice they'd have to make, especially after Lydia hung up the phone on Lloyd when he called to ask if he could come and pick up some of Treasure's things.

"I guess we'll need to take you to the mall and have you pick out a few things, something to sleep in and some underwear and stuff," Cheryl said.

Lloyd stood off in the distance, watching as Cheryl and Treasure grabbed more things than he intended to buy. When they got to the checkout and the total came to well over a hundred dollars, he gave Cheryl an annoyed look. He reached inside his back pocket and pulled out his wallet. He only had three twenty-dollar bills.

Cheryl quickly reached inside her purse and pulled out a credit card. "Here," she said, handing it to the cashier.

The first swipe declined.

"Try it again please," Cheryl said, embarrassed.

"All right," the cashier replied with annoyance. Cheryl avoided the look on Lloyd's face.

"Sorry, miss. It's declined again."

Just as Lloyd was ready to step forward and ask the cashier to try it a third time, Treasure spoke up. "Dad, I don't need all this stuff. Maybe we can just get one outfit for now."

The wrath inside Lloyd seemed to quiet down as soon as he heard Treasure's soft voice.

• ◆ •

"Are you all right?" Donald asked Lydia one day after he returned home from work and found her in the kitchen, crying.

"Yes, I'm fine," she said, hurrying to wipe away the tears.

"You know . . . I've been wanting to talk to you about something," Donald said cautiously.

Lydia reached into the cupboard and pulled out two pots. She waited, keeping her back to Donald.

"Well, I know you've been upset about what happened between you and Treasure, and it upset me, too." After pausing for a moment, he continued. "Well, I'm gonna just say it." He took a deep breath. "I think maybe you should send Treasure to a boarding school or something. She needs to be somewhere with more structure and discipline."

"Have you lost your mind?" Lydia asked. The words were out before she had time to fully digest what Donald had said.

Donald stiffened, forcing himself to remain calm. "No, I haven't lost my mind!" he said.

"Would you send Victoria or Blair away if this were one of them?"

"This isn't about Victoria or Blair."

"Like hell it isn't! It's been about Treasure and Victoria and Blair for a long time now."

"Victoria and Blair aren't like Treasure. This has nothing to do with them."

His words surprised Lydia. "I don't have to listen to this," she said. "I'm tired of your selfishness and your self-serving ways." She stormed past Donald, grabbed her keys and jacket, and left.

· ◆ ·

Shortly after Treasure moved in, Lloyd told her he would see about getting her transferred to the local high school, but when he didn't mention it again, she didn't remind him.

Even though the sofa where she slept was nowhere as comfortable as her old bed, Treasure was ready to trade such comforts to be able to breathe the same air as her father. With Cheryl gone most of the day, she got to spend uninterrupted time with Lloyd, just the two of them. They talked and laughed and shared moments that were once only wishes in her diary.

But by the second week, Treasure quickly learned that her presence only stirred up more commotion. She didn't like the way Lloyd was beginning to treat her and the way he took his frustrations out on Cheryl, calling her bad names and slapping her around for no reason. Treasure tried hard to avoid each explosive situation. One time when Cheryl and Treasure were alone, Treasure got up the nerve to ask Cheryl why she allowed Lloyd to treat her that way. Cheryl sloughed it off as normal, leaving Treasure to realize it was a *normal* that she never wanted to know. Suddenly, all of the rules and structure her mother had imposed on her didn't seem so *abnormal* after all.

Cheryl had been jittery since they'd left the apartment that morning, after she and Lloyd had exchanged some harsh words. Lloyd's anger had been collecting all day and was lessened only for the short time they spent with his mother. By the time they set out for home and reached the bus stop, Lloyd could no longer hold back the rage that had been snaking through him. Before Treasure had time to react, he had already struck Cheryl, knocking her to the ground.

"Please, Dad. Please don't hurt her again," Treasure cried,

trying to pull him off of Cheryl. Lloyd turned and struck Treasure across the face so hard the bruise started to rise before Treasure heard herself scream.

After Lloyd ran away when he heard someone threaten to call the police, Treasure tried to help Cheryl, as she struggled to lift herself up off the ground. When the police came, Cheryl told them she and Treasure were fine and that it was all a misunderstanding.

Seeing Treasure still sobbing, the officer turned to her. "Are you okay, miss?"

Treasure stared at Cheryl for a long time before nodding her head in agreement. "Yes, I'm fine," she said quietly. It was hard for her to believe that Cheryl was willing to cover for Lloyd, even after he had turned his rage on her.

"I'm going to call my mom," Treasure told Cheryl when the bus finally came.

"Are you sure?" Cheryl asked.

"Yes, I'm sure," Treasure said. Cheryl couldn't help but notice the confused and sad look on Treasure's face as the bus slowly pulled away.

The crisp November air carried Treasure, as she walked briskly in search of a phone. She found the black-and-blue telephone booth and reached into her pocket to grab one of the quarters meant for the bus. She dialed the numbers as though each one held the key to her fate.

"Hello," Lydia said in an even tone.

Silence.

"Helllooo?"

More silence.

"Helllooo?" Lydia repeated. "Who is this?"

Just when she was about to hang up the phone, Lydia heard a small voice.

"Mom, it's me . . . Treasure."

Lydia closed her eyes, feeling the hard edges around her heart melt. Her lips trembled as she listened to her daughter's sad voice. "What's wrong? Are you all right?"

Hearing her mother's voice, Treasure already felt safe, loved. She struggled to find the courage to say what she had to say. "Mom, I want to come home. Can you please come and get me?"

No sooner than she hung up the phone, Lydia was on her way.

When she pulled up to the corner where Treasure was standing, the look of brokenness in her daughter's face told her everything she needed to know. Lydia stretched open her arms as she walked toward her daughter. Treasure sank into them and felt them wrap around her.

They held each other, wanting to take back all that had happened between them. Deep down, Lydia knew Treasure had needed to taste the ripeness of life; she needed to learn life's lessons, even if it left a dent in her.

Lydia forced a smile through her tear soaked face. "I love you, Treasure."

Treasure felt something inside of her go warm as she let her mother's words serenade her.

"Let's go home," Lydia said finally.

There was nothing more gratifying to Treasure.

43

Wilson Park had a dreary look in the early morning dew, with the polluted snow lining the banks of the sidewalk. The sound of cold slush slid about as cars whizzed by. Mattie had bundled up in layers, knowing the commute would be a long one. She and John had finally saved enough money to buy a home in suburban Philadelphia, and it took an hour and a half on two buses and a train to reach her mother's house.

Mattie had been taking this journey every morning for the past year, since she first learned of her mother's cancer. She would bathe and feed Eloise, tending to her early morning needs, all before she set off for work. At the end of her long workday, Mattie returned to fix dinner and help get her mother to bed before she made the long trip home. Deller had come to stay for several months to help out as well, and when she had to return home, their brother Walton moved in with Eloise to give her a hand.

Cold, steady flakes fell as Mattie made her way down the final block before reaching Eloise's front door. She paused as she pulled the screen door ajar and knocked.

"Good mornin'," she said, as she stomped her feet against the concrete, loosening the ice and snow that had caught on her boots.

"Good mornin'," Walton greeted her. "I tried to feed Mama, but she won't eat nothin'. She says she don't want nothin' I cook for her."

Mattie took off her overcoat. "Is she sleeping?"

"I don't know. I woke her about a half hour ago. I'm not sure if she fell back to sleep. The TV is still blasting."

"All right then. I'm gonna go upstairs and see what's ailing her," Mattie said, filling the teakettle with water and putting it on the stove.

Eloise sat in a small chair next to the window, looking out at the trees, watching the melting snow. If not for the frailty of her body from losing so much weight and the gaunt look of her once-smooth brown face, she still favored herself even though her eyes had long since lost their glint.

"Hey, Mama. How you feelin' today?" Mattie asked. "Do you want me to fix you somethin' to eat? You think if I fix somethin', you might try to force it down?"

Eloise remained silent and stoic, her face portraying little emotion.

"Mama, I know you hear me talkin' to you. Now, I know you ain't been feelin' good lately, but you still gotta force somethin' on your stomach. How about I fix somethin' for you? You think you could at least try and eat?"

Eloise shifted slightly in her chair.

"Now Mama, I know you hear me talkin' to you. Ain't no sense in not talkin'. How are we supposed to know what you want if you ain't gonna say nothin'?"

Eloise turned, giving Mattie a stone look. "That boy don't know how to cook. All the food he been cookin' taste like dust, and I ain't eatin' it no mo.'"

"Now Mama, you've *been* eatin' his cookin'. Why do you think it ain't good now?"

Eloise rolled her eyes. "I been eatin' it before these medicines done take away my appetite," she said, jabbing her right finger toward the mounds of brown bottles with orange labels sitting on the nightstand. "I was fine til' those doctors got hol' of me. Now I'se sick all the time. Don't know what ail' me now."

"Well, I'm gonna go on downstairs and fix a pot of grits. You think you can hold grits on your stomach if I make it?" Mattie asked calmly.

A slight grunt was the only answer Eloise gave.

Even though the doctors had warned Mattie the medications would make Eloise feel sicker, it was difficult to watch her mother wither away. Every morning, she prayed it would be the last day she would have to see her mother suffer. She hoped that maybe the next round of chemo and radiation would be the final dose that would reverse the cancer. But the more treatment they gave her, the worse Eloise got, and the whole family was witness to the way the disease was devouring her.

Soon, Eloise was too weak to even sit upright. And one

day, Mattie called the doctor and then an ambulance. The hospital kept Eloise for more than a week, and when they released her, Mattie had made up her mind—Eloise was coming home with her.

• ◦• •

Lydia headed straight to Mattie's. It upset her to see how the life had been stripped away from her grandmother and the way her mother seemed to be slipping along with her. She felt bad about all the time she had missed with her mother and her grandmother, wallowing in her own pain, but her heart and mind were stretched too thin with Treasure.

"I didn't expect you till tomorrow." You could hear the joy in Mattie's voice as soon as Lydia arrived.

"I know, but Mama sounded so sad when I talked to her on the phone last night. I wanted to come and see her today."

"Well, that's good," Mattie said.

"Where's Mama?" Lydia asked.

"She's in her room. She's been in there all day." Lydia could hear the sadness in Mattie's voice. "I don't think she likes it here much. I think she's mad at me cause she had to come and stay with us."

"Ma, don't blame yourself. I just think she misses her own house."

Mattie nodded and bent down to check on the chicken roasting in the oven. For a moment, all the sadness in Mattie's eyes made Lydia want to hold her, to ignore the unsaid rule they shared about affection. "Well, I'm going to sit with Mama for a while," Lydia said, her voice trailing off.

Lydia cracked the door open to her grandmother's dimly

lit room, illuminated mostly by the gray light coming from the television. Eloise looked so very small, lying there wrapped in a tan comforter. Her face looked pale, her eyes tired, as though she had aged overnight. She turned her head slowly toward the triangle of light that flashed through the cracked door. Her face lit up when she saw her granddaughter standing there. She patted a spot next to her, willing Lydia to sit down.

Lydia sat in the small space on the bed next to her grandmother. The bed squeaked as she bent to kiss Eloise on the cheek. She took her grandmother's hand in hers, felt Eloise squeeze her fingers.

"Hi, baby. How you today?" Eloise asked.

"I'm fine, Mama. How are you feeling?"

"I'se feelin' a little betta' today. My legs been feelin' numb though. And my scalp itchin' me somethin' ter'ble."

"You want me to brush your hair for you?"

"That'd be real nice," Eloise said, as she forced herself up on one elbow. "Reach in that drawer over there and get my hair grease and brush."

Lydia walked over to the dresser and took out a black, wide-tooth comb and a bottle of Vaseline. "Here, Mama, let me help you sit up."

Eloise sat upright, resting against the headboard. Her shoulders relaxed as Lydia combed her soft cotton hair, the color of silver. Eloise closed her eyes and drew in her breath as she leaned her head back. The Vaseline soothed her itching scalp, pushing all her worries and pain away.

"Don't be afraid to comb it, baby. I ain't gon' break," Eloise told Lydia.

"I know, Mama. I just don't want your scalp to be sore later."

Eloise shrugged her shoulders, frowned her face. "Uhmmpp, it ain't gon' be no more sore than everything else on my body."

"Well, maybe now that you're staying with Mommy, things will be a little easier for you," Lydia said softly.

"Yeah, but I'se really tired. I feel like the more medicine I take, the worse I feel. And every time I go and see them doctors, they tell me somethin' else ail' me."

"I know, Mama, but you're gonna get better soon."

Lydia listened to the soft breaths that came from her grandmother, steady and even. Eloise thought about how much she missed her home, missed the time she had with her family. She was tired of fighting, pushing hard to live one more day in pain. She was seventy-five years old and grateful for the life she'd lived, every moment of it. She had come through many storms, had reared eight children, and was the branch to three generations that succeeded her. She had come to accept, had already reconciled with her God, that she was almost through with this life.

"How was that?" Lydia asked her grandmother.

Eloise moved closer to Lydia. The gray light caught her angelic face. "I'm ready to go home, baby. I'm tired," she said, her voice barely a whisper.

"You're not well enough to go home and live on your own, Mama. You need to stay here. Mommy will take care of you. I'm going to help her."

Eloise reached out and took Lydia's hand. "I'm not talkin' bout that kind of home," she said. "I'm talkin' bout *Home*. I'm ready to go Home and be with the Lord."

Lydia went numb. Her grandmother's words frightened her, split her heart wide open.

Two days before Christmas, Eloise died at the hospital with her whole family at her bedside. Though it was a sad day, it was not a day heavy with mourning, because her many children, grandchildren, and great-grandchildren had been touched by her legacy: their Mama. To celebrate her life, Mattie planned a Christmas dinner at her house for everyone to gather and lift up Eloise's name.

"We can't be sad," Mattie told them as they stood around the table holding hands, their heads bowed. The table was covered with every kind of food Eloise had ever made for them: turkey, ham, chicken smothered in gravy, macaroni and cheese, potato salad, yams, collard greens, cabbage, coconut cake, apple pie, lemon cake, and sweet potato pie.

"She's in a better place, and we thank you, Lord," Mattie said, the tears pressing against her closed eyelids. "We lift up her name today, Lord. And we thank you for letting us know her, for giving us a mother who knew not what it was to suffer when it came to her family. We ask you to keep her, Father, bless her, cover her with your goodness . . ."

Everyone kept their heads bowed. The next voice they heard was Deller's: "Thank you, Jesus. We lift up her name today, Jesus. And we pray that our mother is in a better place. We know, Lord, that she is smiling down on us as we gather in her honor today. Keep her, Lord. Bless Her. We ask that you touch each and every heart gathered here today to remove any pain and replace it with joy. The kind of joy that we know our mother is filled with today. We thank you,

Lord, for bringing us together today: every daughter, son, grandchild, and great-grandchild." There was a long pause, and Deller sobbed quietly before she finally said, "And in Jesus' name, we say, Amen."

The silence was prolonged before everyone mumbled *Amen.*

The choir's voices drifted high into the cathedral ceilings. *Why should I feel discouraged? Why should the shadows come . . . His eye—is on—the Spar-row, and I know he watches—over me.* The words rang out across the pews, and in the distance, the organ's sweet sound could be heard for miles on the morning of Mama's funeral.

It was a beautiful church, laced in old walnut and oak and pine, their scents flourishing the air. It had high ceilings with cross-stained windows and lush garlands that adorned the pews. The pulpit stood high on a pedestal with candles that dressed its stairs, and Mama's white and brass casket, surrounded by mounds of scented flowers, sat beautifully at its center.

Not one eye was dry as the pastor preached a sermon that touched every heart and lay every doubt to rest for the few who didn't *believe* and the many who had come to see Mama for one last time. Her children, from eldest to youngest, sat at the

Mama's Funeral

front pew. Their families: every spouse, child, grandchild, and great-grandchild, followed in the pews behind. And when the pastor said a final prayer just before the six pallbearers surrounded and then lifted Mama's casket, they all heard a sound that bounced off the church walls—an anguished cry that pierced every heart—a cry that came from Mattie.

Mama was laid to rest next to her parents, Affie and George, and the rest of her ancestors. Her family had granted her final wish and returned her to the home where she remembered some of her fondest days—a place surrounded by oak trees, the sweet smell of biscuits, and the yellow dress she wore the day Isaac had first noticed her.

Now she lay in her resting place, where the sun shines its beautiful rays, butterflies gather, and birds sing.

The place where a new branch was spawned, a new leaf hung, a family born.

Mama . . .

So stark, there I watched her lay
a legacy of a woman, my Billie Holiday
the core of the family tree
each branch she reared personally
no thing too great, she'd sacrifice
loving each one of us was her life

A Mommy Dearest she was to us all
caring unselfishly, till she received her call
she was the water that filled our sea
the matriarch to the entire family

We miss you Mama, we truly do
don't know how we'll survive without you
and though it's hard to believe that you're gone
it's comforting to know you've weathered the storm
when our hearts ache and sadness appears
we'll think of the good times and wipe away the tears

So go on my Queen, rest in peace
and know that we'll somehow sustain the tree
though you're gone and will be sorely missed
we thank you for leaving behind
a legacy of sentiments

We miss you, Mama
May God bless you!

*T*reasure tapped her legs up and down in tandem with her thoughts, waiting for the phone to ring. She'd been sitting in the same spot for more than an hour. By the time she felt the sweat bead up on the backside of her neck, she was so jittery she couldn't sit still.

"You look very nice," Lydia interrupted. "He hasn't called yet?"

"No, but he's probably gonna call soon." Treasure looked away from her mother, a tactful sign that she just wanted to be left alone.

"I'm sure he'll call soon. He's just trying not to seem too anxious," Lydia said, trying to soften the mood.

Treasure picked up the pace of her leg, a necessary distraction to keep her tongue quiet. Now that she had turned sixteen, both her tongue and her patience with her mother were wearing thin.

A sudden ring of the phone jolted her. She rushed into the kitchen and let the phone ring three times before picking up the receiver.

"Helllooo," she cooed.

"Hello, is this Treasure?"

"Yes, it's me," she answered.

"This is Elton."

"I know who it is." Treasure scrunched her face, wanting to kick herself.

"What are you doing?" Elton asked, as though he'd forgotten he was supposed to have been there over an hour ago.

"Nothing. I'm just hanging out around the house." Treasure shot a look across the room at her mother.

Elton changed the tone of his voice. "Well, I'm callin' to tell you that I ain't gonna be able to make it there. Somethin' came up."

Treasure frowned.

"Are you still there?" Elton asked.

Treasure glanced at her mother, hoping Lydia couldn't see the disappointment written all over her face. "Yeah, I'm still here," she finally answered. "I just thought I heard my mother calling me."

"Are you sure you're all right?"

Treasure bit down on her bottom lip, forcing herself not to sound let down. "I'm fine," she said dryly. "Look, I have to get going. My mom's calling me." As soon as she hung up the phone, she ran to her room.

Minutes later, Lydia leaned into the closed door. "Can I come in?" She waited, and when Treasure didn't answer, she turned the knob and pushed the door open.

Treasure hated the way her mother looked at her with judging eyes, reminding her that she was there to pick her up whenever someone else failed her, whenever she failed herself. Like she was saying in her silence: *"Now look at what you got yourself into, and I'm the one that's gotta bail you out."* She just didn't understand why her mother couldn't see that she didn't need her pity, didn't want it.

"You wanna go do something? Maybe see a movie?" Lydia asked. "Maybe we can go see that movie you've been talking about lately. What's it called? You know, the one with the actor you like?"

"Can you please just leave me alone?" Treasure said with a sneer.

"Fine." Lydia turned and left the room, slamming the door behind her.

A few weeks later, Treasure jumped for the phone before the first ring stopped.

"Hey, baby, how are you?" Lloyd asked, when he heard his daughter's voice. He had been meaning to call for a long time now, and Treasure's birthday gave him an excuse.

"Who's this?" Treasure responded, not recognizing her father's voice.

"It's me. Lloyd."

Treasure gripped the phone and thought about hanging up on him, but something kept her from it. She waited for him to say something, anything to keep her on the line.

"I know you're surprised to hear from me," Lloyd finally said, groping for the right words. "I've been thinkin' about you, and I just wanted to hear your voice."

Treasure could hear her mother moving around in the

kitchen, water running in the sink. She pressed the phone tightly against her ear. She still loved her father; there was no denying it.

"I heard you had a great time at your sweet sixteen party." Lloyd took a long breath. "I wish I could've been there, but I didn't want to spoil it for you," he said, chuckling. "I still can't believe that you're already sixteen. Cheryl told me I should teach you how to drive. You drivin' yet?"

"Yes. My mom taught me," Treasure said tersely.

"Cheryl's been askin' about you, too. She's been tellin' me we should come to see you."

Treasure stayed quiet, thought about how long it'd been since she had last seen her father.

"So, I ain't gonna hold you. I just wanted to say hello." Lloyd paused. "You know, you can call me if you ever need anything. I'm still your father."

Treasure felt a warmth envelope her.

"Well, I guess I better get goin' now. You take care, you hear?"

Treasure shrugged. "Okay," she said.

Lydia felt a knot tighten in the pit of her stomach when Treasure finally told her Lloyd had called. She despised Lloyd for hurting Treasure and how Treasure had turned on her because of him. "When exactly did he call?" she demanded to know.

The uneasiness in her mother's voice made Treasure stumble for words. "He called last Sunday. I didn't tell you cause I knew you'd be upset."

"Well, you aren't going anywhere near him," Lydia countered. "And he ain't welcome in this house. Ever."

Treasure gave her mother a long, contemptuous look. "Why, Mom? Why are you always so mean? What has he ever done to you? He's my father, not yours. And if I want to see him, I should be able to."

"Okay, Treasure. You're right," Lydia said, swallowing her pride. There was nothing to gain by solidifying the wall already between them. "You're sixteen now, old enough to know better. If you want to have a relationship with your father, go ahead. I just don't want you to get hurt again."

Treasure's voice relaxed. "Mom, you gotta let me make my own decisions sometimes. I don't think Dad is trying to hurt me. I think he's really sorry for what he did. He just wants to have a relationship with me without you judging us."

Judging us. Treasure's words struck a chord. "Fine then. If that's what you want. You can see your father if you like, with one condition."

"What's that?" Treasure asked cautiously.

"As long as you don't ask if he can come here. I'm not gonna stop you from seeing him, but he's never to step foot inside this house."

"Okay," Treasure said, a sigh of relief filling her up inside.

Lydia tossed and turned all night, thinking about how much she wanted to tell Treasure she didn't ever want to see that emptiness in her eyes again, or how fragile she looked on the corner of the bus stop that day. It was heartbreaking enough to see the looks Treasure gave Donald when he became overly attentive to Victoria and Blair and ignored her, barely spoke to her.

Lydia remembered how soon Donald had changed toward

Treasure right after they married. She tried talking to him about it on more than one occasion, and his response was always the same: *"I married you, not your daughter."* His words cut through Lydia like a sharp knife.

No matter how painful it was for her, Lydia wanted to ensure her daughter got the love and support she needed, with or without Donald. She was hoping against hope that Lloyd would ultimately come through for Treasure—it was all that was left.

• ◆ •

Treasure surveyed the people standing on the platform as the train slowed and then came to a complete stop. "30th Street Station," the conductor called out. As soon as the doors opened and she stepped off, Treasure saw Lloyd and Cheryl waiting for her.

Lloyd didn't have much to say, and for a while, Treasure wondered what he was thinking. They'd been talking on the phone almost every day for the last few weeks, and he figured that would somehow make it easier. But it wasn't. Everything he had intended to say suddenly seemed inappropriate, lacking. "Hi, baby. How you doin'?" he finally said. His words felt strange.

"Hi, Dad," Treasure said, handing her bag to him. "Hi, Cheryl."

Cheryl smiled. "Hi, Treasure."

Lloyd suddenly moved closer to Treasure and took her into his arms, drawing her close to him.

Treasure stood stiff, not sure if she should hug him back, whether she wanted to or not.

Lloyd filled with emotion as he released her. He took a step back and looked at her once more. Treasure looked more beautiful than ever, so much more mature, so much like her mother. "I guess we should be gettin' outta here," he said nervously and gestured aimlessly. "The car's this way."

"You got a car, Dad? I didn't know you had a car," Treasure said with surprise.

"I just got it. I've had it for about a week now."

"Wow! How did you get a car? I thought you said you were looking for a job?"

Lloyd looked toward Cheryl and gave her an awkward smile. "Actually, Cheryl is buying it."

When they arrived at a large, brick building not far from their last apartment, Treasure couldn't believe it. "Wow! When did y'all move, Dad?" she asked, trying to take in all that was new to her.

"We've been here about a month now. I wanted to get a larger place so that when you come to stay with us, you can have your own room.

Treasure's eyes lit up. "I've got my own room here?"

A big grin gleamed on Lloyd's face. He liked making Treasure feel happy for a change.

Treasure's new room was fully furnished and included all of her favorite things. Lloyd and Cheryl even took her shopping.

When she returned home on Sunday with two new outfits and a gold necklace with a small gold heart around her neck, Lydia was surprised.

"Whoa. Where did you get that necklace?" Lydia asked.

"My dad bought it for me," Treasure said. She quickly

ran up the stairs to her room, leaving her mother speechless.

⟐

Treasure had been overjoyed to be spending time with her father again. Within a few short months she had transformed, letting go of the animosity she'd been carrying around for the past few months. Nothing could please Lydia more than to see how quickly her daughter changed. When she received a call a few days before it was time for Treasure's next visit with her father, Lydia's heart stopped a clear stroke in time.

"Lydia, did you hear?" Roy Jr. asked with urgency on the other end of the line.

"Excuse me. Who is this?" Lydia asked.

"It's me, Roy Jr."

"Hey, Roy Jr.," Lydia said, happy to hear from him.

"Did you hear?" he asked anxiously.

"Hear what?"

"About the Philly bank bandit. They caught him. They finally caught him, and guess who it is?"

"Who?"

"Lloyd. It's Lloyd! Can you believe it?"

Lydia was shocked into silence, letting her brother's words register. "Are you sure it's him?"

"Yes. It's him. They've been running his picture all day on the news. It's definitely him."

"Do you think Treasure knows yet? Maybe she's seen the news."

"No, I'm sure she hasn't heard. I'd know if she had," Lydia said.

"What are you going to do?"

Lydia thought about it. "I need to go and talk to her," she said quietly.

Treasure's hair was still damp from a shower, and the minute Lydia walked into her room, she could smell her scent. "Do you have a minute?" Lydia asked. "I need to talk to you about something."

"What did I do now?" Treasure asked, half joking. "I've already done my homework, and I wasn't planning on going out tonight, so you have nothing to worry about, Mom." She smiled, and Lydia could see in her face the same joy she'd had for the last few months.

"Treasure, I have something to tell you." The tone of Lydia's voice caught her attention. She quickly listened up, looking intently at her mother.

"Treasure, it's about your father," Lydia said quietly. She paused and took another breath. "Your father . . . He was arrested this evening for bank robbery."

Treasure's chest tightened, sealing off the air. The longer she looked at her mother, the more the air seemed to be trapped in her chest. "What? That's not true. I just talked to him last night."

"I know. But they arrested him today."

Treasure's eyes filled with tears. "Can you leave please? I just want to be alone," she said.

Lydia stood there for a minute. "You know, if you want to talk about it, I'm here for you," she said. Then she quietly pulled the door shut behind her, but not before she heard the sobs muffled in her daughter's pillow.

45

*T*reasure lay curled up on top of the yellow quilt, barely feeling the cool morning breeze that swept through her window. She couldn't feel anything. She wasn't crying no more. She just lay there, thinking, her mind wavering between anguish and contempt. She no longer cared that her father had been locked up or that her junior prom was only days away. She had no desire to hear from him ever again, no desire to wear the dress his money had paid for. Bad money. Money that made the dress seem dirty every time she looked at it. She would never forgive him—no matter how pitiful he sounded—if and when he called. She wanted nothing more to do with him. She despised him, even *hated* him now.

She felt ashamed and utterly alone. She wondered if she was as bad as he was. After all, it was his blood running through her veins. She thought about writing him a letter, pouring all of her hatred onto a sheet of paper and mailing it to him. More than once, she'd grabbed her notebook, ripped a page from its spine, and started writing until her hand went limp and her head ached. But then she'd end up with nothing more than a page full of illegible words smeared by her tears.

Each day, she dragged herself to school and then back home to her room. She avoided Elton's calls. It was easier than chancing that her pained voice would somehow reveal she was indeed her father's daughter.

From her bed, she could hear the birds singing in the trees as the morning came alive, could smell its early dew. But she felt lifeless, the same way she'd been feeling for the past few weeks. She had no desire to do anything. No desire to talk to anyone.

Lydia hadn't slept much for weeks. And when the phone rang early that morning, she cringed, hoping finally it would be the call from Lloyd explaining that it was all a misunderstanding, that they had the wrong guy, that he was looking forward to seeing Treasure again. But it was her Mattie's voice on the other end.

"Hi. Did I wake you?"

"Hey, Ma. No, I'm just lying here." Lydia looked over at the clock, realizing the time.

"I didn't wake Donald, did I?"

Lydia turned and looked at the empty space next to her. "No, he's already left for work."

"Oh, good." Mattie went silent for a time, then quietly said, "How's Treasure?"

"Pretty much the same. She still refuses to talk about it."

"Well, she's been heavy on my mind," Mattie said, "and I was thinkin' about comin' to spend the day with y'all."

"Oh, Ma. I would really appreciate that," Lydia said. "Do you want me to come and get you?"

"No, I can catch the train. I figure if I can catch a train to go to work every day, then it's good enough for me to come and see my granddaughter."

Lydia looked over at the clock again. "Okay, I'll pick you up at the train station," she said, relieved.

The streets were unusually void of the Saturday morning hustle and bustle. Lydia slowed the car as she drove up to the train station. She looked carefully, searching for her mother. When she didn't see her, she circled back around to the parking lot, parked at a meter, and waited five minutes before reaching inside her purse for quarters. As soon as she deposited the second quarter and turned the dial, she heard her mother's voice.

"Hi," Mattie said. "I thought you might be over here." She gave Lydia a long look. "You all right? You don't look so good."

"Yeah, I'm okay. Just a little tired."

"You can't let yourself get sick over this," Mattie said softly. "Treasure's gonna be all right. She just needs some time."

Lydia thought about how sad Treasure had been lately. "I know, Ma," she said. "But I'm just worried about her. Sometimes I'm concerned she thinks everything's my fault."

"Treasure knows none of this is your fault. She's just takin' out her anger on the ones closest to her. Give it some time. She's gonna be all right."

They rode in silence, the car bouncing them slightly,

lulling their thoughts. Lydia felt how her mother's presence had already begun to calm her, and she wondered how Treasure would react when she saw her grandmother. She would be surprised, Lydia was certain of that.

Mattie cracked open the door to Treasure's bedroom and peeped her head inside. "Hey, sleepy head. You up yet?"

The sound of her Nana's voice jolted Treasure. She removed the pillow that was covering her head. "Hey, Nana. I didn't know you were coming here today."

"I know. It was supposed to be a surprise," Mattie said.

As Mattie bent over to give her a hug, Treasure could smell her Nana, a faint, clean, musky scent, a sweet scent.

Mattie took a seat at the foot of her granddaughter's bed. Treasure looked pretty, with the horizon of sunlight that cut across the room, giving her face a glow. If not for the sorrow in her eyes, Mattie would have never known that she was so sad.

"So how you been? I haven't heard even a peep from you. You used to call me all the time," Mattie admonished playfully.

"I know, Nana. But I've been really busy lately," Treasure replied, hearing a tinge of dishonesty in her words.

"Busy doin' what? You ain't never been too busy to talk to your Nana before."

"I know Nana, but . . ." her voice trailed off to barely a whisper. "I've just got a lot on my mind."

"You got a lot on your mind? What kinds of things can be so heavy on your mind that it keeps you from your family?"

Treasure blinked back the tears. "He storied to me, Nana," she said, her voice cracking.

Mattie reached out and stroked Treasure's arm. "I know.

I know he hurt you, but you can't let that stop you from livin'. What's done is done, and there ain't nothin' you can do to change that. You're gonna have to learn to forgive and move on."

"But . . . but why did he have to do that, Nana?"

Mattie wiped the tears from Treasure's face. "Things don't always work out the way we want them to," Mattie said. "He's your father, and there's nothin' you can do about that. He's always gonna be in your life, whether you want him to or not. But you can't go around hatin' everybody else cause of what he's done. You got too much to live for to let him take that away from you." She paused, taking Treasure's hand in her own. "I done been where you are. Don't make the same mistakes I made."

Treasure looked at her Nana, and for a moment, she thought she saw the same grief in her eyes that she carried in her own. "What happened to you, Nana? Did your father leave you, too?"

Mattie paused. "Yes, my father left me when I was about your age. And I never forgave him till it was too late."

Treasure remained quiet. From the look on her Nana's face, she knew Mattie had more to say.

"I lived all those years hating him, holding all that anger and resentment inside. And you know what it got me?" Mattie said defiantly. "It got me nothin' but years of wasted time. Time I can never take back. Time I cheated myself out of."

Mattie stood and walked over to the window. She pushed back the yellow curtains to let more light into the room. "You know, sometimes it's easier to forgive than it is to carry around all that anger. I know you're too young to understand that. That kind of understandin' comes with age." She took a seat again next to her granddaughter. "Life's too short, and before you know it, you're gonna be sittin' here talkin' to one of your grandchi'ren."

"I know, Nana, but it's so hard. Especially since I can't talk to my mom about it."

Mattie raised an eyebrow. "Why do you think you can't talk to your mom?"

"Because she's always judging me," Treasure said.

"I don't think that's true. Your mother's just worried about you, that's all."

"No, Nana. You should see the way she looks at me sometimes when I try to talk to her."

"Are you sure you're readin' her right? Maybe you're thinkin' one way and she's thinkin' another."

"I don't know, Nana. I think she's still angry at me and my dad."

"No, she's not. Sometimes mothers just have a way of expressing themselves. I've got my way, and your mother's got her way, and you're gonna have your way when you have chi'ren. You'll see. Wait till you get about my age. Things ain't always so plain and simple. You're gonna thank your mother one day for the way she raised you."

"I doubt that, Nana," Treasure said, chuckling.

"You'll see. One day you're gonna come to me and say *'You know what Nana, you were right.'*"

Treasure smiled. "Okay Nana, we'll see."

Mattie looked around the room. "So let me see the dress you're gonna wear to the prom."

"I'm not going, Nana," Treasure said.

"What do you mean you ain't goin'? You gotta go to your prom."

"But I don't wanna go."

"Why not?"

"'Cause I don't want to wear that dress he bought me!"

"What good is it gonna do for you to miss your prom cause of some dress?"

"I just don't want nothin' that he bought," Treasure said.

"Well who said you gotta wear that dress? Why can't you wear another dress?"

"'Cause my mom isn't gonna buy me another dress when I got a brand new one hanging in the closet."

"How you know? Did you ask her?"

"Noooo."

"Well, if you ask her, you might be surprised by the answer." Mattie stood up, taking Treasure by her hand. "Come on, let's go and ask her together."

"No, Nana. I don't want to ask her. I haven't been talking to my mom, and she's gonna think I'm crazy if I just all of a sudden ask her to buy me a dress."

"Then I'll tell you what. I'm gonna buy it! You go on and get dressed so we can go to the mall and find you a dress. We can all go together."

"Really, Nana? You wanna buy it?"

"Ain't that what I said?"

"Okay, but first I gotta do my chores."

"All right then. Well, I'm gonna go on downstairs and tell your mother."

"Okay," Treasure said excitedly. "And Nana . . ."

Mattie turned and looked at her. "Yes?"

"Thank you."

Mattie took in the joy on her granddaughter's face as she shut the door behind her.

⦁—⦁—⦁

Treasure stood in front of her mother as Lydia put the gold necklace around her neck.

"You look so pretty," Lydia said.

"Thanks, Mom." Treasure stared down at her shoes. "Do you think I should wear the other shoes? These shoes make me feel so tall," she said.

Lydia glanced down at Treasure's feet. "No, they look very nice with your dress."

"You sure?"

"Yes, I'm sure. You're just nervous, that's all."

"Okay. Which bag should I carry? This one?" Treasure held up a butterscotch purse that matched the shoes she was wearing. "Or this one?" She tossed the butterscotch purse on the bed and picked up a tan one.

"I think the butterscotch one really goes well with the whole outfit."

"Okay," Treasure said tentatively, grabbing the butter-scotch purse.

They both turned at the sound of the doorbell.

"Oh no. That must be Elton. He's early," Treasure said in a panicked voice.

"No, you're running late, sweetie. He was supposed to be here at 7:00, and it's 7:15."

Treasure rushed over to the mirror and checked herself again.

"I'll go and get the door. You hurry up and come on downstairs so I can get some pictures before y'all leave."

"Okay, Mom," Treasure said as she took one final glance.

After the prom, Elton and Treasure were inseparable. Treasure confided in him about everything. Elton began to fill the void that had put a sizeable dent in Treasure's heart. And by late summer, they consummated their loyalty to each other in the backseat of Elton's car.

Treasure wanted to talk to her mother about her feelings, but something kept her from it. Perhaps it was because of the way her mother always seemed to turn something good sour, she thought. Or maybe it was because her mother could never understand how it felt to love with passion at such a tender age. The only thoughts her mother ever shared with her about young love were the terrible things that haunted her from her own experiences. Whatever the reason, Elton was something she wanted that wasn't tainted by her mother's thoughts, or shadowed by her father.

A few weeks later, Treasure nearly jumped out of her skin when she heard the alarm go off at seven a.m. The large red numbers on the clock blazed the hour as she pushed the snooze button and lay back down. She had wanted to get an early start with her chores so that she'd be ready by the time Elton picked her up. He was taking her to his family's Labor Day cookout today. They'd been dating for nearly a year, and the only member of Elton's family Treasure had met was his sister. "They're always busy," Elton would say when she talked about meeting his family. Finally, after she kept prying, he invited her to the cookout.

Treasure barely left Elton's side after they arrived at his parents' backyard. She felt uneasy with the way his parents responded when he introduced her, barely giving her a nod.

"What's wrong?" Elton wanted to know, as they took a seat.

"Nothing," Treasure lied.

Elton went over to a group of boys, leaving Treasure alone; and as more and more guests arrived, Treasure made a game out of guessing who they were. She became bored with that and of Elton's inattentiveness and decided she wanted to leave. As she made her way over to Elton and his friends, a young girl caught her eye. She was walking directly toward Treasure. Something in the girl's face, her eyes, made Treasure extremely uncomfortable. When the girl stopped right in front of her, Treasure gave her a perplexed look.

"Are you Treasure?" the girl asked. She was about the same age as Treasure. Her face was daunting but innocent, and it held a seriousness that made her seem much more mature.

"Yes, I am." Treasure looked over at Elton and saw his face visibly change.

The girl took a step closer, not wanting Treasure to miss one of her words. "Well, did you tell her, Elton?" she asked, raising her voice and turning her gaze to Elton as he scurried over to them.

"Tell me what?" Treasure asked confidently.

"Why are you doin' this?" Elton asked, lowering his voice.

"Why am I doin' this? I ain't doin' nothin'. You just need to tell her the truth."

Treasure's stomach churned. "What is it?" She heard her voice rise, and when she looked at Elton, she knew something was terribly wrong.

"I'm pregnant," the girl blurted out, "and Elton's the father."

Treasure felt a sudden thud in her stomach. "What?!" she said, stunned.

"Yes, and he was supposed to tell you weeks ago."

Tears flooded Treasure, and when she realized that everyone was staring at them, she turned and ran. Elton followed her.

"Elton, where are you going?" the girl called out after him.

"Treasure, wait. Let me talk to you."

Treasure stopped and turned. "Leave me alone," she said. "Go back to her. I hate you!"

"Don't do this. Come on, let me take you home," Elton pleaded, grabbing her by the arm.

Treasure pulled away. "I hate you! Just leave me alone. You're like all the rest of them."

"Don't do this. Let me explain."

"What kind of explaining? You want to explain how you've been cheating and how you got another girl pregnant? You want to explain how everybody but me already knew? What is there to explain Elton?"

On the long walk home, Treasure replayed the girl's words over and over in her head. She was thankful when she was greeted by an empty house. Treasure rushed to her room, slammed the door behind her, and wrapped herself in her sheets. She hated Elton, hated them all—the ones that were supposed to protect her, the ones that claimed to love her. Their voices twisted in her mind, voices that sickened her: *I'm pregnant, and Elton is the father,* the girl's timid voice sang out; *I promise I will never do anything to hurt you again,* her father spoke; *If you ever tell anybody I'm gonna hurt you and your mother,* her grandfather's voice suddenly came alive; *I married you, not your daughter,* Donald gruffed.

Her thoughts were hazy, closing in on her. She wanted them all to pay—to feel as she felt, to wallow in her pain. She lifted up from her pillow and slowly walked into the bathroom. She stared at the mirrored medicine cabinet before reaching inside to grab the bottles: Extra Strength Tylenol, Motrin, and a brown bottle with a prescription on it she didn't recognize. Numbly, she emptied the pills into the sink, tossed the empty bottles to the floor, and filled a glass with water. She peered into the mirror with hardly a trace of recognition. The bright lights ricocheted against the walls, making her head spin as she looked at her reflection. "I hate you!" she screamed at the face looking back at her. "I hate you! I hate them!" And then she grabbed the pills and slowly tossed them down one by one.

Lydia fumbled with her keys before opening the door to a dark, quiet house. "Treasure, Donald," she called out, setting the heavy grocery bags on the countertop. When no one answered her, she put away the groceries and took one piece of fish out of the package. A quiet dinner, a hot bath, and a good book was just what she needed, she thought to herself.

She darted up the stairs and turned on the overhead light in her bedroom. She made a mental note to call her sister Eileen so they could discuss the surprise anniversary party they were planning for her mother and stepfather. Leisurely, she pulled off her clothes, wrapped herself in her bathrobe, grabbed the bottle of Vanilla scented bubble bath she kept on her dresser, and headed to the bathroom. As soon as she turned on the light, the empty bottles in the sink caught her eye. Then she noticed others strewn about the floor.

Fear engulfed her. "Trea...sure!" she called out and bolted to her daughter's room.

Treasure lay sprawled across the bed, her eyes closed, her body limp, her breathing shallow. Lydia rushed to her. "Treasure . . ." her anguished voice called out. "Please, baby, wake up!" She shook Treasure relentlessly. She moved her head to Treasure's chest, hoping for sound. She put her mouth on Treasure's, blowing profusely. Treasure didn't respond. Lydia rushed to the phone and dialed 9-1-1.

46

$\mathcal{T}$he paramedics arrived in less than ten minutes.

The man who spoke first was young, not much older than Treasure, Lydia thought. "Where is your daughter?" he asked.

"She's upstairs in her room," Lydia said frantically and moved aside to let him and two others in—another middle-aged man and a young woman. They rushed upstairs, each carrying a tan and black bag.

Lydia stood in the corner, keeping her eyes pinned on Treasure—watching, waiting, crying, praying, as they worked to revive her daughter. After several long minutes, she heard a small gasp come from Treasure.

"Treasure, can you hear me?" the middle-aged man said, kneeling over her. "Honey, squeeze my hand if you can hear me."

Treasure felt herself floating between a thick black space

and a slow peaceful dream. In her dream, everybody was happy. Her mother. Her father. Her Nana. Through her foggy mind, she began to hear strange voices, voices that came from a distance. She felt a tingling move through her body, and her heart thudded as she struggled to open her eyes.

"That's it, sweetie. Squeeze my hand."

Treasure rolled her head back. Her eyes fluttered open.

"Hi, honey. Can you speak?" the young woman asked.

Treasure saw the faces clearly now: three of them, white faces. She could see their expressions filled with hope. Everything moved in slow motion around her. Soon, she could hear small sobs coming from the corner of the room. Her eyes followed the sounds and came to rest on her mother's grief-stricken face.

Lydia sat steadfast in the small, brightly lit room, watching the doctors pump Treasure's stomach, take blood, and run an IV. She massaged the temples of her forehead, trying to keep at bay the migraine headache she sensed coming on. Lydia thought about calling Mattie but decided against it. She needed time to find the wherewithal to tell her mother that Treasure had done what had been haunting their family for so long. She wondered what she would say to Treasure when she was fully awake—anything to let her know how much she loved her.

As the doctors finished up and Lydia was about to call Donald, the child psychiatrist appeared and introduced herself to Lydia and Treasure.

"Hi, I'm Dr. Faulkner," the young blonde woman announced. She had a soft face and trusting blue eyes. Her voice was soothing like it, alone, could heal one's soul. "I was wondering if you feel up to talking to me?"

Treasure kept her back to the doctor and said nothing. She'd hardly moved since arriving at the hospital, had not even looked at her mother.

"I know you're not feeling well, and the medication the doctors gave you probably makes you feel worse. But I really would like to talk to you for a little while if you'll bear with me."

Treasure stared at the wall, felt the tears brewing inside of her. She could feel Dr. Faulkner's presence, and she could hear every breath her mother took.

"Sweetie, I know it's hard. But I really want to help you. Maybe we can talk for a few minutes. How about that? Just five minutes."

Tears melted into Treasure's pillow as she turned and gazed up at the white speckled ceiling, avoiding Dr. Faulkner's eyes.

"Okay, sweetie. That's good. I promise this won't take long," Dr. Faulkner said as she stepped closer to the bed. "Now, I just need to know what happened. Can you tell me what happened?"

Treasure parted her parched lips to say something, but her mind was still cloudy, void of any thought. She swallowed the bitter taste in her mouth. "I hate them," she said with finality, her voice thin and childlike.

Dr. Faulkner looked at Lydia, questions etched on her face. "Who do you hate?" she asked.

"My grandfather," Treasure said, and then thought about it. "My father . . . Donald . . . Elton." Each name fell off her lips like poison.

Dr. Faulkner nodded her head and scribbled something in the folder she was holding. "Okay, I think I understand. But why do you hate them?"

"Cause," Treasure replied quickly. "Cause I do," was the only answer that came to mind.

Dr. Faulkner looked quizzically at Lydia, and then she rubbed Treasure's knee. "Okay. You get some rest now. I'll be back to talk with you again."

Treasure stared at the IV that dripped into her arm and listened to Dr. Faulkner's and her mother's footsteps as they left the room.

In the hallway, Dr. Faulkner got straight to the point. "Whenever a child attempts suicide, I am required by law to do a thorough examination and make a recommendation to Child Protective Services. I would like to admit her for a few days to complete an evaluation."

"Child Protective Services?" Lydia faltered.

"I know this is all difficult to take in, but it's procedure," Dr. Faulkner said in a reassuring voice. "Besides, I think your daughter would benefit from the therapy she'll receive through this hospital. We have an exceptional program for children, and I believe it will help her tremendously."

Lydia swallowed hard. "Okay. I understand. Do whatever is needed."

She signed the papers to admit Treasure and then left the hospital. She had been trying to get ahold of Donald all evening, and she was surprised to find him sleeping peacefully when she got home. As soon as she saw the silhouette of his large frame underneath the covers, she stopped in her tracks. "Did you get the messages I left?"

she said pointedly, elevating her voice to wake him.

Donald stirred. "Yeah, I got your messages," he said, coming out of sleep.

"So why didn't you call me back?"

Donald pushed himself up on one elbow and rubbed the sleep out of his eyes. "I couldn't leave work, that's why. And by the time I got home, I was really tired."

The nonchalant tone of his voice enraged Lydia. Her raw fury snaked across the room. "You couldn't leave work? Treasure almost died, and the only thing you can think about is your job?"

"Look, it wasn't like my being there was gonna change things. So I decided to come home and wait for you."

"You selfish bastard! How dare you treat her like she means nothing to you."

"Look, I'm here now aren't I?" Donald said, raising his voice.

"What good is it that you're here? I needed you *there*. Treasure needed you there. We both needed you!"

Donald searched for something to say that would sound reasonable.

"You know what?" Lydia said. "I want out!"

The venom in her voice caught Donald's attention. "What do you mean you want out?"

"Just what I said. I . . . want . . . out . . . I want you gone." She paused. "I want a divorce."

A week later, Treasure was released from the hospital.

Dr. Faulkner worked very closely with her, and after several sessions, she recommended that Treasure be released back into the custody of her mother with mandatory follow-up counseling. *Counseling that could benefit both the child and her mother,* Dr. Faulkner had written in her final report.

On Tuesday, the morning following Treasure's first night home, Lydia lay in her bed. Sleep had evaded her. The anguished voice on the television, announcing that a plane had crashed into the New York City World Trade Center's Twin Towers, jolted her upright.

Donald was gone. Treasure was in a deep, sedative-induced sleep, compliments of Dr. Faulkner. And the United States was under terrorist attack.

47

$\mathcal{T}$reasure sat erect in the plush sofa, her hands clasped in her lap, her face level. Her gaze was set on the picture frame behind Dr. Faulkner's leather chair. She liked the picture in the frame, the way the young girl with the pale round face and large green eyes seemed to be smiling at her. It made her and her mom's visits with Dr. Faulkner feel less formal.

"So, Treasure, how have you been?" Dr. Faulkner asked.

A gentle smile broke on Treasure's face. "I've been fine." The softness in Lydia's eyes told Treasure she agreed.

"How did the journal writing go last week?" Dr. Faulkner asked next.

"It was good. I did what you suggested and wrote down all my feelings."

"I'm glad to hear that." Dr. Faulkner turned her attention to Lydia. "And how are you, Mrs. McCall?"

"I'm doing very well," Lydia answered. "We both are," she added.

"That's great," Dr. Faulkner paused, jotted something down on her pad, and looked back up at Treasure. "Any news yet from the schools?"

"Yes, I've been accepted to three."

"That's great! Which schools?"

"University of Delaware, University of Maryland, and University of Pennsylvania."

"That is wonderful," Dr. Faulkner said. "You must be very proud of her, Lydia."

"I am. I'm very proud of her. She's the first in our family to attend a four-year university."

"So, have you decided which one you want to attend?" Dr. Faulkner asked.

"Yeah," Treasure said. "But I think my mom wants me to go to University of Delaware so I can be close to home, cause she's gonna miss me."

"That's not true," Lydia interrupted, smiling. "I want you to go to whichever school you want to go to."

"She's going to miss you, Treasure. I can tell," Dr. Faulkner teased.

Lydia nodded in agreement.

"So, let's see." Dr. Faulkner flipped through her notes. "Oh yes, how about the letters? Last week you mentioned that your father sent you another letter. Have you opened it yet?"

"No," Treasure replied sheepishly.

"And that's fine," Dr. Faulkner assured her. "Remember what we talked about last time. You don't have to open it until you're ready. And even if it takes you a long time, he can wait. Take as long as you need."

Treasure lifted her chin and smiled openly at Dr. Faulkner.

"So, how about dating? Any new prospects?" Dr. Faulkner asked.

"Yes," Treasure said excitedly.

Lydia was visibly shaken.

"Don't worry," Treasure said mischievously. "I'm talking about Buttons. We got a cat, Dr. Faulkner."

"That's wonderful. I have two cats."

"We got him so my mom won't be lonely when I leave for school."

"Well, I think that's great. I'm sure he'll make your mom very happy while you're away." Dr. Faulkner looked at her watch and made another note on her pad. "Anything else you want to talk about, Treasure?"

"Yes, there's one other thing," Treasure said quietly.

Dr. Faulkner gave her an encouraging look. "And what would that be?"

Treasure hesitated. For a moment, she looked like a frightened little girl again. "I've been thinking about what you said about Elton," she stopped, thought about it some more. "I guess you were right. There probably were signs all along, but I think I was ignoring them . . . you know, because of how I felt about him . . . how I felt about everything."

Dr. Faulkner nodded in agreement.

"Anyway," Treasure went on. "Now I know why I did what I did to myself."

Lydia's heart constricted at hearing her daughter's admission.

"That's exactly what you needed to do," Dr. Faulkner said. She reached over and squeezed Treasure's hand. "You needed to face the truth. The moment you're able to face the truth and own up to it, you can release it, just like we talked about."

Treasure wiped away a tear that had surfaced without her knowing it.

"You're going to be fine, sweetie," Dr. Faulkner said, giving Treasure's hand another squeeze. "Just fine."

Dr. Faulkner stood up. "Do you mind waiting for me and your mom outside, Treasure? I want to talk to her for a few minutes."

"Okay," Treasure said.

"I'm so proud of you," Dr. Faulkner said. "You've come a long way." She embraced Treasure.

After Treasure shut the door behind her, Dr. Faulkner sat next to Lydia on the sofa. "So, how are you really doing, Mrs. McCall?"

"I'm fine. It's been difficult these past months with the divorce and all. But I'm so thankful to you for all you've done for Treasure. I really appreciate how you took a personal interest in her and the time and care you've taken. Without you, I don't know what I would've done."

"I'm glad I could help, but you deserve all the credit. Treasure is lucky to have a mother like you."

"No, I really can't thank you enough. Treasure is doing so much better, and I have you to thank for that."

"Thank you," Dr. Faulkner said graciously. "But I want you to take some time for yourself, as well. You've been through a lot, and it's important you take care of you, too."

"I am," Lydia said, wiping away her tears with the tissue Dr. Faulkner handed to her. "I'm doing much better now. The divorce is almost final, and I'm looking forward to helping Treasure get ready for college. I think once I know she's okay, then I'll be all right."

"And she will be okay. She's a strong girl. And I think the change in scenery at college and the friends she'll meet will make all the difference in her young life."

Lydia reached over and gave Dr. Faulkner a long hug.

Treasure was outside letting the sun warm her face when Lydia found her. "So where would you like to go for dinner?" Lydia asked.

"You know, Mom," Treasure hinted.

"I know. Pizza, right?"

"That's right."

When Lydia and Treasure returned home, Lydia went straight to her bedroom. The room was dark except for the red blinking light that illuminated the nightstand, an indication there was a message on the answering machine.

Lydia pushed the message button.

"Hi, Lydia. This is Eileen. Give me a call when you get this message." Lydia noticed the urgency in her voice. "The caterers called to say they won't be able to get the food to the hall until seven o'clock, so you may have to call them back to make sure they'll get there on time. Okay, call me right away." A click and a loud beep followed.

If one more thing goes wrong, I'm going to scream, Lydia thought, as she picked up the phone and dialed Eileen's number. The twenty-fifth anniversary and life celebration they were planning for their mother and John was less than three months away.

Mattie and John

• ◆ •

Treasure awoke to the bright sunlight streaming down on her. She could hear her mother moving around downstairs, could smell the bacon frying. She sat up and stretched. Her white dress and the gold cap and gown were already pressed and hanging in the closet, where she had put them the night before.

"Treasure?" Lydia tapped on her door.

"Yes."

"I've made us some breakfast. I think you should eat something before you get dressed. It's gonna be a hot one today, and you don't want to get sick sitting out in that sun for three hours."

Graduation was being held at Howard's football stadium. A little over two hundred students would be graduating, and if everyone that received an invitation planned to attend, the stadium would be packed.

Following Treasure's graduation, Lydia had the summer all planned out, ensuring she and Treasure spent as much time together as they could before she left for college. In June, they traveled to Miami for a week, soaking in the sun and spending lazy days together, just the two of them. They celebrated the Fourth of July at a cookout Mattie had hosted. In August, they started shopping for the things that Treasure needed for college: sheets, blankets, a small microwave.

The night before the anniversary and life celebration, Treasure sat with mixed feelings as she helped her mother wrap the last two gifts. Part of her was excited about her Nana's celebration; the other part of her was apprehensive because on Sunday, the day following the party, she and her mother were driving to the University of Maryland. Early registration was to begin on Monday.

•—◆—•

Beautiful lavender and white lilies sat atop every table. A large sheet cake covered in white and lavender iced roses and inscribed with "A Life Celebration—We Love You" sat on a table in the middle of the room. Silver-framed photographs of Eloise, Isaac, Roy, and Angie were strategically placed on top of a table with a white tablecloth. Smaller frames held pictures of all of Mattie's children and grandchildren.

The room was bursting with all of Mattie's loved ones. Children, grandchildren, and siblings from the eldest, Deller, to the youngest, were all there. Even Aunt Alma, Eloise's only surviving sister, and Uncle Otis were in attendance.

"They just pulled up in the car!" Eileen said excitedly. "Shush . . . quiet everybody. Remember, don't say surprise until Lydia gets out of the way."

Eileen hurried to turn down the lights. The room became so still that only the two-inch heels Lydia and Mattie were wearing could be heard clacking against the pavement outside. "We just need to stop by the hall to pick up a gift one of

Eloise's daughters, from left to right: Mattie, Deller, Charlene, Paulene, and Leona.

Lionel, who passed away in 1996.

Rollie

Walton

my friends got for Treasure," Lydia said to her parents. "Then we'll be on our way to dinner."

As soon as Lydia opened the door and moved to the side, Eileen flipped on the lights and they all bellowed *SURPRISE!*

Mattie covered her mouth with her hands, as her eyes skimmed the room, looking at each face. When she noticed the silver picture frames of Eloise, Isaac, Roy, and her daughter Angie, she broke down. Every eye in the room became moist, as her family stood and applauded her.

"Congratulations, Ma," Lydia said, hugging her mother.

"How could y'all have kept this from me?" Mattie cried with joy.

Roy Jr., Eileen, and Anthony walked up to her.

"You are the reason for keeping this family together," Roy Jr. whispered into her ear, as he embraced her and handed her a rose.

"We love you, Ma, and we thank you for all you've done for us," Eileen said, folding Mattie into her arms.

Anthony smiled at his mother and handed her another rose.

Then, each of her grandchildren—from eldest to youngest—paraded up to her and gave her a hug and kissed her perfectly aged face.

•—◆—•

Buttons lay perched on Treasure's bed. He watched her every move, as if somehow he knew it would be the last time in a long time he'd be able to cuddle with her. He purred when she walked over to rub his head.

Lydia peeked her head into the room. "I thought I heard you moving around in here," she said.

"I couldn't sleep, so I decided to just get up and finish packing."

"Well, that's good. I'm gonna make us some breakfast, then we can get an early start. Okay?"

"Okay, Mom," Treasure said.

They rode in silence, each absorbed in their own thoughts. Two hours later, Lydia pulled the car up to a large brick building. The campus was crawling with students, parents, and administrative staff. By nightfall, Treasure was fully unpacked and settled into her dorm room, and it was time for Lydia to say goodbye.

A light drizzle fell as Treasure walked her mother to the car.

"Well, I guess this is it," Lydia said.

"Yup, this is it," Treasure said, smiling and holding onto her mother's hand.

"Your roommate seems really nice. I think you two are going to get along very well," Lydia said, stalling.

"Me, too."

Lydia looked around the parking lot. "Well, I guess I should be going now. It seems like I'm the only parent sticking around here."

"I know. I noticed that, Mom," Treasure teased.

Lydia smiled again. "You know I'm going to miss you a lot."

"Yes, Mom, I know. I'm gonna miss you, too."

Lydia reached out and took Treasure into her arms, and they stayed that way for a long time. "I love you, baby," Lydia said, finally letting go of Treasure.

"I love you, too, Mom."

"All right. You be good," Lydia said.

"I will."

"And you call me if you need anything."

"I will, Mom."

Lydia smiled through her tears, grabbed Treasure's hand again, and chuckled. "All right, I know. I'm going."

Just as Lydia was getting into her car, Treasure called out, "Oh, Mom, I almost forgot." She reached into her pocket and pulled out three warn-looking envelopes. "Can you hold onto these for me? I don't think I'll be needing them while I'm here."

Lydia took the envelopes from Treasure. Each one was neatly addressed to Treasure with a return address from the Harrisburg Correctional Center. "Okay, baby, I'll hold them for as long as you need me to," she said.

Lydia backed out of the parking spot. She looked in her rearview mirror and waved to Treasure one last time.

As she made her way up 95 North toward Philadelphia, Eloise's words suddenly came into her mind. *"You gotta turn one corner, baby, to find another,"* she remembered her grandmother saying.

She sunk deeper into her seat, taking in the lush green trees, the gray sky, the road ahead. She let her grandmother's words sink deep into her heart, and for perhaps the first time in her life, she felt at peace.

Images of her grandmother, her mother, and her daughter came to her all at once, and her face lit up. "Oh yes, Mama," she whispered to herself, as a smile broke across her lips. "We have finally turned that corner. We have *finally* turned that corner!"

• ◆ •

I'm colorless, cocooned in my skin
and I don't know when
things turned so bad
but suddenly . . . I'm sad

I done cried me a river
prayed when I had no voice
even found me some courage
when courage was not my choice

Now I'm ready to surrender
Leave the tears from my cries behind
Ready to spread my wings
Color Me Butterfly

I've had days with empty thoughts
nights when I couldn't sleep
Sundays when I'd pray all day
and Mondays when I'd just weep

It's sometimes hard being who I am
there are days when I don't exist
at times I just can't go on
can't let this life persist

Now I'm ready to surrender
Leave the tears from my cries behind
Ready to spread my wings
Color Me Butterfly

I am a beau-ti-ful woman
laced with substance and so much more
bred from a legacy of goodness
something so rich, something so pure

I have a strong voice from within to speak
I have hopes and desires and dreams
and though much has been stripped from me
yet I still have my self-esteem

Now I'm ready to let go of the past
Leave the tears from my cries behind
Ready to spread my beautiful wings
Color Me Butterfly

       Color Me Butterfly

         Color Me Butterfly

Mattie's family at the 2006 family reunion to
celebrate Eloise. From left to right: John, Lydia,
Anthony, Mattie, Eileen and Roy Jr.

Acknowledgments

I am first and foremost thankful to my grandmother and my mother, who made it possible for me to share our story with the world. Without you, there would be no butterflies.

I am deeply indebted to my editor, Gail Kearns, whose meticulous and brilliant editing made it possible for the story to come alive.

To the eight women from the book club—my greatest friends—who read each part as I wrote and shared their insights and their tears.

To my daughter, whose wisdom and inspiration is so unabashed and real that I sometimes am left breathless.

And finally, to my partner, my soul mate, who allowed me the time and space to craft my writing and encouraged me to remember the 'core.' I love you!

Author's Note

The fondest memory I have of my mother was the day she kissed me on the cheek, said she loved me, and encouraged me to stop crying and to let go of the pain.

I was lying on her bed, drenched in my tears and begging God to remove me from this day. Remove me from this pain. Remove me from this earth. I remember having a nagging headache that felt like blisters were bursting inside of my head. That was the day of my eighteen-year-old sister's funeral. It was a day that no one thing or person could have prepared me for, a day I will remember forever.

I remember this day not because of the finality of my sister's death. Not because I would have never expected to see my mother crying over a closed casket that contained the remains of her youngest child's dismembered body. And not because my sister's death was a result of her having taken her own life. I remember this day because it was the only time I ever remember my mother kissing me and saying three words: I Love You.

My grandmother, Eloise Washington, met Isaac Bingham in Kingstree, South Carolina, in 1941. After a short courtship, they married, and within the first four years of marriage, they had three children—two girls and a boy. My mother was the second child. By the time my mother turned three years old, my grandparents had moved north and settled in Philadelphia, Pennsylvania.

My mother is a loving, giving, nurturing woman. She is and always has been the type of mother who would take the food out of her own mouth and give it to any one of her children if they were hungry. The type of mother who would go barefoot before she let any of her children go without. The type of mother who would scrub toilets before she would allow her children to live with no roof over their heads. Her love had no boundaries.

Oftentimes, I reminisce about the care she provided to each of her five children. And although at times she was a stern and strict mother, she instilled values that are still embedded in my heart and soul to this day. She is and always will be the epitome of motherhood. She is love. She is grace. She is my mother.

If she were all these things and more, then one might wonder why it is that my fondest memory of her is the day that she kissed me on my cheek and expressed her love. Why is it that this memory surpasses all others? It is because—although my mother illuminates genuine care and love—she is a woman, a mother, who displayed neither physical nor vocal affection. I can't recall ever witnessing my mother being demonstratively affectionate to her children. In other words, I can't recall, other than the day of my sister's funeral, ever having received a kiss from her. Ever having enjoyed a hug from her. Ever having heard her say *I Love You*. To understand her, you must come to know who she was as a child, a wife, a mother, and a woman.

This book is a reflection of memories suffered, survived, and shared by the women of my family. Like all powerful memories, let alone those that span more than sixty years, the inconsequential facts surrounding those experiences are often forgotten or lost, and substituted when the story is retold, without compromising the integrity of the emblazoned memory. It is the sole purpose of this book to create a dialogue with and between women about suffering, hope, and perseverance. So while I can almost guarantee that in some instances a rain cloud might have been dry and a milkman might have been a mechanic, I can equally assure you that other inconsequential liberties were taken to effectively communicate and connect our unforgettable experiences. Just as the ten-inch knife scar on my mother's leg will forever sketch a portrait of my father in my mind, so too will all the true-life accounts of abuse beared by four generations of women in my family—often suffering in silence; surviving in darkness.

This is our story . . .

An éL publishing Readers Guide to

Color Me
Butterfly

A true story of courage, hope, and transformation

L. Y. Marlow

QUESTIONS FOR DISCUSSION

1. Was it surprising to you that Isaac suddenly changed after the family moved to Philadelphia? At what point and for what reasons do you think he changed?

2. Why do you think Eloise chose to stay with Isaac, even after he'd mistreated her and their children for so long?

3. What was the primary thing that helped Eloise to survive and cope with her life? What impact did this have on generations to come?

4. What impact do you think Isaac had on Mattie? What quality did Mattie pass down to her own children because of her relationship with her father?

5. Eloise, Mattie, Lydia, and Treasure grew up with strong-willed mothers. Were you able to identify with these mothers and daughters? If so, in what ways?

6. *Color Me Butterfly* presents the reality of intergenerational abuse that exists within families. For example, Eloise married an abusive man, and then Mattie found herself married to an abusive man. Later, Lydia became involved in an abusive relationship, and Treasure clung to her abusive father. What do you think about intergenerational abuse that's passed down from generation to generation? How do you think this family's life resonates with other families' lives? Do you know a family that has similar experiences?

7. Why do you think Deller finally decided to forgive her father, even after all that he'd done to their family?

8. Why do you think Roy became so abusive? Do you think Mattie's experience with her father had anything to do with her choosing Roy for a husband?

9. Why do you think Mattie decided to stay with Roy? How do you think Roy's death ultimately changed her?

10. Eloise and Mattie were the epitome of old-fashioned mothers that exist in most African-American families. How do you think the values they embraced resonate with most African-American families?

11. What impact do you think John had on Mattie and her five children? Have you ever had a father figure in your life who wasn't your true father? If so, discuss the impact this person has had on you or someone you know.

12. While writing *Color Me Butterfly*, L. Y. Marlow had to dig deep within her soul to confront and move past emotional turmoil. What did you find most intriguing about the way she told her family's story? Did you find the story believable? Upsetting? Worthy of being told?

13. Do you believe *Color Me Butterfly* presented African-American men in a negative light? Why or why not?

14. Do you think each of the women made good choices in their lives when they chose to stay in their relationships? Could they have handled each situation differently? Discuss.

15. The bond between mothers and daughters in this story was very strong. Each mother had a significant impact on her daughter's life. What impact do you think Eloise had on Mattie? Mattie on Lydia? Lydia on Treasure?

16. Lydia confronted the issue of skin color in her family when she was only nine years old. How do you think her portrayal of her light skin compared to her siblings' dark skin resonates with similar issues of skin color in other African-American families and communities?

17. Do you agree that Lydia was the one to finally break the cycle of physical abuse and push beyond a miniscule life? What do you think was the reason behind her strength and determination?

18. How would you describe Lydia and Donald's relationship? Were you disappointed in the end, when Lydia decided to leave him? Why do you think she made this choice?

19. What do you think compelled Treasure to call her mother a *bitch* and spit in her face? Do you think Lydia handled this properly? If not, how would you have handled it?

20. In addition to abuse, mental illness played a significant role in this family's life. How do you think Mattie was able to cope with her daughter's disease and, later, her suicide? How do you think Lydia was able to cope with her daughter's attempted suicide?

21. Eloise had a way of "crafting words to make them make sense." What do you think she meant when she told Lydia to "*let the past rest itself*"?

22. In the end, Mattie lost so many—her mother, father, husband, and daughter. How do you think she was able to cope with all of this loss? What was the significance of her strength?

23. After Lydia dropped Treasure off at college, Eloise's voice suddenly came into her mind. "*You gotta turn one corner, baby, to find another,*" she remembered her grandmother saying. What do you think this meant to Lydia?

24. Which of the four women would you say most inspired you? How does she compare to your life or the life of someone you know?

25. L. Y. Marlow chose the title *Color Me Butterfly*. What do you think motivated her to choose this title? What does the title *Color Me Butterfly* mean to you?

Readers who want to learn more about domestic violence, and those wishing to assist battered women or domestic violence organizations, may contact and make charitable contributions to:

National Coalition Against Domestic Violence
1120 Lincoln Street, Suite 1603
Denver, CO 80203
Phone: 303-839-1852
Fax: 303-831-9251
TTY: 303-839-1681

The National Domestic Violence Hotline
1-800-799-SAFE (7233)

The Color Me Butterfly Journal Series

With its unique and stylish design, and a collection of themes that are sure to inspire and impel, the *Color Me Butterfly journal series* is designed to guide women in self discovery and empower them to find more meaning, purpose, and joy in their life through the art of journaling. Whether at a place in their lives that requires **Courage**, **Hope**, **Love**, or **Reflection**, these journals enable women to find their voices, reach new heights, and enhance their lives.

Chock full of inspirational quotes, an elastic pen holder for easy writing, a satin bookmark ribbon, and a keepsake pocket, this celebration of four beautifully sculpted themed journals offers motivation and inspiration and a way for women to capture their most provoking thoughts.

Courage
A Woman's Inspirational Journal
ISBN-13: 978-0-9787320-6-6
ISBN-10: 0-9787320-6-5

Hope
A Woman's Inspirational Journal
ISBN-13: 978-0-9787320-7-3
ISBN-10: 0-9787320-7-3

Love
A Woman's Inspirational Journal
ISBN-13: 978-0-9787320-8-0
ISBN-10: 0-9787320-8-1

Reflection
A Woman's Inspirational Journal
ISBN-13: 978-0-9787320-9-7
ISBN-10: 0-9787320-9-X

Available wherever books are sold.